TRAINING TO BE MYSELF:

An Indulgent Odyssey of Obsessions, Confessions, and Curiosities

JAKE JABBOUR

Published by Inkshares, Inc., Oakland, California
www.inkshares.com

Cover design by Andrew Martin
Interior design by Kevin G. Summers

ISBN: 9781950301317
e-ISBN: 9781950301324
LCCN: 2021937713

First edition

Printed in the United States of America

This book is dedicated to
Colonel Nicholas Jabbour
With love and appreciation for sharing his life with me

CONTENTS

This book chronicles sixteen days on multiple Amtrak trains for a nationwide improv podcast tour following the dissolve of three of my most significant relationships in Los Angeles. It examines the trials, tribulations, and occasional triumphs that landed me here at thirty-three, untethered from my roles as boyfriend, roommate, and grandson, and setting out on my dream enterprise to tour the country on my art, specifically comedy. It's everything I hoped for, and feared, all at once, just as I imagined it and without any familiarity. It is, at times, an autopsy of self, and at others, a PI's investigation of me relating to the expansive American landscape and its accompanying zeitgeist. I'm my own coroner. My own dick.

The trip starts in LA, rolls through nine cities, and wraps up in New York. There's a little of what you might call getting my affairs in order up top, and a pinch of unwinding at the end. It's exchanges with friends, travelers, and strangers. It's the thoughts and feelings I have when I'm left to my own devices. It's dissections and comparisons and diatribes and rants. It's me considering the accuracy of my own sensibilities. In short, it's a road trip with me.

Like any road trip with someone, you will get to know not just what I am like, but what I like. Because what I like is important to who I am. Or at least, that's what I need to believe. Nick Hornby writes, in *High Fidelity,* that "...what really matters is what you like, not what you are like." Or as described by Chuck Klosterman, obsessing over things is "... an extroverted way to pursue solipsism. We are able to study something that defines who we are; therefore we are able to study ourselves." If you need proof of this, consider that in a book about defining myself, I'm only a couple paragraphs in and already quoting nerdy, white, culture-obsessed writers.

As my relationships with others evaporated, I leaned hard into my relationships with culture, books, movies, TV shows, music, and improv. Since they remain fixed, my swaying relationship to them should clearly point to my developing identity. For that reason, there will be plenty about *Die Hard,* Jay-Z, prestige TV, *Terminator 2: Judgement Day*, HBO, geographic rap genres (dirty south, midwestern backpacker, New York), long-form improvisation theory, and sprinkles of other personal cultural touchstones.

The only mention of sports is as analogies for other things, and one anecdote involving watching golf. *Teach For America* and education come up a lot. You'll likely be surprised by how far backward I'll bend to connect any seemingly banal interaction to the education drought in this country. The *Upright Citizens Brigade* and improv heavily influence the text, but there's no mention of proper theatre or *Who's Line Is It Anyway?* I'm snooty about the lowbrow and blind to the high. You might say I'm the undesirable unibrow, growing thicker with age.

There's special education, and *Infinite Jest* (a novel by another nerdy white male author, surprise surprise), the Tim Allen extended universe (this was legit surprising to at least me), and just a tease of pornography (a surprise to no one).

Expect mention and magnus on television shows shot in LA, train travel, and more about movies. Not train movies, however. I can't possibly invest in a story where the train is the villain.

Last listed, but not least mentioned, there will be a lot about fatherhood; motherhood; other familial hoods; maternal influence; best, last, and first friends; flawed heroes, disappointing relatives, and relative disappointment.

This is a sad book. There's no way around it. Writing necessitates rewriting, which requires reading and rereading, and every time I return to these pages, I find it a little more sad. Which is to say that my life now is ever more present with joy. The distance between writing it and reading it has shown me that. I don't think I would have written this book had I been in a sunny place, and I'm not sure I would be in a better place had I not written this book. There's a saying in improv that life is a Harold, a specific form of improv we'll get into momentarily. But basically it suggests that where you end should be a reflection and improvement of where you started. This is my Harold. Something my improv teachers will be proud to hear, and something everyone else will be baffled to hear.

I'm here to unpack my life one tiny engagement at a time. I'm not looking at any one subject in its entirety, but at my relationship to the subject as it is—incomplete. I have done all the research for this through living and thinking. Often passively. Sometimes compulsively. Frequently both. If I can zero in on what emotional or social nutrition I get from chewing on the relationship between my mom and John McClane, I can hold that up to other people's interests and look for overlaps in our lifestyle lenses. One of my favorite things is to spend time with someone while they passionately enjoy something I have no interest in. Which is probably why I'm well-versed in sports analogies, despite not having a clue what a triangle offense is.

Lastly, this book is a failure. It fails to represent me accurately. It has succeeded in helping me understand an earlier version of me, but the further I grow from it, the less relatable I find the version of me who wrote it. He has helped me come to this conclusion because the knowledge I gained from this experience has helped me to navigate in the present. I wouldn't have been able to have the revelation that I am no longer him without him. However, as a book written to help me know myself—the self writing this very sentence, the self you may very well know, the only self that exists—it does not succeed, because our lives change and we grow. That is a good thing, a beautiful thing. It, like so many failures, has been educational, prescriptive even, but not descriptive. So the Jake in this book only lives in these pages. And what he saw and said can't be fact-checked because that version of the world has changed, too. This is a snapshot in time from an unreliable narrator. It's the verbal description of a Polaroid that was lost in a slow burn.

John Steinbeck, not a cultural nerd, but an American author who traversed the United States, wrote, "I cannot commend this account as an America that you will find. So much there is to see, but our morning eyes describe a different world than do our afternoon eyes, and surely our weary eyes can report only a weary evening world." So the world in this book may not ring the same bells for you or me, but it's the world a self-conscious, grieving, culture-curious, wide-eyed introvert witnessed.

I THINK I CAN.
BECAUSE I CAN'T.

I am taking a train trip across the country because I am a failure. It is one of my fundamental traits. In elementary school, as part of the Presidential Physical Fitness Exam, a program designed to make non-athletic kids feel un-American, the fourth graders were tasked with kicking a soccer ball, then they were given a grade based on the distance. They gave each student three attempts, and Mr. Foley, our PE teacher, would average the distances. I, like clockwork—or more aptly, counter-clockwork—kicked all three balls backward over my head. My average score was negative, and that would be the first time, but not the last, I would let down my country.

For a long time, failure really sucked. It would take me a while to get the hang of failing well. Really nailing failure takes practice. But now when I fail, I really fall on my face. I mean, I go all in. The fall breaks my nose, and on the way down I usually manage to clip my balls on a hand railing. Failure is a skilled teacher, and I am it's enthusiastic student showing up after class, during office hours, and on weekends. If there was a clip show hosted by Rob Dyrdek about failing in life, my calamities would be in the top ten countdown. I've become good at failing because I know that as long as I get up, I get to stare down the barrel of an opportunity. In this case, a cross-country train trip and two weeks of teaching and performing improv comedy with one of my closest friends and comedic mentors.

I am taking this train trip because, for the seventh time in eight years, I auditioned for a UCB Harold team and didn't make it on. If that last sentence reads as nonsense to you, then you are not alone. You probably make up 99.99999 percent of the population. But don't worry, I will catch you up.

Improv might not interest you, but I owe this tour, this book, much of my happiness, and finding my voice, if not my identity, to the art form. What follows is a brief crash course in long-form improv and the Upright Citizens Brigade.

AN INCOMPLETE
IMPROV GLOSSARY
(by estimation)

Base reality: The foundation and rules of the world for your improv scene. It establishes what is to be expected.

Batman is in the bat cave with Alfred.

Beat: A scene with a game that will then be heightened. First beats establish the game. Second, third, and beyond will heighten the game.

In the first beat, Alfred tells Batman he needs to stop hanging out in the bat cave because he smells and is covered in bat shit. In the second beat, Batman can't strike fear into the hearts of criminals because they can smell him coming.

Character: The persona an improviser takes on in a scene.

I am Batman.

Frame/label: An explicit title, sentence, description, or prescription of what unusual thing is happening in the scene and what will continue to happen, so as to be both surprising and inevitable.

> *Batman is disgusting because he spends too much time in the bat cave.*

Game: An unusual behavior, idea, or concept that can be repeated in various locations and with multiple characters, almost always for comedic effect. Should have some structure or rules so it can be patterned, allowing for the audience to have expectations that can be met in surprising ways.

> *Stinky Batman can't do his job.*

Harold: A specific structure of long-form improvisation where an improv team performs an opening to generate premises to perform three scenes, then a group game. Then they revisit the ideas generated in the first three scenes, hopefully heightening them through time dashes or analogous beats, followed by a second group game, and third beats of the first three beats, ideally threading all the games together in a satisfying conclusion.

> *The first scene of the Harold was a beat about Batman smelling. The second scene of the Harold was a beat about a man who is overly confident about his tiny penis.*

Heightening: Playing a game more by raising the stakes through changing the environment, the characters, creating tension and/or consequences.

> *Batman can't see out of the windshield because it's covered in bat shit, and he accidentally runs over Robin.*

House team: A team selected by the theatre to perform there regularly. A coveted spot that rewards its performers with free beer, comedy clout, and occasional TV appearances.

> *I saw the theatre's house team, Flap Jackson, do a very funny set where Batman was a part of The Real World and he got kicked out for smelling like bat shit.*

Improv: Abbreviation for improvisation. Improvisation is the act of making something up or acting without a script. When abbreviated, it's a performance without a script. I have performed somewhere around ten thousand improv sets. I have been paid for three.

> *I have committed most of my adult life to improv, while my peers have gotten married and bought houses.*

Improvise: The verb. You improvise. You don't improv.

> *Even someone with a rigid work schedule improvises, because you can't predict everything about their day. Everyone improvises. No one improvs.*

Improviser/player: The person making stuff up. A group of them make an improv team (see next term).

> *I am an improviser.*

Improv team: A collection of improvisers who dedicate any-where between two to six hours a week to make stuff up in a living room or theatre space.

> *I have been on no fewer than twenty-five improv teams. No improv team lasts forever. Even the ones with clever names like "Too Fast, Too Curious."*

Improv coach: The person you pay to tell you and your team how to be funny and if you are.

> *Our improv coach thinks we should play more characters.*

Improv teacher: The person you pay more than your coach to tell you and your classmates how to improvise and be funny.

> *Our improv teacher never learned my name.*

Logic/justification: The reason for a character's unusual behavior. It doesn't have to be bulletproof, just enough reason to keep playing.

> *I'm Batman. And to strike fear into the hearts of my enemies, I must be authentic. I must under-stand what it is to be a bat, which means living in a bat cave. The bats must be there, too, or else it's just a cave.*

Long-form: A style of improv. An improv team usually gets a suggestion from the audience, and then they create a series of scenes to create a form or world, and each game played is inspired by the suggestion, created from an opening, or discov-ered organically within the scene.

> *No one wants to hear you recap a long-form improv set you saw, but watching one unfold live in front of you can be magic.*

Mapping: Taking the specifics of one world and laying them over the specifics or environment of another.

The Justice League Real World. When superheroes stop being super and start being real.

Peas in a pod: Two characters who share a point of view.

The Peguin also smells like shit because of choosing to live with penguins.

Premise: An idea for an improv scene/game.

Batman smells like, and is covered in, bat shit because he spends too much time in the bat cave.

Scene: Consists of a who, what, where. Active in either dialogue or action. Similar to a movie, play, or TV show. An effective scene has a game. An ineffective scene lacks a game, a who, a what, or a where.

That scene worked because we knew it was Batman and Alfred in the bat cave, and Batman smells.

Short-form: A type of improv where games are told to the audience before the players start the scene. For example, "cocktail party," where one player hosts a fake party, and the audience is told ahead of time who each of the attendees will be. Perhaps one will be a lobster. One player arrives at the party pinching their thumbs and fingers together, and the host must guess that they are a lobster.

Think 'Whose Line is it Anyway?'

Tag: Patting your teammate on the shoulder to relieve them from the scene, and allowing yourself to enter the scene. Usually used to change the environment and character in the scene.

> *Batman was in the scene with Robin until Robin was tagged out, and a player from the back line took Batman to meet with Commissioner Gordan.*

Voice of reason: The character in the scene meant to remind everyone what is reasonable behavior in the scene, so the unusual behavior continues to stand out. Often a surrogate for the audience.

> *If Batman is refusing to clean up, Alfred, the Justice League, even the Joker could be the voice of reason.*

Walk-on: An improviser on the back line walks on to the scene as a character.

> *My teammates walks on as Poison Ivy.*

Yes, and: The foundation for a successful improv scene, and arguably life. You agree or accept what is offered, and you add to it. That doesn't mean you blindly consent. It just means you listen, recognize what was offered, and add to it, either by calling it out as unusual or building on to it for your base reality. The reason I'm here writing this book on an Amtrak train touring across the country.

> *I am Batman and you are my butler, Alfred. Yes, and you smell awful.*

UCB is the abbreviation for Upright Citizens Brigade. And true, U comes before Y, but this definition is more of an encyclopedia entry. The UCB is a comedy foursome whose historic imprint on the zeitgeist was a short-lived Comedy Central sketch show, and are now mostly known for opening an improv theatre school whose alumni include actors from *The Office, Silicon Valley, Parks and Rec*, and Ben Schwartz, who is only a minor character on *Parks and Rec*, but is pretty well-known.

The UCB has schools and theatres in both LA and New York. The school teaches long-form improv and sketch, while the theatre itself puts up improv, sketch, and stand-up shows. These shows are produced, written, and performed by current students of the school, former students, and outside high-profile comedians. The tent pole of the school and the theatre is the Harold, and its accompanying Harold Night.

Del Close, a pioneer of long-form improv, from Chicago, and rumored drug addict and friend of L. Ron Hubbard, developed the Harold. The Harold is performed primarily on Monday nights in LA, by teams that comprise current and former students hand-picked by the artistic director. This would be like if you went to college to study law, and the school had its own law firm that tried weekly cases, and the best students from the school were selected by the dean to be in the law firm. Wait, that actually might be how law firms work.

UCB is great, and I owe much of my happiness to it. Harold Night is also great, and I owe much of my despair to it. The difference between the fictional law school I've fabricated above and the UCB, is the law school based on a university which has degree programs that graduate you. But for the UCB, you can cryogenically freeze yourself and remain a perpetual student with an arrested adult development; unable to have a career because you're too busy playing make-believe and unable to "succeed" at make-believe because it costs $500 every eight weeks, and you don't have a career to support that. Why the sacrifice then? Why volunteer yourself to sit firmly between an exciting rock and a stifling hard place?

Coolness.

Coolness is not measurable, but it is identifiable. And while you can separate it from its cousins' physical prowess and potential, you can't prevent it from wielding influence. So in the land of the comedic, the UCB performer is king. Or jester. But the jester is the king. And how do you become king? You audition. And those who make it get to perform regularly on the UCB stage. And those who don't make the cut question spending $3,000-plus dollars on improving their ability to make stuff up. And some of us, not satisfied with our ability to, once again, just make stuff up like children, will drop another three grand. *Maybe half of my paycheck will unlock the secrets of improvised scenes about farting presidents*, I hope, as I enter my credit card information.

Auditions for Harold Night take place once a year in the fall. When I started, two hundred people auditioned. Now, it's over seven hundred. It's intensely competitive and stressful. Which was half the reason I stopped playing sports and just tried to be funny in the first place. The other half is I am bad at sports.

The first time I auditioned for a Harold Team was the same weekend in 2009 that I interviewed for Teach for America.

Teach for America is a program in partnership with AmeriCorps, which, if you're not familiar, is like the Peace Corps right here in the US of A. AmeriCorps programs range from educational to environmental to humanitarian, and the math works out such that your air of superiority is considerably diminished because it's not as recognizable as the Peace Corps, so you can't off-handedly mention it at parties to seem noble, but you can still live in a first-world country and talk about the latest Noah Baumbach film over caramelized pork belly pops at a gastropub called the Bees Knees.

Teach for America is probably the most high-profile arm of AmeriCorps, as it takes college graduates, trains them over the summer in research-based education methodologies and strategies, and in the fall, places these trainees in high-need schools all across the country. And it was mentioned on *The Office* as having hot women who are nuts. The commitment to TFA is two years, at the end of which you come out with a master's degree at a heavily discounted rate, and a preliminary teaching credential. It's a program to offset our failing education system. It's a meaningful program, but it's mostly a glaring indicator of how bad our schools have gotten. After all, you wouldn't let someone with six weeks of training be a doctor.

I learned of it in 2005, on an episode of *The Colbert Report*, and thought it sounded awesome and like a good way to be of service. But with my history of failure, and their highly rigorous applicant demands—primarily Ivy League graduates—I could see the writing on the wall and didn't bother.

Cut to four years later. It's a Friday in the Fall of 2009, and I have a TFA interview during the day, and my first Harold audition in the evening. I aced my interview and was accepted as part of the 2010 Corps, a position I applied for because I had failed to find another social services job in LA.

I tanked my Harold audition and thus began the yearly cycle of sharpening minds as a special education teacher during the day, and sharpening my imagination at night.

Through lesson planning, IEPs (legal documents drafted between a school and a family, ensuring individuals with learning disabilities receive equal access to an education that their typical peers receive), year-end field trips, dating, writing, weekly visits to see my grandpa, weddings, and just standard life fare, I continued to improvise and I continued to fail. Once, I even left a wedding I was a groomsman in to go to my callback in a tuxedo, only to shit the bed and return to the wedding in time for the mother-son dance.

I became infamous. A peer who had been around in the community for a while, and did poorly in an audition, said people had said he was the new "Jake Jabbour." My name became synonymous with failure. I was the post-*Seinfeld* Jason Alexander of improv.

Now, I'm speaking about a specific type of failure. As a teacher, specifically a special education teacher, you become well-versed in two types of failure: effort-less and effort-full. Effort-less failure is when an individual—say for example, an eighth-grader named Juan—puts no effort into taking his test, and instead throws his desk at you. Effort-full failure is when an individual—say a ninth-grader named Lucia—pours every ounce of energy into a book report on Mary Shelley's *Frankenstein*, but does not meet the teacher's standards for proficiency, and therefore fails the assignment, even though it's the best work she's done. Both students receive Fs on their report cards, but the lessons they take away are much different. Juan learns he doesn't feel stupid if he doesn't try. In fact, he feels strong for being able to throw a desk. Lucia learns effort and improvement don't count for shit. Both students drop out. And if you're wondering, these are true anecdotes, and both students dropped out. We've got a genuine problem in this country, and chief among them is me not getting on a house team!

I have dabbled in both types of failure, as most of us have. But my percentage of effort-full failure, I suspect, is far higher than the average; thus, the comedy community's recognition of my name as a shorthand for effort-full failure.

Before I go on, let me say this: I am aware of how all this talk could be perceived as a backhanded way to list my accomplishments. That perhaps I'm being over-the-top, disgustingly humble. And perhaps I am. I am proud of what I've accomplished, but I wouldn't have accomplished any of it without lots and lots of failure to keep me going. And I can't seem to focus on one without the other. Every time I fail at something, I water down the bitter taste of disappointment with a chaser of success. Conversely, every success comes with a chip on my shoulder from the last defeat. I sit squarely between a successful failure and a failed success. I'm Larry David post-*Seinfeld*, pre-*Curb Your Enthusiasm*.

I failed to get a practical degree in college, which led me to nonprofit. I failed to get a job in LA, which led me to TFA. I failed to get on a Harold team, which led me to write a sketch show. I failed to get on a sketch team, so I co-created a late-night talk show. I failed to get representation from my late-night talk show, so I poured myself into education reform. I failed to reform education, so I started coaching improv. I failed to get on a Harold team again, so I created a podcast. I failed to get back into graduate school, so I wrote another sketch show. I failed to get the sketch show green-lit, so I took my podcast on the road. So yes, there is a lot to celebrate in this. But if it weren't for inadequacy, disappointment, and falling short, I would have just been a management-finance-contractor-business-suit guy making $75k a year, plus benefits. Instead, I owe the federal government $80k and only wear suits when I co-host a talk show where my friends and I eat chocolate molds of our penises. And let me posit, you may learn nothing about yourself from eating your own chocolate phallic, but have you lived if you haven't?

Failure didn't make me who I am. I am a failure, and trying not to be only made me more of who I am. And being who I am, follies and all, brought me more fulfillment than success ever has. This presents an odd predicament regarding the publication of this book. I desperately want this book to succeed, but experience has taught me it's failure would likely prove to teach me more about myself, which is the ultimate goal of writing this book. So in order for me to succeed at learning about myself, I need this book to fail commercially. Which is something I could have done by not writing it at all or giving up halfway through. And this is what I mean when I say I crush at failing. I am putting my full weight behind this literary effort in the anticipation that its failure will reveal who I am. If it becomes a hit, I guess I won't know anything, which puts me right back where I started. Except with maybe more followers. Or at least more trolls.

Going on tour has been one of my most coveted aspirations. It's the original antecedent for writing a book. To write a book that garnishes attention means to travel the country, reading part of my book and answering questions. It's not glamorous, but it is subtly engaging. No rock shows, no improvised routines or choreographed numbers. Just a read-aloud. My desires have always been more MTV's *Unplugged* than *Fuck Yeah Fest*. I'm not looking to tear the roof off this motherfucker. I'm looking to tuck in and read a bedtime story. Hunter Thompson I am not.

Rather than wait to see if my book is a flop of existential importance or a hit worthy of a tour, I went on the tour first, using the only tools I possess that are sharp enough to cut a path—improv and isolated conversation. I'm Jerry Seinfeld coasting on *Comedians in Cars Getting Coffee*.

Ba-dum-dum-dum-boing.

TILL DEATH
DO US DEPART

A wedding, a funeral, a break-up, a departure

Wedding

It is May 2017 and I am packing, but not for the train trip. I will do that in two weeks. Right now, I'm packing for a weekend wedding in Portland with my girlfriend, Em. Her brother is getting married. My life is about to significantly change because of important choices I have to make. And so as I stare down at the two types of dress socks in my hand, I give up and throw them both in the bag. Luggage space I can spare, but I need to conserve any brain real estate for more life-altering choices.

The reason this wedding is significant, beyond two people pledging their love to one another—the reason this wedding carries some emotional weight for me, a stranger to the happy couple, by most definitions—is that it is the first time I will meet Em's entire family. And for her family, being brought to a wedding to meet everyone means something. It means I have risen past the ranks of brunches, rides to the airport, and holiday meals. I am meeting everyone because the expectation is that I am on my way to becoming a permanent fixture. The trouble with this is that is not the plan. My introduction to Em's family is also my farewell.

Em and I met through a mutual friend, Maddy, who shockingly makes another appearance all the way in Chicago later in the book, back in 2014. We both knew Maddy through our time in San Diego. I worked with Maddy, and Em did improv with her. The exact introduction is lost to the countless nervous greetings I've made in my life, but there are at least half a dozen photos out in the world as evidence of our mutual friendship. Every time Em and I would see each other, we would take a picture together and send it to Maddy. Less because Maddy would be delighted to see two of her friends hanging out, although I'm sure she was. She is very sweet that way. But more because it was an opportunity for us to flirt.

Somewhere in between pictures three and four, Em and I bonded over a bowl of ice at a house party she threw. She was one of the rare people in Los Angeles who lived in a house, and she would share her riches by throwing improv house parties. An improv house party is just like a house party with everyone drinking and goofing around, except the goofing around is put on display, shared, and timed. And the best at goofing usually go last.

Em and her roommates would book three or four improv teams and clear the furniture out of their living room to make a stage. Teams would perform in front of a full house of partygoers seated in folding chairs and standing around the kitchen island in the open floor kitchen. I was one of the party attendees scooping ice out of a bowl for my next cocktail, and Em came up and started playfully shushing me. I, of course, then spent the rest of the night being actively, yet subtly, disruptive in hopes of getting some flirtatious admonishing.

From there, we started texting and she asked if I wanted to hang out, adding explicitly that she wasn't looking for another friend, so this would be a date. She also made it clear that she was openly dating a couple other folks, and that she understood if I wasn't okay with it, but she would still like to date me. I said I was fine with it, because I thought I was. Later, I would learn that I was not okay with it. I didn't have the self-assuredness or self-confidence to be in an open relationship. But at the time, I was so smitten with this beautiful, funny, and no-nonsense person, and shocked that she was interested in me, that I would have agreed to open dating, closed dating, me dating her dates, just about anything for a chance to spend some quality time with her.

We had some rocky moments up top, navigating an open relationship alongside just trying to figure out each other's communication style—and yes, eye-roll—but absolutely subscribing to love language. I was, and am, someone who speaks through gifts and acts of service. Ironically enough, I find it easier than finding words that express my adoration. If I thought I could afford it, I would have happily just sent every potential reader a gift to express how I feel, as opposed to writing a hundred thousand words.

Em expresses her feelings verbally. Our differing love languages did not always translate. But we weathered those early storms and built a shelter of admiration, attraction, and affability. We grew strong together, supporting each other through career transitions, improv exploration, and plenty of trips to Disneyland and ramen restaurants. We made it our mission to go to Disneyland at least ten times, and to find the best ramen in Los Angeles. I'm not sure we ever achieved either, but the attempt proved more fruitful than the goal.

She was the first girlfriend my grandpa ever met, and when we went down for the introduction, Em swept him off his feet with glitz, glam, and grace. My grandpa, not to be outdone, wooed her with songs and stories. One of my favorite pictures of Em is her walking alongside my grandpa, taking his arm and steadying him as they walked down the hall of his retirement home.

My relationship with Em was my first adult relationship, in that we were both past our formal education and focusing on finding our roles in this world as individuals but also as a couple. My prior relationships took place while I was in some variation of a school setting and the luxury that comes with it—others doing the life planning for you. You sign up for the role of student, and they give you a syllabus with what you'll be doing for the next four months. You get a part-time job, so no serious commitment there, and the rest of the time is yours to devote however you'd like. It made relationships easy. Or at least, easy to prioritize. After college, I didn't have any relationships, in part because I'm an insecure introvert, and also because I was pretty focused on trying to devise my own syllabus for life.

Em and I were together as we entered our thirties, the imaginary threshold into adulting. I remember having these deep, often funny, and sometimes uneasy conversations with Em about what we would do with our lives. She was my confidant and supporter as I struggled with failing at improv—something I loved and thought I was good at—and succeeded at teaching, something I discovered I was good at but often dreaded because of the stakes. And I like to think I was there for her as she transitioned into commercial acting and improv, finding her footing in Los Angeles after moving from San Diego.

Life can be hard; no great epiphany there. But having someone there to tell you that your wants are not foolish and your perspective is valuable, can make the difference between throwing in the towel or settling for *This'll do*, and waking up and going, *There's more out there for me.* Being in a relationship with someone as magnetic and passionate and fiery as Em made me believe in myself a lot more. If someone with her character and intelligence saw something in me, then there must be something there. I attribute a lot of the drive I mustered during those weird years in between teaching and comedy to her. I don't much care for the idea that someone "completes" someone else, because I think it implies it's unlikely that an individual on their own can be complete. But I will say that Em was there to point out all the pieces and show me I could be complete. Back when I thought I might have lost some pieces of my puzzle in the move to California, Em was there to point out that they were all there; I just needed to look a little harder. In Em's confidence and brilliance and beauty, I could see my own. That's nearly the best thing I could ever ask from anyone.

Em and I have been together for over two years, and it is almost certain that sometime shortly after the reception, but shortly before I arrive at Union Station to board the Amtrak for two-plus weeks, Em and I will break up. I know this because we have talked about it. Talking about it has been helpful, but naturally, more troublesome as time rolls on. The details of our relationship are perhaps of interest, but they are not mine to share because the relationship belonged to both of us, and so making them public seems like a joint effort, and that is not in the cards.

What I feel (un)comfortable sharing is that our planned uncoupling is hollowing me out, but it's necessary. We have a fundamental disagreement about how we should spend our time as we grow old. Neither of us recognize the other as being wrong, and perhaps time will reveal that I am, and she is simply being kind. But for now, the least heartbreaking route appears to be to move forward with a thoughtful and planned breakup sooner rather than later, as opposed to being blindsided or demolished by an unkind and regretful separation down the road.

I can disclose that I do not want kids. That is my current feeling, and as far as I can see down the road, the route never changes. But I hope that I am wrong. Everyone seems to think I am. "What a great dad you'll be," someone will present as a compliment, despite me seeing it as evidence for the prosecution.

"My kids were the best thing to ever happen to me…you don't know how much it will change you…how much it will reveal about your ability to love." These are but a few of the many responses I have received when I present my position. And I am sure all of those sentiments are true. In fact, it's those truths that keep fatherhood at bay for me. I believe parenting to be the most important, labor-intensive career a human can embark on, and I want no part of it. I do not want to spend my life worrying about the safety and joy of a person I brought into this world. I do not want to inevitably traumatize or scar the most important human in my life. I do not want to bring someone into this world and then watch helplessly as the world bullies and intimidates them. Or something worse. I'm certain my heart couldn't take it. And I'm rarely certain about anything.

Few of us get out clean. Which is a coward's way of saying that I'm culpable in passing along misery to my fellow humans. I suspect we all are. Men more, much more, than women. But that's what people do. People hurt people. And that does not make it okay. Admitting to it doesn't make it okay. But neither does not admitting to it. Apologizing doesn't make it okay. Nothing makes it okay. That's why we don't want to do it in the first place. But admitting to it, and apologizing for it, and learning to be better helps it to stop. Which is the goal because it spreads so easily. Ubiquity does not equate to normalcy. We should be better. And my parents tried. They made a conscious effort. They were deliberately thoughtful in trying to raise a kind and thoughtful human. But still we stumble and skin our knees and leave scars. It's not okay, but it's expected. And that expectation is not something I'm equipped enough to shoulder. And so for that very heavy and somber attitude, Em and I are blueprinting an exit strategy.

While that cloud looms heavy over us, we do our best to spot rays of sun and soak up our time together. We arrive at an exquisite Airbnb with a hot tub, a sixty-inch TV, and six bedrooms. By all typical measurements, it is a luxury family home. Except for the garage. The garage has a bar, a disco ball, and a floor-to-ceiling pole for exotic dancing. Sure, the pole could be for something else, but there is a pin in the bottom that can be removed so the pole spins, and there is also a collection of dirty magazines, and a coffee table with cut-outs of naked women placed under the glass. This fascinates me. The natural habitat of dirty magazines is hibernating under mattresses, or roaming out in the wild on train tracks and in dumpsters on the path an eighth-grader walks home. The closest they get to domestic living is when they're purchased at the airport and stuffed in a carry-on next to a Toblerone or a souvenir Yellowstone postcard reprinting a rare photo of a moose. It's not often you get sexuality right there butting up against domestic living. We usually celebrate each independent of the other.

Em and I go for a walk and get coffee, and we both feel a little under the weather. It could be our weak stomachs (not uncommon), or maybe we are in knots about spending our fleeting moments together while trying to celebrate eternal love. It's a hard spot to be in. I can't help but question if I'm the reason she and I are destined to be *Em and her plus-one*, and not bride and groom ourselves.

Now I know that, based on the earlier paragraphs, it would seem as if yes, I am definitely the reason. But I guess what I'm wondering is if it's my destiny to be alone because I, in fact, am too afraid to give in to caring without limit. Limitless affection is an idea about letting go, which opens me up for the potential to lose something with no way of getting it back. It's about giving over to love and giving up control, and I'm afraid of that because if it hurts, I won't be able to stop it. Logically, I can unpack and understand the adage that it is better to have loved and lost than to never have loved at all. But with the passing of my grandpa, someone I came to love without limit, and this inevitable separation with Em, the heartache is enough to throw logic out the fucking window and then close the window and lock the door.

I'm writing on the plane back to LA, post-wedding but pre-funeral. I'm yada-yadding over the event because it's not my event. To report on the ceremony feels like a violation. Know that it was magical. Know that love was in the air. And know I hope to never have to take a catering job to support myself, as the stress of pleasing people would most likely cause me back pain and pit-stained shirts. But if I do, I think weddings would be my choice event. It's hard not to be moved by people traveling from afar to toast to the love of a friend or relative. Also, weddings might be the one place you can witness parents uncharacteristically dance. And not briefly or to appease a crowd chanting them on. When music plays at a wedding—even Sir Mix-a-Lot—the same parents who would frown at the off-color joke in the best man's speech about pegging, will bust a move for the butt-obsessed MC. It's really something spectacular. I'm grateful for every wedding I get invited to.

The Funeral

My grandpa passed away in October 2016, but my family opted to have the funeral in June because so many of us are teachers and that's when summer break is. I hate this choice. I feel like I'm putting my grief on hold. But grief doesn't hold well. It doesn't sit patiently for its turn. It's in the waiting room, pestering the other feelings (happiness, curiosity, love), and it's screaming while everyone's trying to get work done, and it smells like booze. Instead of attending to my grief, I just pick at it, knowing I'm going to have to tear open the wound again in eight months. But I'm contributing almost nothing to the planning, so I bite my tongue.

I have been labeled repeatedly by both sides of my family as *sensitive, emotional,* and *over-thinking.* I am the youngest member of my family on both sides. Or at least, I *was* for the better part of ten years. Then my sister had kids, but they somehow were always kids, while I remain the frozen baby. Reasons for this include, but are not limited to, my crying at a little league game, throwing a fit over no one coming to my college graduation, and crying after a haircut at the tender age of fifteen. My dad has said, in print, that he's thankful there was never a draft for my generation, as I am too sensitive and would not have survived war. All of this is to say that my family doesn't really consult with me because I have a history of being an emotional bummer. Except for my mom. My mom always considers me, even when she undoubtedly loses points with the rest of the family. This makes me a momma's boy who loves his mommy very much. And his grandpa.

When I was a kid, my grandpa and I would walk on the beach, and we would walk backward, so if someone were following us, it would look like we were walking in the opposite direction. It didn't make much sense, but for a kid it was sure fun to see an adult be silly and walk backward with me.

When I was growing up, we'd exchange letters. On my birthday, he'd send a card that would say, "Here's a few bucks to live a little," and *a few* always meant fifty dollars. I'd write him detailed accounts of my adventures through elementary, middle, and high school. I can't imagine how self-indulgent and pointless those letters must have been. Much later, my mom said she visited him once, and she saw that he had filed all my letters away, and had highlighted and underlined all the important details.

When I went to college, he got an email address, and we would keep in touch about our living situations (For me, the dorms. For him, a new house he bought with his new wife, who he met on eHarmony). He was encouraging, even when I didn't know what I wanted to do. And he was vulnerable when—alone again—he had to move into a retirement community. We were both going through transitions, and I like to think the comfort I felt was mutual.

When I was twenty, my dad and I stayed at his place for two weeks one summer because we were helping my mom, who lived nearby, build a pantry in her house. For two weeks, every morning, my eighty-five-year-old grandpa would get up early and pack us sack lunches with sandwiches, fruit, and mini candy bars.

When I moved to San Diego, he was eighty-seven and only thirty miles away, so we started going out to lunch on Sundays, as often as every week. He still drove but didn't like to, so I'd park my car at his place and drive him and his girlfriend around in his. Nine years later, and after moving from San Diego to Los Angeles, one hundred miles farther away, I don't think a month went by where I didn't see him at least once for lunch. I could always count on consistent uniqueness from him. He'd sing to the server or hostess, or in the elevator to his girlfriend. When one of his children or grandchildren would come for an overnight visit or vacation, there would be slippers and robes with our initials either ironed on in felt or written with permanent marker.

For most of the time that I knew him, he lived alone, but his house was stocked for family. Coloring books for the youngest, Bill O'Reilly for the oldest, and Boogie Boards and Oreos for everyone. He'd routinely make efforts to bring his family closer together, often sending his two sons and his grandson the same Hawaiian shirt or leather vest (his taste was not always impeccable), and insisting we get together to take a picture in them. For Christmas, he would send a package addressed to The Jabbours, and in it would contain a multitude of presents with no names on them, and an envelope with a handwritten letter and a stack of one-dollar bills. This was the Guessing Game. We'd each get a chance to guess what each present was, and if you guessed correctly, you'd get three dollars. And until I was about eleven, I'd get two guesses, as I was the youngest. He'd ask me if I was happy with work and if I had any ladies in my life, and he'd pick up the check. I'd thank him for lunch, and he'd tell me it was his pleasure, and that I didn't know how much my visits meant to him.

If I'm honest, I started visiting him because I felt it was something I should do. But now it's clear it was something I needed. Aside from my roommate and a couple other people, he was the person I grew closest to during my time in California. For twenty-three years of my life, he was my grandpa. For the last nine, he was my friend. But perhaps that's not even accurate because I've never had a friend who, in exchange for clearing out his inbox, would take me out to lunch at *Islands* because of their excellent bottomless fries.

When I moved into my own apartment for the first time in my life and needed a deposit but hadn't got a paycheck from my new job yet, he sent me a check and wrote, "Your ace in the hole." That's more than friendly; that's paternal. But he was more than a parent. He used to get mad at me for not saying "sir," or for tucking my hands in my sleeves. All of that fell away the more we hung out. He'd ask for dating advice and give his own, telling me I "should always send a card."

Our time together never felt "he" focused or "me" focused. It was "us" focused. He would inject little sayings into every outing. Some I'd heard elsewhere. "You've got champagne taste on a beer budget." But others were Nick originals. Once, when we walked down the hall of his retired living apartment complex, he said, "Welcome to the hardware store. Screws on the left, nuts on the right." Or when something surprised or delighted him: "Nina Ross, the kickin' hoss with the golden hooves (or tits, depending on the company)." To this day, none of us, his family nor a Google search, could provide any insight into who Nina was, or if she was a woman or a horse.

He would sing to hostesses, steal cookies from the dining hall, and always gift a crisp fifty-dollar bill to "help with gas." He was always so aware of the people around him, so conscious of his impression on them, and as he got older, so determined to ensure that impression was a positive one. For nine years, I saw him weekly—roughly 450 times more than I saw anyone—and so it's impossible not to see my immigration to the West Coast as equal parts adulthood exploration and a study in aging and generosity.

I have anxiety over this funeral. It feels like I'm in middle school English and the teacher said "Jake, stay after class." Except class has been eight months. My stomach is turning, and I can't be present because I know something dreadful is waiting for me. How can I possibly enjoy now, when later will be worse? That's the rub with death. It's coming later, and is usually a straight-up bummer.

I fucking hate death. Who doesn't? As a society, we remain shocked and destroyed any time anyone we love or admire dies, even when they are old and it is their time, or they just happen to be humans, and all humans die. It's one of our defining traits. How is it that death still gets us every time? It's like re-watching *The Sixth Sense* and doing a spit take every time Bruce realizes he's a ghost. I mean, you knew it was coming. How did it surprise you? And why have a drink before the reveal?

I should have known my grandpa would die. It literally happens to everyone. We all see dead people. We all love dead people. We all die.

The funeral is today, but my recording of it will be sparse, and as a result, the recounting of it will also be light. You're getting the stuff I felt emotionally present for, or the stuff that hit so hard it left an imprint—the ordinary and the overwhelming. I'm sitting in the La Quinta Inn in Riverside, while Em showers. She is here with me, and I am grateful for her company. Aside from her love, she is providing a comforting constant that I can tether myself to as the winds of loss thrash me about.

After the wedding and before the break-up, this will be the last event she and I share. It's funny, despite the circumstances, we act according to routine. No pauses for reflection or moments of epiphany as we rustle from our slumber. For someone who likes to look for the extraordinary in the ordinary, all I want in this moment is the ordinary.

I meet my dad in the lobby, and we talk about *Homeland*. My adult relationship with my dad consists mostly of talking about what TV shows we both like. Not shows he likes and shows I like, but shows we both like. There's not a lot of room for listening to one another. It's mostly him talking to me about a show I like, that he's watching. It's like show and tell, except it's eternally his turn, and we brought the same thing.

We could also talk about my grandpa and his dad being dead. But we don't.

Aside from a visit here to a friend almost twelve years ago, I probably haven't been to Riverside since my grandmother's funeral, and I certainly haven't been back to the cemetery since then. I left the Air Force Cemetery in Riverside over twenty years ago, probably not thinking about whether I would be back. Even though my grandmother is buried there, I'm not sure it ever occurred to me to visit her. I'm not sure how often my grandpa did. But I sit in this hotel room, wondering if I'll ever be at the La Quinta again. I may not. I will probably be here in Riverside again because I would like to visit my grandpa. That's the thing I'm thinking about most.

As I try to project out to my last days, looking back on the life I lived, my memories and time with my grandpa will have to share more and more space with new experiences and memories and relationships, and I hope that the space for him is always protected. I read cards he sent me ten years ago, and he wrote me much more as a grandparent fulfilling his role, saying things like, "It's been nice to get to know you," and, "I enjoy your visits." And then when I look on more recent letters or think of things he said during our weekly lunches, he really saw me as someone close to him, obviously as a grandson, but equally a friend. A companion of sorts to usher him into his final years with some positivity. It has to be so hard to get old, to lose loved ones, to be left to wonder, to be idle, to miss and to love. I see now, we probably made it easier on each other with my transition to California, and his to old age. We were both on our own in ways we didn't quite plan for, and we were there to make sure we had love and support along the way.

When he died, I fell apart. We knew it was coming, and he went peacefully, but it didn't make it any easier. My sadness feels like selfishness because I am absolutely torn up by how my life will be more vacant without him. He has passed away, his life is over, and yet I can't stop thinking about how it will affect me going forward. He made California feel like home, and his love was so warm. I feel cold and without a home. He lived a glorious life and went out as easy as one can. Shouldn't that be something to celebrate?

I always thought grief was about the person being gone, but right now it feels like the person who is left—me. When I was adrift, my grandpa made me feel like someone with something to offer. I wasn't a person gone overboard, but one of those round flotation devices for someone to hold on to. But without that person holding on, am I just trash? I hate feeling like trash, and I hate feeling like his death is somehow more about me than him leaving this earth.

The last meal he and I had together, he sang in the hallway, he asked about my job, and he told me how much he adored Em. When the check came, he instinctively went for his wallet, even though he hadn't been carrying one for some time. I got to pick up the tab for the first time in our relationship, and he said how generous *I* was (I'd have to buy him a chain of Red Robbins, pay Guy Fieri to invent a burger and name it the Ol' Nick after him, just to break even). I told him it was my pleasure, and that he didn't know how much the visit meant to me. It was the first time our exchanges were swapped. And it would be the last time either of us said them.

At my grandpa's funeral, his friend Rutledge told a story of my grandpa going to impressive lengths to recognize and honor the men in his ROTC. The Reserve Officers Training Corps is a university-based training program for the armed services. My grandpa taught the corps members of Colorado State University. It was a prestigious position for him, and a noble commitment from the students, but it wasn't exactly the pride of either the university or the armed forces. As Rutledge tells it, there was an annual competition between different university ROTC programs to presumably inspire and motivate. When my grandpa's unit won, they were notified, and that was about the gist of it. So my grandpa took it upon himself and his pocketbook to have 24"x 24" plaques designed and produced for every member of the unit. The plaque hung on his own wall until we packed it up after he died. My grandpa didn't feel that simply winning was enough. He felt that people should be recognized for their efforts, not just their achievements.

I'm sad to say that it took this story at his funeral for it to click for me. My grandpa did that in his professional life, and he did that in his personal life. When my dad wanted to open a cabinetmaking business, my grandpa subsidized him. And when that didn't work out, and my dad wanted to open a bookstore, there was my grandpa. My grandpa even enlisted my dad to make an altar for a church that he and my uncle would visit in San Diego. My dad is decidedly agnostic, while his brother is a devout Christian, and my grandpa somehow found a way to recognize each and marry their passions.

Not one of his children or grandchildren went into a career in the armed services, despite his hope and desire that they would. And yet he supported our passions. Even when we failed. He applauded me for graduating, even if it was with a degree in philosophy (seemingly useless), and beamed with pride when I got an apartment by myself in the Inland Empire to be closer to improv classes (seemingly useless). He supported my dad through every one of his entrepreneurial pursuits, even though my grandpa was a company man and my dad's efforts met more of his internal needs than they did produce income and fanfare.

My grandpa celebrated our efforts, not our victories. He applauded our passions, even when they weren't aligned with his. And I realize, not in that moment, but in writing this book and after hundreds of hours of therapy, that that practice is what's most important to me in my relationships: to support and appreciate the efforts others make on their path to self-fulfillment.

He never measured us on our ability to succeed or to follow in his footsteps. He saw our passions as our triumphs and wanted us to know that he had our backs, so long as we put in the effort. Until now, it was never intentional, just a product of being Nick Jabbour's grandson. But now, it's how I intend to honor him: to appreciate and acknowledge the value in others.

It's something, of course, I think we all want to do, but the threshold for it relies heavily on our own limitations or priorities. It's why we can assume everyone wants to do this, and yet people irritate each other, take advantage of each other, and step over one another. It's not personal or conscious, but a product of prioritizing self-acknowledgement over outward appreciation. And then, of course, it's easy to value others when they make our lives easier, or to appreciate those who appreciate us. But what of the people who make our lives difficult? That's where my grandpa shined. His children, his grandchildren, never set out to make his life difficult. But they, like all future generations, concerned themselves with…well, themselves. It can't always be easy for a World War II vet entering his twilight years to know he is not always thought of, and yet he thought of us. Unconditionally. Perhaps that's the role of grandparents. Or perhaps they've just been around long enough to see the importance of that.

The Breakup

Em and I spend our last day together getting brunch and lying on her bed, crying on and off. This feels like the healthy thing to do, but fuck if it doesn't feel like it's killing us. I would love to say I could see myself wanting kids to extend our time together, but the truth is I don't. And so I can't start a life together with someone on what I perceive to be a lie, even if I don't know myself well enough to know how I'll feel in the future. Like I said, I'd love if I was wrong about this. But if we get three years down the road, and she asks if I want kids, and I say, "I was hoping I would, but I still don't," then I have failed us both. It's too soon to tell if orchestrating a breakup is a bad idea or a good idea. In fact, there's nothing definitive about it except that we set out to do it.

I have never been in a planned breakup before. I mean, I guess to some extent most breakups are planned. One person feels a shift, sudden or subtle, and they start the strategizing—to minimize casualties, to minimize the pain. But this one, this was a joint effort. Not unlike a divorce. We didn't have property or children to think about, but we still had each other and the unanswerable question of *What are we doing?*

All days end. Some will be wonderful, but only one will serve as the last day you spend with someone. On that day, Em is beautiful and kind, and she is sure to make this day better than most, despite knowing we have to crack our hearts open at the end.

She drops me off at Josh's. I walk to Josh's door and turn around, luggage in hand, and race back for one more hug. I am crying in the middle of the street like a character in a movie, so absent of self-awareness he wins a Daytime Emmy. To say I'm not good with goodbyes is generous. I'm barely farewell competent. Anything from seeing someone off on a new chapter of their life to just leaving a BBQ early, I always botch it. My preferred method is to not do it at all. I envy the people who own their salutations. I see people who leave by saying bye to everyone, and everyone loves it, or at least appreciates it. But I get caught up in handshakes versus hugs and what to say, and the whole thing is awkward. And I know people take awkward over rude, nine times out of ten, but not me. I don't think not talking is rude. I think it considers other people's feelings just as much as polite conversation. Extroverts lead this world, so it's common to think the nice thing to do is reach out, tell a tale, give a pat on the back. But in the eyes of the introvert, a squeeze on the shoulder is reserved for waking someone up on a sinking ship. Otherwise, hands off.

So a planned breakup is maybe the thing I fear most. Because it plants a goodbye out in front of you, navigates the route, and delivers you an ETA. You can take a couple detours, but the destination remains.

You have arrived, my emotional GPS alerts me. It's supposed to be the end, but I find us in the middle. In the middle of the street, in the middle of me completely falling apart, and in the middle of not knowing what to say or do next.

Em and I agree to "work on our shit." Well, I said it and she nodded. As I said it, I realized I didn't know what I meant by it, but by then it was too late. She had nodded, and I felt ridiculous asking what she thought I meant, when I didn't know what I meant. Perhaps I meant that there was something that we could do to "fix" this. To return to a happier time. It just felt too sad to say, "Well, we tried. Goodbye." Or maybe it was just the breakup version of *Let's keep in touch*. Not meant to be binding, just meant to ease the separation. A little morphine as we drift away.

I wipe my eyes, clear my throat, and drag my luggage across Josh's doorstep.

Departure

There are social contracts most humans agree to when out in public. The most notable: don't get emotional. Take the metro, or fly Delta, and you'll see everyone doing their best passport photo pose. No smiles, no frowns, refrain from the obscene, and especially no crying. People break these contracts by yelling at their significant other, or drunkenly ordering another round. And when this happens, their peers are granted permission to stare. It's in the fine print. Don't stare unless someone shows emotion.

There is no more public place than Union Station, and no more unsettling emotion than crying, so I discreetly march ahead down through the lobby to the Amtrak window to get my tickets. A man playing a loud boombox is rapping and shouting, and I've never felt such relief for someone causing a scene. I pull my hat down over my eyes as they swell with tears, and stress-purchase thirty-eight-dollars-worth of snacks from the convenience store inside the station. I am overcome with the feeling that I want to be alone. It's not exactly the perspective one wants before embarking on a countrywide storytelling and improv tour, but one doesn't always get to choose how one feels.

I take the next few minutes to stare out the window as we pull out of the station, and I reflect on being a crying man departing from Union Station Los Angeles, whose next destination is improv in Maricopa, Arizona. I had an active imagination as a kid, but no amount of creativity could have predicted a version of adulthood that would incorporate such an imagination into a cross-country tour about comedy, sadness, and existentialism.

MEAT PACKING WITH JOSH

Inventory: improv, podcast, stories, and friend

Before we go any further, I want to go on the record here. And I know this entire book is *the record*. Believe me, it haunts me. But if I'm to regret everything in here, I want to make sure I regret my sincerity and not my detachment. I love improv. Improv literally nourished me, taught me to provide for myself, and restored my belief in myself and my belief in belief. I am embarrassed by how much I love improv. I feel I need to say that because I give it a pretty hard time in this book. Part of the reason is that I am a child, and my adoration for it is so great that it makes me self-conscious, and consequently, I will spend a lot of this book teasing it the way a grade-schooler might tease their first crush. Notice me the way I notice you, give me any form of attention, but you mustn't know that my efforts are sincere, because if you reject me, I fear I might explode all over the playground.

Expressing affection and being rejected is another form of effortful failure, and so I will choose to disparage improv, still granting it my full attention, still pleading for its acknowledgment, but if it turns its back on me, I will at least be at a safe enough distance not to feel the coldness from its shoulder.

The other reason I'm tough on it is because of its potential to help and to harm. I love improv because it has done so much to give me confidence, a career, a community, and above all, it's made me laugh harder than the funniest episode of *The Simpsons* or *30 Rock*. In fact, in some ways, it's ruined sitcoms and comedies for me. I remember once hearing that someone in the improv community who was very funny didn't watch comedies on TV. I couldn't understand it. But after a decade laughing on stage until it hurt, until I went dizzy from lack of oxygen, I got it. Improv took the best moments you have with your friends at a sleepover, and the giggles you get during a lecture, and the incubated inside jokes you still have with your high school friends and compressed it into fifteen-to-twenty-minute doses performed in front of a live audience. It was like freebasing an orgasm dipped in grain alcohol. Okay, maybe not, but it had the power to strip you of all your insecurities and anxiety and depression, to make you forget about all your debt and despair, to bring levity to your heartache and loneliness.

Improv is magic. It has its lovable magicians who make you question what you've come to accept as reality, and whisk you away to a land of fantasy and escapism. And it also has its pickup artists, its wieners and turds who use it to trick and deceive and manipulate status. And that shit sucks.

I have realized so much personal potential out of improv, from performing to writing, to directing, to producing, to letting D'Arcy Carden pick out a tattoo for me to get on stage, that I truly wish the benefits of it on anyone and everyone.

So when some slimy dude or group of dudes uses it to make anyone feel less than by telling them they're not funny, or withholds opportunities or self-expression and exploration by engineering a hierarchy or exclusivity to the whole thing, I get unreasonably angry and want to cast the whole thing into the pit of Mordor. I should admit I'm not well-versed in *Lord of the Rings*, but I've seen enough improv scenes to be fairly confident in that analogy.

That's another thing improv has done for me. It's taught me about *LOTR*, *Harry Potter*, the risks associated with sitting for too long, coding, fracking, edging, bee migration, snow-balling, Maine Coons, meditation, behind-the-scenes celebrity gossip, and what a wood humbler is. Just kidding. I learned that from a BDSM catalog and taught it to improv. The bottom line is improv should be used to expand and include, not to retract and exclude. It should be made accessible to every-one and anyone because it literally costs nothing and produces nothing tangible. But I suppose anything is corruptible. So I'm often critical of my darling for how it's made me feel, how it makes others feel, and how it attaches a price tag to those feel-ings. And so enter *The Meat Improv* podcast. A weekly respite to remind and restock me on all the joy and fulfillment improv is capable of.

At the time of writing this, there are over 150 episodes online of *The Meat Improv*, a podcast where my comedy part-ner, Josh (I'm using his real name because the podcast exists and his name is in it), and I invite comedians on to tell true "meaty" stories from their lives, and then we improvise off those stories. We created it to have some control over what improv could be for us and for others. It's our own small-town movie theatre where we can screen *Porky's* if we want. Let's be honest, we're *Porky's III* at best. It's our own music label where we get to record fifteen-minute meandering melodies not meant for radio play. It's our underground zine. Too punk rock for Barnes & Noble, and not at all profitable.

On top of that, it has been one of the best formats for my preferred interactions. It's concentrated conversation and structured goofing. We invite two guests on to tell us meaty stories from their lives, anything personal to them, and then we use those stories for inspiration for long-form comedic improvised scenes. We typically record for two hours in one of our apartments to no audience, making each other laugh as we pretend to be jewel thieves covered in snot. We then edit it down to ninety minutes and upload it to the Internet, where in one week, more people will hear it than will ever see me improvise live.

But that's all about to change because Josh and I are taking it across the country.

BEFORE DAY 1: UCB SUNSET, LOS ANGELES

Population: about three-fourths capacity, friends, lovers, idols

Our first show of the tour is one week before departure. It's a kick-off event at the Upright Citizen's Brigade Theatre on Sunset Boulevard in Hollywood, California. The UCB has two theatres, Franklin and Sunset. Franklin is a sort-of black box, bursting with sweat and energy, and the best stage to perform on in Los Angeles. Sunset is a brand-new theatre with tall ceilings, a crow's nest, and it's attached to the training center. It's seen as the more polished, theatrical stage.

Our guests for the show are Heather Anne Campbell and Ian Roberts. We're sitting in the green room with Heather and Ian, and I'm shitting my pants. Heather is an improv legend, a quick and explosive chameleon, and someone I had admired since first arriving on the scene in 2007. Ian is one of the founding members of the UCB. He was in the first show I ever saw at UCB. It was their long-running ASSSSCAT, a collection of all-star improvisers doing scenes inspired by a guest monologist (if that sounds like *The Meat* structure, that is no coincidence).

His performance in that first show was probably par for the course for him, nothing memorable, but it was the reason I started taking classes. I wanted to make people laugh the way he made me laugh. This show is a big deal for us dopey meat-balls. It's a testament to how far we've come, even if just in our eyes.

My relationship with Josh started as idol, then mentor, then teammate, then friend, then collaborator, and finally landing somewhere between improv husband and platonic life-mate. I first saw Josh on the UCB Franklin stage performing with his then Harold team, Flap Jackson. He and another guy, Joe, were my favorite performers. They looked similar, and for the first handful of shows I saw of theirs, I got them confused. They were so playful on the stage. They really seemed to have fun, not only with the form but also with each other. I found myself impressed with their ability to construct joy out of nothing. Josh made doing improv seem like a no-brainer. Have fun play-ing make-believe for an audience of comedy nerds? I couldn't believe it was something anyone got to do. And if so, why wasn't everyone doing it? This would be the first of many times Josh inspired me and lifted me from my own expectations of what I was capable of.

Josh became my coach for over two years. He taught me how to take my sense of humor and season it so it was digestible and desirable to an audience. He pushed me to keep audition-ing when I got rejected time after time after time. He directed my first sketch show and asked me to join his team Puddy and host a bimonthly improv show. Then we started *The Meat Improv* podcast.

I remember the first time Josh and I hung out outside of a "professional" setting. I put professional in quotes because it just means I was paying him to tell me if my jokes about bonking my head on dumpsters were any good. Not exactly corporate finance law. We were on his patio after a practice and he said, "You're funny dude." He added that I went blue often (meaning indelicate, gross, or profane), which should come as no surprise to you. But that I earned it, which is probably a tremendous surprise. I went home that night and wrote down everything he told me. I was so elated that someone of his comedy prowess had taken the time to see me and single me out.

The next day we got burritos, and I'd thought I'd made it. Here I was with Josh, a member of Flap Jackson, eating burritos and talking comedy. What could be better? Aside from financial stability, love, self-actualization, and societal contributions. A few months later, Josh would ask me to join his indie improv team, Puddy.

For the first few weeks of performing with Josh and my other idols, Wayland and Clay, I was so in my head, and consequently, so bad that I thought for sure they would rescind their offer. I was a ball of nerves oscillating between being frozen and making no moves, or coming out and making outlandish untenable moves. I kept waiting for the conversation to happen after a show or over lunch or even over email. They had decided I wasn't quite ready. Because I wasn't. But that conversation never happened. I don't know why. They were just patient with me until I was ready. And the catch is, I might have never been ready had they not given me the chance to fail with them. I pushed myself hard, as hard as you can for an art form that requires no memorization or homework, and I became determined to fail less. And slowly, surely I did. And when I would get a loud giggle from Josh, or make Wayland break his commitment in the scene, or watch Clay wipe tears of laughter from his eyes on the back line, I knew I was getting better. Or making them worse. But I didn't care. I was having the time of my life making my comedy heroes laugh.

When Josh and I started the podcast, a decision we made after I was rejected by the UCB theatre for the seventh time, it was just so we could have ownership over our comedy. We wanted to perform, and it seemed like we should be able to. After all, it was just make-believe. The UCB has limited stage time. There are only so many hours in the day. Coupled with it being a business, it made sense that they had to be highly selective about who they put up on that stage. But what made less sense was the idea that if they said no to you performing, that you couldn't perform. It wasn't brain surgery. It was pretending to be brain surgeons, and we could do that anywhere. All we needed was to sit in the same room and pantomime, or in the podcast's case, describe operating on a brain. We had all the power to do what we wanted. The greatest lesson Josh ever taught me was no one is going to anoint you to create. You do that on your own. Ironically, this was him anointing me, but I got the message, and everything from our podcast to this book has resulted from that lesson, and I owe much of my creative fulfillment to him.

Our podcast got accepted into the Del Close Marathon in New York, and with listeners all across the land—or at least, a listener in a part of the land—it made sense we tour the country, perform live along the way, and end in New York. Josh found a blog that detailed traveling by train from coast to coast for under $300, which seemed like a steal. Plus, the train seemed like a good way to see the country. More research revealed it would end up costing us closer to $500, but by that time, we'd fallen in love with the idea. And Josh, a detailed and organized man, set out to plan our destinations and schedule our shows and workshops. I set out to support this idea and be suitable company during the planning. Oh, and I would handle lodging. Or wing it when we got to the city. I am easy-going, but at the cost of not contributing much.

All aboard! First stop, UCB.

Josh and I take the stage to a mostly full house, and I can hear the tremble in his voice. This ignites my nerves because I look to Josh for guidance and I've never known him to be nervous. Of course he gets nervous, but I craft my heroes in the image that makes them the most heroic. In my mind, he also never farts, and he knows how to speak seven languages.

We sit at a table, pick up our microphones, and introduce our guests. I can't believe this is happening. We stick to our regular format, chatting up top with our guests, usually to help put them at ease, but in this case, to put us at ease. And then we do what we call a warm-up scene, something equivalent to an ice-breaker or a lap around the gym. This particular warm-up scene is based on an anecdote I share about being a kid and worrying that my parents would sneak into my room at night and stab me. It was a totally baseless fear. My parents never spanked me, never even put me in time-out, so it makes for good improv pulls.

The scene that follows is about Ian worrying that his wife, Heather, is trying to kill him on their anniversary. Josh and I are barely in the scene, a strong indication that we're nervous if we're not even playing in the show we host. It was a hilarious scene, and I had front row seats. Ian then tells a story about some unusual neighbors he had once, and Heather tells a gruesome story about the untimely passing of some animals. I find my groove about two-thirds through the second scene with help from a familiar laugh in the audience. Em. Remember, this show happened a week before we left, so a week before Em and I would part ways. She came and supported and laughed extra loud. With her laughter from the audience, and Josh's playfulness on stage, and two improv hall-of-famers believing in Josh and I enough to accept our invitation and play, I was feeling incredibly supported. They, like you, gave their time to listen to me. A powerful gift that made me feel ready to take on the world for myself in search of myself.

DAY 1: MARICOPA

Population: Audi test drivers, manifest destiny-ers, and Pamela Anderson

This trip is not messing around. Our first leg of the trip is seven hours. I would love to regale you with a beautifully constructed paragraph detailing the interior of the Amtrak car, the passengers with their distinct characteristics, and the wise gray-haired train conductor with a silver pocket watch given to him by his grandmother, the first female lead conductor, but I can't. Because I am asleep. From "All aboard," I am all snores.

I have always been a good sleeper. As a youngster, just put me in a car, or really any cushioned seat, and I'm out before the ignition turns over. It made me a great travel companion. Or at least, an easy one. As I grew older, it made me a less-than-great travel companion. Or at least, an unhelpful one.

When people travel with partners, they do so to share the experience, share the work of navigating. In short, to experience the act of sharing. But I am not a sharing vagabond. I am a thief, robbing my partners of their companionship in the middle of my night-night. People notice my burgling less when the trip is good, but when the trip is bad, people want company for their misery. So Josh and I are off to a rocky start because this first leg was bad. So I'm told. I wouldn't know. I slept great. Josh, however, was kept up not only by the sliding door they seated us next to, but by the smell of the bathroom, and the incoherent chatter of our train mates. But not me.

In 2008, I accompanied my sister Michelle to India to adopt a child. She was adopting. I was co-adopting. That's being gracious, too. I was...there. My mom has raised three pretty outstanding children, with me picking up the rear both in age—I'm the youngest by at least fourteen years (we have different fathers)—and in life experience (they are two hundred years my senior). I don't have many memories of them rearing me or showing me the ropes, as they were both grown and out of the house before I could put pants on all by myself. But they would guest star for seasons, sometimes moving back home, or for the holidays, sporadically showing up in my arrested development.

My sister Nicola has the self-confidence, style, creativity, and boldness of Dennis Rodman. I mean this in the most complimentary sense. She has always followed her own path, a story I will not tell for her. But growing up, she would come into my life with a new passion, partner, or pursuit, and she would wear it as effortlessly as she did her cool hoodies and Ts. Any points for style I got growing up were slid to me under the table by her.

My sister Michelle, as of this writing, is the mother of seven children—five adopted (and there's a chance this is inaccurate, as I may have miscounted, or she has adopted another)—has worked extensively in social services, the Navy, foster care, and basically any organization that puts *non* in front of *profit*. If you look at my years in AmeriCorps, displaced youth service, TFA, or special education, and then you look at my sister, it's easy to see who I'm modeling after. Although, she's effectively at the Met Gala, and I'm in the back of the *PennySaver.*

Generosity and kindness is not a competition. Because if it were, we wouldn't have an exponentially widening wealth disparity. My sisters have always led by example, making me want to strive to be cooler and kinder.

So it was 2008, and I was feeling full of myself, having just completed a year of AmeriCorps, working with youth on probation and getting paid so little it was basically a volunteer position. I had finally achieved something to earn the title of our mother's favorite child. This is an inside joke between us. My sisters call me the little prince because by the time I came around, my mom had softened on some of her rules, and I was allowed cookies or ice cream for dessert instead of the graham crackers they had to pretend were a treat. My mom will only go so far as to say I'm her favorite son, still allowing for some technicalities. So this was it, I thought. But my reign on the top was short-lived, as three months later, my sister completed the paperwork to adopt a little girl from India. She asked me to go because I don't make much of a fuss. Which would be a problem because when a fuss was needed, I was sawing logs.

On the plane trip back, her new daughter, my niece, got a fever of 104, and I slept through my sister's natural and expected panic as she contemplated having the plane land somewhere in Russia. My hibernating abandonment likely upset her, although she never said so explicitly because her kindness is boundless. I would have liked to have been a better brother, and it pains me I wasn't, but I was at the mercy of too many sleep agents. Besides the soothing rhythms of transportation I knew so well, stress is a natural Ambien for me. I've exited many arguments by lying down and dozing off, only to wake up to my opponent still seething.

My niece would need emergency surgery when we landed in LA. It was not an easy journey, and my sister and niece braved the worst of it. But everything settled into their comfortable place, and they are living their best lives in Northern California. However, I have always felt that I let my sister down, and now I am letting my friend down, because he went to a lot of trouble to plan this trip with his best friend. But instead, he's pinned awake on this red-eye train to Arizona with a two-hundred-pound baby. I'm sorry, Josh. If my ailing niece couldn't keep me awake, you never stood a chance. Good baby. Bad copilot.

We pull up to Maricopa, Arizona, a little before 8:00 a.m. It is a small reservation with a remodeled Harrah's Casino as its biggest landmark. There is a sense of neglected rusticness. Some towns feel rustic as a product of their central business. Take, for example, my hometown of Idaho Springs, Colorado. It's maybe three miles long and a half-mile wide, with a mine at either end, and pubs and ski rental stores peppered throughout. It feels rustic by necessity. Maricopa feels rustic the way a grandparent's garage does. Valuable, sure. But overlooked, and therefore never realized. Waking up here, I feel stuck out of time, which feels appropriate, as Arizona doesn't subscribe to daylight savings. While the rest of the country falls back and springs forward, Maricopa stands firmly in place. If you start old, how much can you really age?

I'm having an out-of-time experience. No longer an improviser, a modern-day profession, I feel like a miner heading West, hoping to strike it rich. Less than twenty-four hours ago, I stood in the thoroughfare like Wyatt Earp and said farewell to the woman I love, never knowing if I'd see her again, and set my sights on a new frontier. However, unlike a miner, I have no delusions about the fortune I will not find. And I'll probably eat better. And be much safer. So aside from the certainty for healthy arrival, the relative comfort, hot meals, and lack of any real risk of fatal disease or bear attack, I'm just like my ancestors, forging ahead and pursuing my manifest destiny. If my forefathers lived *The Revenant*, then I'm living *The Revenant* when it comes on TNT and all the violence is edited out.

Anthony leads our manifest destiny. He is our first Lyft driver of the trip, and he is driving us from Maricopa to Phoenix. I do not know how we would do this trip without ride-sharing. I can't imagine figuring out how to get a cab out to a distant and desolate Amtrak station at 8:00 a.m. in the middle of a near desert, and taking us to Phoenix without it costing us $200. Thank goodness for ride-sharing. Even if I find it uncomfortable to ride in a stranger's car and not talk to them because I'm introverted and they are, in fact, a stranger.

Besides driving for Lyft, Anthony test drives VWs and Audis. He owns two cars and has been to Japan. Anyone who thinks ride-sharing perpetuates a class system never met Anthony. He whips us through desolate highways, and maybe it's all in my head, but I feel like I'm in capable hands. Unlike other ride-share drivers, Anthony gets paid to drive on top of getting paid to drive. Over the course of this trip, it will be the ride-sharing experience that most exemplifies the contrast between the Coasts and Middle America.

Josh and I arrive at our Airbnb, a quaint one-bedroom apartment with no personality. There is a futon in the living room, a dining room table, and a little calendar on the wall. Nothing about it screams home, and nothing about it screams hotel, either. Every Airbnb I've been to feels like a house abandoned during a zombie apocalypse. Everything of value and sentiment has been taken, and all that remains is a fridge full of butter and one Corona, a small flat-screen TV, and a sewing basket filled with obscure DVD titles like *Horrible Bosses 2* and *Pearl Harbor*.

Josh and I immediately take space from one another—Josh in the bedroom, me in the living room—and we fall asleep. We nap before going to teach a workshop at noon. I doze off, wondering if I should move to Maricopa to test drive automobiles. I can't help but consider trying on someone else's life when they seem outwardly happy about it.

When I wake up, I look up the improv theatre where we'll be teaching, The Torch Theatre, and learn it's only a mile away, so Josh and I decide to stretch our train legs and talk about the workshop. This is an immediate mistake. It is one hundred degrees outside, and it feels like the surface of the sun. It's hard to talk improv theory when your body is worried about maintaining a living core temperature.

Josh and I decide that I will teach the first lesson. Then we will go to lunch, and Josh will teach the second. This will be our model for the entire trip. Josh has done a superb job of making me feel like a comparable and trustworthy teacher, despite his having years more experience. He often reassures by bringing up that I have a master's degree in educational instruction. But regardless of my education, putting me on the same plane as him comes down to trust. And it's Josh's trust in me, more than anything else, that makes me more qualified.

On the walk, I am struck by how modern Phoenix feels. There are lots of gastropubs and cantinas that promise happy-hour cocktails and sliders on their sandwich boards. It seems every town in America is hip now. I bet it rules to be a teenager. I suppose it always did, minus the raging hormones, being surrounded by other teenagers, and the lack of autonomy. But I can't imagine growing up with access to sweet potato fries, a practically limitless library of stand-up specials, an actual limitless music catalog, and somewhat easier access to quality marijuana. I suppose the only upside my generation had was that *Playboy* showed vaginas. Although with the

Internet, the vagina has become as exotic as earlobes. They're not always on display, but there is certainly no mystery as to what they look like.

I suspect the youngest generation's relationship to pornography will soon mirror my generation's relationship to junk food, in the same way my parents' relationship to drugs and alcohol was much more casual than my own. To hear my parents talk about that time, or to watch it on *Mad Men*, everyone was a little drunk all the time. And usually driving, too. Often to get more drunk. And cocaine was pretty much on the food pyramid in the '80s.

More rational heads eventually prevailed, and now having a "nooner" or a road soda is frowned upon, and coke is mostly seen as something people do to slip into another decade of their life. Teenagers do it to feel in their twenties. People in their twenties do it to feel like they're in their thirties. People in their thirties do it to feel in their twenties. And people in their forties do it because it's highly addictive.

My generation missed those days of drinking and driving, but we sidled up to the table for Happy Meals, Surge as a beverage, and candy that was chemically closer to plastic toys than food. Remember Fun Dip, and Dunkaroos, and Gushers? Packed in our brown bags for lunch in place of something that required photosynthesis to exist? Now, kids eat apples and dried seaweed for snacks. Soda has been replaced with coconut water. And I suspect the same will be true for the Internet. No one wants to censor it, but I wouldn't be surprised if adult erectile dysfunction doesn't hit us the way diabetes has.

Maybe it's not such a bad thing to limit what people, especially those with growing minds and libidos, have access to. I used to masturbate to pictures of Britney Spears in *Rolling Stone*. She was in an outfit that revealed her midriff. Now, using that image for arousal would probably qualify me as a carnival attraction. "Come watch the man turned on by nothing more than bare breasts!"

"Freak! Freak!" they'd yell.

Ah, to be young again.

The last time I stayed in Phoenix was with my aunt on a road trip to California. My aunt doesn't drive out of state lines alone. She was coming to California from Albuquerque, so my mom asked if I would drive with her. I agreed, and after an unremarkable two-hour flight from LAX to Santa Fe, I was in the car with my aunt, headed back to California. We stopped at a Burger King, and my aunt ordered a large root beer, no ice. The gallon of Barq's tested the strength of the plastic cup and my aunt's forearm as she hoisted it into the car. She talked about going to see Cesar Millan, the dog whisperer, at a casino on a reservation and loving it. My aunt used to train dogs, so it's pretty cool to think there was a famous dog trainer she could go see.

There's a celebrity for everything. The rest of the country is slowly catching up with Los Angeles. When people ask what I like about LA, I say it has so much variety and diversity, you can really laser focus on your niche proclivities. Not only does LA have long-form improv, but it also has three theatres with different philosophies. You don't have to settle for the only place in town that serves ramen. You can go to the one with lobster, or fried tofu, or black oil dip. Thanks to the expansion of the Internet and TV, my aunt doesn't have to settle for the only live act touring through her town. She can see a famous dog trainer.

America has delivered on its promise of pursuit of happiness. In fact, we plowed past pursuit right into silver platter.

We stayed at a Motel 6 in an unsavory part of Phoenix, and throughout the night, there was shouting and tire peel-outs. And once, someone even banged on our door. At least, that's what my aunt said. I slept through it all. I wonder if during those alarming moments through the night, my aunt thought, *I am no safer with my nephew than I would be with a baby.*

Good baby. Bad security.

We are at The Torch Theatre, and despite committing myself to improv for the last eight years, this is the first time I've been in an improv theatre outside of Southern California or New York. Out front, the storefront seems underwhelming—a poster or two on the windows, and a standard sign listing business hours. When you step inside, it's not so much magical or visually overwhelming, but the passion inside is like a thick fog. It feels like the comic book shop Coyote Comics, in my hometown. Children would be overcome by the possibility waiting inside. It leapt out at them, grabbed them by the heart, and whispered, "Your dreams await." But for an adult—or more accurately, a parent—it looked like a handful of humans running their fingers over boxes as if they were typing.

The Torch gives off the same feeling. There's a few DVDs and books for sale, mostly related to improv and comedy. They are the same ones in every improv space. The art form isn't yet that big to showcase variety. Then there's the box office, a stack of business cards, and a dry-erase board listing the shows. Everything an eager improviser could want, and nothing an outsider would even classify as noteworthy. It's a feeling of ignored intensity. The proprietors and regulars are deeply passionate about what it houses inside, while most of the population just knows it as the place next to the place that used to be a Radio Shack. There is so much passion and joy packed into this compact business space in this strip mall, and yet next door is a joyless H&R Block that probably does three times the business. If only the patrons knew what the return on improv is. Emotionally.

Financially, there is very little return. But for someone feeling lost, or disconnected, or voiceless, it is the Amazon of creative stock. The principle of *Yes, and* extends beyond the stage. It inspires in its players a welcoming and collaborative attitude toward hanging out before shows, grabbing a beer after, creating a sketch, reading each other's scripts, acting in shorts for one another, and recommending people for jobs and career opportunities. The reason so many improvisers found themselves on TV in recent years (Mindy Kaling, Tina Fey, Amy Poehler, Adam Pally, Mary Holland, Donald Glover) is as much a result of their talent as it is their ability to say, "Yes, and," to themselves, the industry, and each other. If you can learn to accept an offer instead of deny it, you are much more likely to heighten beyond your station. And that makes teaching improv incredibly rewarding. By creating a space for people to be heard both by improvisers and their scene partners, you are creating a space for people to find their voice and surprise themselves at what they can do when they are encouraged.

I will not go into depth on my improv lessons. But I will share a simple lesson, just so you know what goes on in an empty room with four chairs and a bunch of immature adults. One I will teach on this tour is "The Firing Exercise." Two improvisers take the stage—one is the boss, the other the employee. I instruct the boss to invite the employee to take a seat and start by complimenting the employee on all the ways they excel at their job. The purpose of this is to give the employee value (all effective scenes have characters who value one another), and to tell us what business this is and what the duties are. This establishes a base reality with expectations so we know when they are broken.

> *"Sister Cathryn, you are an excellent teacher at this Catholic school. The children love you, you're always on time, and you always come prepared with interactive and engaging lessons."*

Then the boss will get to the firing. They will say they have undeniable proof or evidence of the employee doing something totally unusual and inappropriate.

> *"Unfortunately, though, I have to let you go. It was reported to me that you are arriving early and defecating on our property. I didn't believe it, but then I went out to the schoolyard and saw fresh human feces."*

The employee will then admit that they have been doing the unusual thing, and then they will provide their justification, and it must be for a reason that they think is good for the business or organization. This is to express the power of good intentions. I call it "good intention island," and it is the island you swim to when you are accused of something evil, stupid, inappropriate, or destructive. You don't have to know what is on the island, nor the exact reason for your behavior, but you have to swim toward it, insisting that you had the best of intentions. This creates the "Walter White" principle, which is, you want the audience to understand and even root for your behavior.

Breaking Bad was extremely popular, in part, because it was a meth dealer working to provide and protect his family. The writers on the show kept elevating his dastardly deeds to see how long people would be in his corner. If he were just a villain, people would have tuned out immediately. So you give your "well-intentioned" reason:

> *"Catholic schools are getting a reputation for being stale and boring. So I thought I'd inject a little taboo into my lessons, while still being educational. We're studying biology, so I'm showing them how humans fit into the ecosystem by consuming and producing."*

Then I let the scene play out however they like. The boss can try to understand this more or frame the behavior: "So you're trying to be more taboo to keep Catholic school more relevant?" And the employee can continue to explain or play the frame they were just given: "That's right. Which is why you'll notice I've taught the dance team how to twerk."

It's a simple exercise that establishes a clear base reality, an unusual behavior, a logic, a frame, good intentions, and a significant amount of "Yes, and-ing."

Okay, that's it for the lesson. I hope I didn't bore or offend too many of you. A common risk with improv.

I teach my first workshop, and I do so effectively and easily. It feels weird to boast about that. I've never been great at selling myself, and as this book expands with every word, few sentences feel as foreign as the ones where I talk about my strength in something. But I am trying to be better at being myself, and I can't do that if I willfully ignore my strengths. So there. I am an adept teacher. And I should be. The amount I borrowed for grad school, $70k, will turn just about anyone into a decent anything. That kind of money would have made Kimmy Schmidt a competent family therapist. Loyola Marymount, one of the top-rated education universities in the country, took my money and molded me into an effective educator. And not just any educator. A special educator. I am a special education teacher. Or at least, I was one. I suppose I still am, so long as I am educating in some capacity.

I haven't taught in a classroom setting in almost a year, but I teach improv now. And while my "students" are not in special education, every technique I've implored to help some twenty-something take their rudimentary fart joke and make it a colossal windbreaker is a special education tool. The misconception is that special education only applies for a small percentage of individuals. That the rest of us do not require, nor would benefit from, special education. The truth is most of us require special education, and it's only a select few who don't.

Special education is a term used to describe a branch of education in which the students have identifiable learning challenges ranging from auditory processing deficits, to autism-like behaviors, to being visually or hearing impaired. Down syndrome would classify as special education, as would attention or hyperactivity disorders. Special education targets learning challenges and accommodates or adjusts for them.

A small percentage of the population is innately equipped to learn through any means, whether it be auditory, visual, or kinesthetic. These people are highly intelligent, near geniuses, or at the very least, have stools with their name embossed on them at the Genius Bar. The rest of us have our learning strengths or learning challenges, and depending on the skill set of our teachers and schools, we may receive instruction in the modality that fits our learning style, or we may not.

If we are unfortunate enough to go to a public school where the demand is so great that we are placed in a classroom with thirty-five other individuals, it is unlikely that the person positioned in the front of the classroom has the time or aptitude to teach to thirty-five individuals, each with their own unique learning proclivities. And if we go to a private school with smaller class sizes, then we probably have the money and resources to compensate for any lack of educational variety.

So often, money is the determining factor, and being rich or poor doesn't affect your biological make-up for information processing and conceptual understanding. It just eliminates the distractions or improves the conditions for learning. So when you think of special education, I encourage you not to think about the classroom isolated from the rest of the school, the short bus, or the student with an accompanying adult, but rather, the teacher who got you to love reading by giving you a copy of *Choke*, or reinforced the periodic table through skate-board brands, or used The Roots to explain social injustice. That was special education, and you're smarter and better off for it. The moment we recognize education is about accessibility, and not superiority, is the moment we might actually save ourselves.

Perhaps you're wondering, *if we all have learning challenges, then how come so many of us are educated with no help?* To which I would say, most of us have help, even if that help is just having a parent who has the time to sit with us. Furthermore, the number of us who are actually educated is not that high. The educational bar has been lowered into the basement, and even then, a shit ton of us weasel our way through, anyhow, only to rise to the ranks of bankers, politicians, and academics. And that's the problem. We rank any position that makes money higher than any position that enriches. Which, in the end, will leave us bankrupt. I don't care much for bumper stickers, but if you can read one, thank a teacher. And then donate to your local school. This has been a public service announcement brought to you by me, a public servant.

For lunch, we walk to Shake Shack, which, two years ago, would have been such a treat for me. But since we are living in the time of ubiquitous gratification, I've lived next to a Shake Shack for months and have eaten there a dozen times.

When I first moved to LA, I sort of became obsessed with this quest to try all the great cheeseburgers. Taking advantage of the previously mentioned abundance of LA, I would drive all over the city, trying different ones, ranking them, researching, and talking with others. I also gained an easy twenty pounds. A lot has happened in those eight years. For starters, I'd have to work to eat a bad burger. Not really, but most burgers in LA are very good. Food is excellent right now. And so is TV, and rap music, and books. Even movies are making a comeback. And it's all at our fingertips. We are in the golden age of just about everything. Everything except equality, social justice, immigration, and education. But those shortcomings aren't coming at the expense of our Grub Hubs or Hulus, so we haven't exactly been moved beyond tossing some humanitarian breadcrumbs into the lake of social media. But I got news for ya: Breadcrumbs aren't enough to feed a duck, let alone a country. Life has called on us less, and we still let it go to voicemail.

For the record, the Shake Shack burger was the best burger I've been underwhelmed by. Sometimes I think our manifest destiny is so ingrained in us that it's not the perfect burger I want, but the quest to find one. It's not a sequel to Star Wars we want. It's the yearning for one.

In 1995, I was twelve. I, like a lot of budding teenagers, was attracted to, and spent a lot of time thinking about, women. Specifically, women who seemed particularly dialed in to being attractive. The Internet wasn't quite what it is today, and *Playboy* still ruled the roost, and its golden goose was Pamela Anderson. I don't recall my first introduction to her; it seems now like I always knew about her. I never watched *Baywatch*, but perhaps it was just that *Baywatch* was a thing. Pop culture used to be objective. Or at least, the understanding that *pop* meant *popular*. I'm not so sure now. It's much more subjective. What one might classify as popular, might not even ping the radar for someone else. We should probably change it from pop(ular) culture to sub(jective) culture.

For most of my life, people sort of all knew about the same TV shows, movies, music, sports, and celebrities. So regardless, wherever I first encountered her, I quickly made her a staple of my daily daydreams and fantasies. It was a smooth integration. She was attractive, naked in magazines, and I was thinking about sex a lot.

At a sleepover once, some friends and I rented *Barb Wire*, the action movie she starred in, because we had heard she appeared naked at some point. We were all very disappointed. The nudity is brief, and the fun even briefer. Nevertheless, the pursuit to see her naked remained. And it seems weird to type this out, but the act of seeing her naked aided my imagination of having sex with her, which is what I wanted, even though I don't know that I ever directly said it to anyone, or even myself.

And then a videotape of her having sex was released. And by *released*, I mean someone stole it from a safe in Pamela and Tommy's house and sold it to an adult video production company. It's horrendous, when you think about it. The '90s were rich with public dehumanizing. But I was twelve, and I wasn't thinking about that. I was thinking about sex with Pamela Anderson, and suddenly my deepest sexual fantasy came true as much as it ever realistically could. It was like I had jerked off into a magic lamp.

There was no way I would ever have sex with Pamela Anderson. The obstacles were too many to name. She was older than me, and rich and famous and cool, and on and on and on. So the idea that I could watch her have sex made me believe that if the world wasn't my oyster, it was at least my clam, which turned out to not be so good.

I got my hand on the video and watched it. Wow! It was authentic, which is not to say it matched my fantasy, but it was Pam Anderson having sex, so it was great. What's that novelty T-shirt: "Skiing is like sex. Even when it's bad, it's still good." Yeah, well, Pam Anderson having sex is like Pam Anderson having sex. Even if it's bad, it's not, because it's Pam Anderson having sex. But then, like any pornography, it eventually lost its allure. I mean, how weird would it be if that video was still in heavy rotation for me? But its impact has been everlasting. I got exactly what I wanted, and it didn't really change my life, except that it changed my life. That experience taught me that wanting something is often more powerful than having something. So be careful what you wish for lest you get it, and then you have nothing left to wish for.

Josh teaches his lesson, and then we chat with the proprietors for a few minutes before going back to the Airbnb. Josh's lesson didn't go as he intended, and he's self-critical on the walk back. He says I did a much better job. He vows to make some adjustments for the next one. I don't like comparing our lessons because it feels unnecessary and counterproductive to our mission. But I admire him for being reflective and striving to make improvements.

When we get back "home" (a definition that will become more loose as the days go by), we both re-up on sleep. Remember, Josh didn't sleep well. And I, well...I like to nap. Then we go out to eat again. I could get used to this life on the road. Sleep, eat, goof, repeat.

Josh is looking for romance on this trip so he sits across from me, swiping away on his phone. My generation has made it so you don't have to lift a finger for dating and casual sex. It's hard to not see this as the next step before intercourse with robots. That's not to say the dating from these apps can't be fruitful or loving. But I imagine it's only going to get easier. And what would be easier than falling in love over a connection made through a computer? *Fucking the computer.* I suppose people do that now with VR POV escorts, but the online part is still leagues behind its action-adventure counterparts. You can create a soldier who looks just like you, and then go whoop Nazi ass in World War II or dominate Peyton Manning in the Super Bowl. It is only a matter of time before we'll be customizing our avatars with our same faces, better bodies, and more generous genitalia. Then we'll undress our little Sim and let Peyton Manning dominate us on a whole new field. Sure, people are looking for connections, but they can do that on Reddit. We're just going to strip down and outsource all the parts of being in a relationship to different aspects of the digital age. I fuck my robot, go to message boards to talk *Game of Thrones*, and take a vacation with my Instagram followers. Life has never asked less of us.

Our first live show starts with us sitting in on The Torch Theatre's popular storytelling/improv show. And while I'm listening to the monologist tell a story about meeting her last boyfriend in a diner, I realize that I'm hundreds of miles from home, doing improv with strangers in front of strangers. It's easy enough because there is no script, but it's also ridiculous because there is no script. It's not like we're *Hamilton*. We're not even a community theatre's reimagining of *Hamilton*. We're two idiots making each other laugh, and we somehow got enough people to listen to us that we can travel the country. Not enough to make it profitable, but enough that people will volunteer their free time to listen to us. It's an amazing thing. And while I'm thinking about this, I forget to take part in the show I came out for, effectively making this a seven-hour trip to watch a show. Life asked for too much.

Fortunately, I get a second chance to improvise. We record a live episode of our podcast, our second of the tour, but our first from the road, and it's a blast. We test the mics with what will be our running bit for the trip. Shortly before I left for this trip, during my dad's visit for my grandpa's memorial service, my dad fell on the beach and dropped his phone in the beach. Notice I didn't say sand. That's because he marvelously got it in both the sand and the ocean. So before every live show, we test the mics with a variation of this incident as a tongue twister:

"My papa propelled his PalmPilot off the pier."

"My daddy dropped his device in a divot."

"My father fell on his phone."

"My daddy dons the Donald's dressings." (This one refers to my dad's Trump attire.)

Funny enough, my dad has a history with beach and phone calamity. It's also impressive because he doesn't spend much time at beaches or with phones. But once, he and I were at the beach, and two young couples came up and asked if he would take their photo. I took this personally because I was much closer to their age group and couldn't figure out why they would ask him and not me. Don't we all gravitate toward generational proximity? Especially when it's regarding technology?

It would prove to be a catastrophic error on their part. It took my dad so long to figure out how to operate the camera function on the phone, that while the couples were posing with their backs to the ocean, a wave snuck up behind them and splashed against one of the dude's calves. It startled him and he flinched, which knocked his girlfriend's purse onto the ground just in time for another small wave to break right into her purse, drowning her phone and glasses. She yells at him, and he yells back at her. They collect their phone before my dad ever even snapped a pic. So while they will have nothing to remember that moment by, I most certainly will never forget it.

Our first guests that host us are Jacque and José, the founders and proprietors of The Torch Theatre. José took the workshop, and it's amazing that I could have anything to teach someone who owns and operates a small business. That's leagues above where I'm at. But I guess, while he was busy investing in his future, I was learning how to heighten a second beat of an improv scene by taking the character to work, home, play. I guess you could say both Jose and I work, and live in a home, and play. But only one of us "works" as a chatty astronaut, who, at "home," is also chatty, and for play, he's on the golf course being…tight-lipped because you have to stay ahead of the audience.

Jacque tells us a story about a DUI and the infamous Arizona Sheriff Joe who mandated tent prisons—outdoor tarp-covered confinements for prisoners. José tells us about a near-death experience as a kid, that put him in the hospital, and he missed out on the NBA All-Star game or something. If you want the full stories, I will point you in the podcast's direction because, a) they are not my stories to tell, and b) we could use the listeners.

One thing I like most about our podcast is the structured socializing. There's storytelling up top, where I get to ask questions. Then we have about twenty minutes to goof around then another story, and then more goofing around, and then we go home. It's turned me into a compartmentalized fun guy.

Fun guy should probably be in quotes. One of my most pressing issues, and the reason I don't go to parties often, is my struggle to get out of a conversation, or to join one. When I smoked cigarettes, that was my tool. I'd join or leave conversations by either going for a smoke or finishing up a smoke. But since I stopped smoking, I float through a party like one of those bobbers in the ocean, bumping into occasional schools of fish or two dudes lost out at sea, talking about representation. When I tell people this, they advise using the excuse of having to use the bathroom or getting another drink, and they insist this is universal and widely accepted. But if it's universal, then it's no better than just saying, *I'm tired of talking about this subject*, or *I'm tired of talking to you*, or both. People are always going to the bathroom and getting another drink when I'm talking to them, and I took them at their word. But now that I know the code, I'm wondering, *Are people "peeing" with more regularity when talking with me? Is there a horde of people in the bathroom, hiding from me? When I legit go to the bathroom, are people wondering why I lost interest?* This code is hurtful and confusing. We should all just wear name tags, but instead of our names, it should list the last three opinions we've had, and you just approach the people whose opinions interest you, and then you go down the list, dissecting each attractive opinion, at length, and then you say, "I guess that covers it," and then you move on.

After the show, Jacque takes us to the local bar for a couple of beers. This bar could be the bar in my hometown. Have I traveled across the country only to find myself back home, minus the familiar faces? We talk about the improv scene, and Jacque says she took improv classes in other cities before moving to Phoenix to start The Torch Theatre. She seems to be pursuing her manifest destiny with a spirit I envy. She's living her dream, even in hundred-degree heat. And I guess that's the point. Living your dreams isn't about meeting your expectations. It's asking from life as much as it asks from you. Our dreams aren't realistic, but that doesn't mean we can't live some version of them. After all, no one dreams of going through a breakup and losing a loved one, and then riding a train to play make-believe with strangers. When we're kids, we all dream of being on *SNL*, or owning a home in the country, or living in a major metropolitan city and making major metropolitan money. But those dreams come with compromises, and mortgages, and public shaming all the same. And what kid is going to dream realistically. They should. It would make life more palatable. But kids are idealistic idiots. And that's fine. It's the only time in life when you get to be one and be happy. Unless you're Adam Sandler. He seems to be the anomaly. The rest of us adults, with our idiotic idealism, find our fates closer to Jimi Heselden, the millionaire owner of the Segway company, who rode one off a cliff. Careful about flying too close to the sun on wings made of mall chariots.

After a pitcher of beer, Jacque brings us to our Airbnb, and I crash hard for the third time in a day. I am exhausted. It takes a lot of work to distract myself from heartache. Although the heartache probably would have wiped me out just the same, so it's hard to say what the culprit of this fatigue is.

Josh elects to walk across the street to a bar and try his hand at some local romance. I fold out the futon and think about how, in setting my sights on the future, I am closer to a life as a comedian and further from a life with companionship. So while Josh goes out to ask more from life, I wonder if I have asked too much or gotten exactly what I wanted.

DAY 2: PHOENIX, ARIZONA

Population: sex techs, baseball non-fans, retired instructors

I am, at best, having an allergic reaction. And at the very worst, transforming into a werewolf. I wake up and rub my eye, and it's that feeling where a part of your body you've come to know so well feels foreign. It's swollen. I say *werewolf* because once, when I was eight, I had an unknown allergic reaction in the middle of the night. I could feel my lip heavy and bloated. I didn't get out of bed, but instead pulled the covers up over my face. When my mom came in, she said, "What's wrong," and I mumbled through fat lips, "I've turned into a werewolf."

"Don't be silly," she said. "Everything's fine."

We had recently watched *Teen Wolf,* so she assumed I had a bad dream. But when she pulled the covers down to reveal my plump smoochers, she later said it took every ounce of her not to scream in horror, which would have surely fanned my flames of panic. That's my mom for you. Even in the midst of mythical beasts, she keeps her cool for her little wolf boy.

If my mom, Claudia, ever sweated being a parent, she never let me see it. She's like John McClane in the fourth *Die Hard* film, *Live Free or Die Hard*. She's seen it all before, and she can launch a car into a helicopter or take down a jet on foot, just as easily as she can throw me a pirate-themed birthday party with actual buried treasure, or calmly receive a phone call from the police in the middle of the night, informing her I was picked up for streaking. This, I suspect, is because my sisters served as the prequels. They were her first run-ins with danger and deception. This book is not about airing their dirty laundry, so just know, even if I wasn't born into this world a rule follower, anything less than swiping some of my parents' private stash of glamour drugs would have seemed derivative. My mom is also like John McClane in that she is my everyday hero. Here come the accolades.

Before I really dive into singing my mom's praises, let me give you a little history lesson on *Die Hard* and my relationship to it, as it might be helpful for context, and as I might never get another chance to have an audience for my affection for one of the greatest movies of all time.

The plot of *Die Hard* is simple. John McClane (Bruce Willis), a New York cop, flies to Los Angeles to be with his family on Christmas. He and his wife Holly are separated, but they're working on it. John goes to visit her at work for the Christmas party, and then bad guys show up, take over the building, and hold Holly and her co-workers hostage, leaving John no choice but to defeat them and save his wife. It's one unprepared, improvising good guy versus fifteen well-organized bad guys with machine guns.

Die Hard was the first action movie I ever saw, and it was with, guess who...my mom. We were on a road trip and stayed in a motel, and it must have been on HBO. I was maybe eight. Here's what I remember. We were both watching from the bed, and every time something violent happened, we would pull the blanket up over our eyes. Then one of us would peek to see if the coast was clear. Omitting violence from that movie left us with about thirty minutes of a man arriving to LA and then running around lost in an office building. I'm surprised I gave it a second chance. But even though I didn't see John McClane shoot a guy through a conference table, or run across broken glass with bare feet, or hang a guy using a heavy chain, I knew this movie was delivering on heroics. And what's better, it was adult heroics. I used to brag about this to friends: "But I've seen *Die Hard*, and I was seven." This was usually said in my defense when I was too scared to go on a roller coaster, or try a backflip on a trampoline, or smoke a Black & Mild stolen from a 7-Eleven. No one cared. I still got duct-taped, pants-ed, and thrown in the neighbor's yard.

As of the publication of this book, there are five *Die Hard* films. None match the quality of the first, but some come close and are pretty fun. What they all have in common is John McClane, a ruthless bad guy, a family member in peril, a side-kick, and an attitude of annoyance from McClane. What four of the five movies have in common—and this is the key—is that they were not written as *Die Hard* movies. *Die Hard* was initially a sequel to the movie *The Detective*, based on a book series. *Die Hard 2* was based on a book called *58 Minutes*. *Die Hard with a Vengeance* was originally a script called *Simon Says*. *WW3.com* was the title to the script that eventually became *Live Free or Die Hard*.

This all matters because those were stories written without John McClane in mind, which is why they work. The plot isn't about John McClane. It's about what the villains are trying to do, and then you just plug crotchety McClane in there to stop them. Which is why *A Good Day To Die Hard* sucks. It was an original *Die Hard* script, so the focus was too much on John

McClane's plan. The dude flies to fucking Russia in it. You can't pack a bag, water your plants, book a plane ticket, and ask a friend to take you to the airport, go through security, eat a cinnamon roll, and still preserve the attitude of not wanting to be there. And it's in that attitude that McClane's true heroism lies. He's a "fly in the ointment, a monkey in the wrench, a pain in the ass," because he has no choice.

Superheroes choose to be good guys because they feel it's their duty, or it makes them feel good, or they're trying to impress someone or live up to their legacy. Anything that makes them get up in the morning and lace up their boots with the gusto of kicking ass. But McClane…McClane would rather be at home with his family, drinking a beer with his feet up. Give him the choice of the simple life versus the heroic life, and he'd choose the simple life ten times out of ten. But he can't because he knows what needs to be done, so he does it.

There's a line in the fourth installment, where Justin Long's character, Matthew Feral, points this out. McClane says he's not a hero because if there was someone else to do it, he'd let them do it. But there isn't, so he's got to do it. And his sidekick, Feral, corrects him, saying, "Doing it when you don't want to is what makes you a hero."

The misconception is that John McClane is an everyman. People say Bruce Willis changed action movies because he didn't look like Arnold or Sly, and that he reminded people of themselves or their neighbor. But the truth is if saving the day were easy, we'd all be heroes. It's precisely because it's hard that makes McClane far more heroic than his muscle-built, com-mando, ex-marine, superhuman peers. Those are all average heroes. McClane is anything but average, and everything that makes a hero hard to be. The reason all the iterations of *Die Hard* that were spun out of previous scripts work is because true heroism isn't about the hero's self-interest. It's about preventing the threat that imposes itself onto others. The hero isn't focused on themselves. The hero is focused on others.

Before we go any further, I think my mom—my hero—would appreciate it if I devoted five hundred words to our favorite antagonist to hate: the best villain, Alan Rickman. My mom and I love Rickman's performances as a villain. He's most known for Hans Gruber in *Die Hard*, but he also played the Sheriff of Nottingham in *Robin Hood: Prince of Thieves*; and Elliott Marston, the racist Australian rancher, in *Quigley Down Under*. Mother and son love these movies because of their simplistic stories, one-ish man (he always has some help from sidekicks, wildcards, and merry men) against a barrage of thugs, always under the command of Rickman's arrogant, sharp, suave, and humorous big bad. We enjoy his screen time as much as the hero's, because, as loathsome as his characters are, they are also where so much of the comic relief comes from.

Over the course of every movie, whatever character Rickman plays becomes frustrated, humiliated, and sloppy with every victory by the hero. In *Quigley Down Under*, he plays a vile ranch owner who hires Tom Selleck's character to hunt Aborigines. When he's making his disgusting proposal at dinner with all the muster of a pompous scumbag, the movie cuts to the outside of his home, and Rickman is thrown through the window. He gets thrown out of his own house in front of all his men. And in *Die Hard*, his entrance is magnificent. He rolls up with henchmen, dressed in an Italian suit, and there's orchestra music playing. By the end, when Holly Gennero McClane reduces him to nothing but a "common thief," he lunges for her, his hair a mess, and screams like a child, "I am an exceptional thief, Mrs. McClane!" Then he gets thrown off a building.

As the Sheriff of Nottingham, Rickman kills his cousin, cancels Christmas, and orders women to his room every fifteen minutes, adding that the next one needs to "bring a friend." At the end, he's trying desperately to wed Maid Marian. Running out of time, and in a panic, he orders the priest to skip the vows, and when he tries to wield a sword, it's too heavy for him. He gets stabbed by his own dagger.

Rickman's vileness makes his characters despicable, but his humility makes him relatable, which is what you need from a bad guy. He plays villains that are so easy to despise, yet there's a magnetism about them. You likely can't relate to their nature or their desire to exert their will, regardless of the law or the cost, but that feeling of exhaustion and frustration is always humorous, if not a little relatable. My mom and I appreciate him because we know how crucial he is to a story. In order for a hero to rise and pull up others, there has to be a worthy foe keeping people down.

Claudia and I have always been students of the hero genre. As an elementary and literature teacher, my mom knew all there was to know about the hero's journey. And me, a comic-book and action-movie junkie, was born into the world of heroes. I was doing some astrology research because my friends had said I was too nice to be a Scorpio and that my rising must be something else. So I asked my mom when I was born. "Seven fifty-eight p.m.," she said. "I remember because *Magnum P.I.* was on."

Magnum P.I. was a television show—or I should say *is*, because it's been rebooted—about a private investigator in Hawaii. The original starred Tom Selleck, and from what I can remember, it was mostly about car chases, Hawaiian shirts, and occasionally a helicopter. And so, the first thing my mom and I did together was watch a slightly campy story for adults, about a good guy catching a bad guy.

On drives home up a windy, two-lane mountain road, my mom would tell me we were being chased by bad guys like in

Magnum, and she would take the turns just a little faster to make it feel like a chase. She would ask me to look and see if we had lost them, and we always had. Although, sometimes I would say I thought I saw them, just so she would speed up.

There we were, mother and son in hot pursuit. Or I guess, being pursued. It just occurred to me, we likely would have been the villains under this dynamic.

My mom has said, "You always loved heroes rescuing people. You had a homemade Superman cape, and you'd fly around the house, going 'I'll save you, Mom.'"

I'll be honest, I had forgotten all about that. But when she said it, I had a memory of blocking the door from invaders and phantom-fighting imaginary bad guys. My mom said she wasn't sure where it came from, but she encouraged it. And there's no better method of encouragement than modeling.

My mom has John McClane'd her entire life. She was the oldest of three, and while my grandma worked, my mom stepped in as matriarch. At twenty, Claudia started her own journey as mother, giving birth to Michelle. And two years later, she brought Nicola into this world. In her thirties, she became pregnant with future bestselling author and all-around good boy, Jacob, ensuring that she would be a maternal figure from seven to seventy.

I know a parent's job is never done, but from a practical standpoint, parents clock in at their child's birth and clock out when that child reaches eighteen. But my mom started when she was only a child herself, and she hasn't taken maternity leave from maternity in over sixty years. Now, she differs from John McClane in that she chose to be the provider and protector for so many, whereas John McClane didn't elect to be the hero at Nakatomi, or Dulles International, or New York City, or DC.

But besides her parenting tenure, my mom went back to school, got her teaching credential, taught for seventeen years, grassroots campaigned for Obama, got arrested in protest of George W. Bush, and simultaneously wore the hat of grandma and caregiver as her eldest daughter had kids and her own mother required more emotional, financial, and physical support. That's at least worth the dispatching of a dozen European thugs.

My mom has always done the job that needs doing, even when she didn't want to. How do I know this? Because every job worth doing has parts that suck. If they didn't, the job wouldn't be worth doing because everyone would do them. And not everyone is a stable sibling, a lifelong parent, a parent to their parent, and certainly not a public school teacher.

Now, my mom has said frequently that being a parent was the most rewarding and fulfilling part of her life, and I believe her. But I also know that not every aspect of that role, or the role of educator, has been rewarding or convenient. And still, my mom did it every day. Putting yourself in the position of caregiver and guardian is putting yourself in the position of willing and unwilling hero twenty-four-seven. Being a hero isn't about comparing yourself to others, nor should it be quantitatively measured or evaluated. But if observing heroics is important, there is no better model than my mom. Yippee-ki-yay...

Leap off Nakatomi Plaza and back into our Airbnb, with my infected peeper. As I study it in the mirror, Josh bursts out of his room and starts our day by regaling me with a near-fatal texting mishap he had late last night. It's not the details of his story I'm thinking about, either. At least, not for long. Something once happened with texting mishaps that was so outside my realm of expectations, that I am transported back to that event any time I'm even in the vicinity of texting misfires.

It was 2016, and I was lying in bed, in the early hours of the morning, when I received a message from my friend Marv. It was a video message and the freeze frame was blurry, but it looked like maybe an up-close photo of a hand giving a peace sign. I opened the message to see that the fingers in the peace sign were legs spread apart. Marv had an erection and was masturbating. The reason it looked like a hand gesture was because Marv was lying down and holding the phone up over his head, angled toward his legs, giving him the best angle for size. His moans pierced my ears, and in an unreasonable panic, I screamed his name, as if he, in the video, would hear me and stop. When I closed out of the video, there was a flurry of texts pleading me not to open it, explaining that it was for a girl, and asking politely for me to kill him: "Kill me!!!! Pleeeease!!!!" And then I guess he calmed down, because he offered his masturbatory mistake up as a segment for *We're Gross with Gilli Nissim.*

We're Gross is a late-night talk show I co-created with my friend Gilli, and I serve as the Andy Rictor to her Conan. The show is a response to glossy, polished celebrity culture that is supposed to make you feel incomplete so you'll buy whatever the ad executives are peddling during the break. Our show is about the filth and shame that binds us. But instead of casting it off, we own it and celebrate it.

Past segments have included reading emails and messages we've sent to crushes online, having a guest match pictures of our bowel movements to facts about us, sharing how much we have in our checking account, or pasting googly eyes above our genitals and having them perform scenes from *Dirty Dancing* and *A Few Good Men*. There is also a confessional segment where we and the audience share something we've kept to ourselves that burdens us, and we shout, "You're gross" and "That's okay!"

As much as the show is entertaining, I'm fairly certain I've grown to use it as a polygraph test for social acceptance. I hook my friends up to a chair in the audience, and instead of probing questions, I show them a slideshow of sixty pictures of my penis taken over the course of two months, set to Green Day's "Time Of Your Life," and then ask them if they still like me. Or I confess the things I want people to say at my funeral (that I'm a good improv coach and funnier than I gave myself credit for). I read their faces, trying to decipher the response. *Are we still friends?* Every time, the answer has been yes, even if it's a yes wrapped in pity.

I'll probably continue doing the show until the answer is no. And then I'll call them all frauds, move back to Colorado, substitute teach at my old high school, and push improv on the uninterested community. That's assuming it's not too extensive a background check. Which I'm sure it won't be. I've been drug tested for every job I've had, except for washing dishes and being a public school teacher.

We're Gross is cathartic, and so Marv's video made sense. Here's a deeply personal, embarrassing moment we can't take back, but that doesn't mean it devalues any of the involved parties. To protect people from feeling violated, we projected a screen grab and just played the audio. People groaned. A few people muttered, "Oh, come on." And you could hear bodies squirming and tightening up in the seats. It was quite a visceral production and produced quite the audible reaction, which is somewhat funny considering it was a pretty basic and relatable activity. I'm speaking of masturbation. Not sending videos. imagine if most of us masturbate, only like 85 percent of us send evidence of it. But sex and technology have always gone hand in hand, or genitals in hand.

Just as often as technology has increased accessibility (planes, trains, Segways), added convenience (iPods, Postmates, every episode of *Blue Bloods*), or expanded the exchange of information (Reddit deep dives on whether Stannis Baratheon from *Game of Thrones* is a praying mantis), it has been used just as often to help people get their rocks off, and usually that came first. Online payment systems and Blu-ray both owe their ubiquity to pornography. Right now, there are scientists actively working to connect us to life on other planets...probably so we can fuck it. Sex encourages the advancement of technology, and technology helps sex permeate the culture.

I was once sent a best-of compilation of something called the "running butthole challenge"—and that there were enough challengers to make a best-of and someone was up for collecting, editing, posting, and sharing said cut signals. If technology isn't paving the way for mainstreaming sexuality, it's at least setting a camera up on a bed so someone can run and jump and bop the screen with their fanny. It seems like orgasms are the proverbial carrot for advancement. And the stick...the stick is also the carrot. It depends on your kink.

Josh's close call wasn't this vivid, nor did it lead to mass entertainment. But somewhere out in cyberspace, an erotic image of my comedy partner drifts about, never to reach its intended destination.

I go to splash water on my face and realize there's something (more) unsymmetrical about my face. My eye is swollen. I can't tell if it's pink eye, but it's droopy and I wonder if I'm having that face paralysis people get when they're overworked or stressed. Someone told me Angelina Jolie has it. I often conflate my minor ailments with those of people who have accomplished much more, and I pair everything down. I have a few gray hairs. Gray hairs I'm sure came from the stress of teaching. Me and Obama have that in common. We both went gray from stress. He had to lead the free world and be the first black man to do it. I had to teach kids about the Pythagorean theorem.

And to do that, I had to re-learn the Pythagorean theorem. So you know, tomato, tomato.

Josh and I have plans today, so like the President, I throw on some shades and roll up my sleeves. No amount of bacteria in my eye will keep me from brunch and a baseball game. We are being treated to both by Josh's aunt and uncle. I'm thirty-three and still getting treated to meals by my friends' parents and relatives. I don't treat many people to meals, outside of girl-friends, an occasional student, and my grandpa. In fact, if I'm being embarrassingly honest, I've had former student-teacher lunches, both as student and teacher, and I was treated both times. My entire generation will be forever children staying over for dinner. I get a meatball sub at brunch. It is delicious.

At the baseball game, it's free bat day, but apparently the Arizona Diamondbacks don't subscribe to the notion that my generation is locked in arrested development. They refuse to give me a bat because, although I am as responsible as a child, I do not look like one. They might as well have said "we're only giving these out to humans who might not know better than to hit someone with them."

Nothing happened until the bottom of the seventh, which is the worst kind of baseball. It's like ordering a steak for dinner and waiting forty minutes only to get a house salad. Baseball is boring. If they had introduced it today, it wouldn't stand a chance. If improv was four hours at this pace, it would seem needlessly cruel.

The highlight was when *The Lion King* Cam surveyed the crowd. The gimmick here is that the camera will find some-one with a baby and play the score from *The Lion King* as the adult holds the baby up, replicating the famous scene from the Disney movie. Josh and I joked about what type of cam would find us, and we landed on the Pumbaa Cam, both of us accus-ing the other of being a Pumbaa—a stalky, chubby warthog.

Neither of us relents, and we settle on our new team name: Two Pumbaas.

I've never been much of a fan of baseball. Or any ball. I played little league, but not because I wanted to. My mom would insist I try a different sport every summer. I didn't have to stick with it the following summer; but I had to try it. And for reasons I can't place, I did little league maybe three or four summers. I was a pretty good batter. I remember having the highest batting average on the team, and this pissed off these twins Will and Bill Arnold. One reason it pissed them off was because I was so uncoordinated in every other aspect of the game, including waddling when I ran.

It wasn't a little waddle, either. In fact, my mom, so worried about it, filmed me flopping around and had my PE teacher review the tape like a referee. You know what he told her? It wasn't that I had bad joints or anything. I wasn't taking full strides. I was basically half-assed running because it was physical work. Also, I didn't really have a sense for how to move my body. I couldn't visualize fluid movement. On top of that, I was a little afraid of the ball. For all these reasons, I was always dumped in the outfield. I tried my best to catch any fly ball because if I had to chase it and throw it, I flopped around like a stick of string cheese that someone had whipped across the field.

My fondest memories of baseball were the games I went to with my mom. I grew up in Colorado, and neither she nor I were real baseball fans, but she would go in on season tickets for the Colorado Rockies with the other teachers from her school because it guaranteed a solid outing for the two of us at least a few times a year. It was nice that we weren't fans, when I think about it. There was no pressure to enjoy the game a certain way, and even when The Rockies lost, we still had an excellent time. We had our favorite parking lot, one that was cheap, but not too far of a walk. And we'd usually have time to browse Tattered Cover Book Store, and we would buy waters from street vendors and smuggle them in. But my favorite part was when we had the money to get these Domino's baked chicken wings. They were so good. Not too messy and just the right amount of crisp. I can't recall a single home run or a winning catch, but I can tell you that we'd get four drumsticks and four wings, and my mom would clean the drumstick to the bone and insist I was missing plenty of chicken by only eating the wings. My mom and I spent multiple summers driving an hour to eat a box of chicken wings, surrounded by twenty-five thousand people. I loved those games.

My only other experience with professional sports is once in LA, I went to a Dodgers game and sat in the all-you-can-eat seats. So basically, my relationship to sports is mostly food. And that's all the sports you'll get to read about in this book. Actually, there's a bit about golf later.

After the game with Josh, where I drank a big beer and had nachos, we go to Native Grill & Wings, a semi-local chain, or a local semi-chain. I'm not entirely sure. I've never seen one before, but it definitely has that feel of a restaurant that wants you to know if you have one in your hometown, this one will feel like that one, even if it's not. You're home, even when you aren't. That's the appeal of chain restaurants. You know what you're getting.

I do wonder, though, if food will go the route of TV and music, individualizing your meal based on your preferences and eating history. You like a burger and fries, so here is a dipping ramen that tastes like a cheeseburger and is vegan, and a beer that tastes like sweet potatoes and is gluten free. Then the individualized experience will become routine, and people will want a shared experience the way the Super Bowl keeps getting more popular because it's a live event. Will people line up and pay twenty-five dollars for a bite of one big meatball so they can taste what everyone else is tasting? I think I just described Los Angeles pop-up restaurants. And yes, I would shell up the cash for a taste of that behemoth of beef.

As the server politely takes our order and diligently fills my ice tea a half-dozen times, I wonder, *Who lives in Maricopa?* I'm constantly fascinated by why people live anywhere. I'm self-conscious about how pretentious that makes me sound, but it's rooted more in ignorance than entitlement. LA makes that question easy. It's obvious. Seventy-five percent of people in LA live there because they want to be in the entertainment business. The other 25 percent are there because they were born there, and if you can or can't afford it, there's no reason to leave. The weather is always nice, and every band tours through the city. Plus, movie stars.

I suspect the population of Maricopa lives here because it's inexpensive and the burdens of being part of a community are light. No one seems interested in what you're doing. I can imagine taking immense comfort in that. I will ponder the intentions of almost every populace we encounter on this trip. I will never ask a single soul about it, because I can't figure out how to do it without sounding like a jerk. Fortunately, I'll come upon a few verbose folks who volunteer their reasons.

We go to Harrah's Casino, and I lose five dollars with the naturalness of using the restroom. A win for me. Gambling is not my thing. I don't enjoy it. I'll stupidly spend money I don't have, but I don't feel comfortable risking the money I have. I recognize that if I win, I have arguably free money to spend. But I wouldn't make that argument, because the suspense that is entwined with the nature of gambling makes me uncomfortable. I'm not forking over money to feel vulnerable. I use money to purchase things that make me feel safe, like clothes and food and headphones that cancel noise so I don't hear the outside world, even when it's an oncoming car or a mugger. It's an imperfect system, I recognize. It is also the disposition of an introvert. According to the book *Quiet*, introverts are risk-averse, and extroverts are reward sensitive. I am soundly an INFJU—introvert, intuition, feeling, judging, unlucky.

Now, most personality questionnaires don't test for luck, but if you're curious, here's what you do. Divide the number of times you've won money by the number of times you've been attacked by a wild animal. If the answer is greater than zero, you're lucky. Most of my friends have a story of winning a lot of money. That's never been the case for me. I don't have the confidence to be a gambler. I have the confidence to be a folly.

Once, as a child, we stumbled onto an elk farm (this is not a thing I thought existed until we were at a rec league soccer game, and next to the field was a fenced-off area with a bunch of elk in it), and an elk charged me and knocked me down. And once, in Paris, a pigeon flew into my face, smashing its greasy wings across my cheeks. And finally, once, while walking to work, a bee flew into my mouth. I don't think a guy who has those kinds of stories also has a story about how he won $500 playing Craps.

Josh and I take a dip in the large Roman-style outdoor pool because I am a pool fiend. As I am getting in, a woman, who later reveals herself to be a retired teacher, instructs me on how to climb down the ladder so I don't slip and hit my head. It makes sense she would correct my form. Not because it was wrong, but because educators often have trouble allowing for variation.

I've met very few teachers who don't have some strong feelings about being in control. But as classroom occupancy continues to balloon, it's harder to know if it's the nature of the educator or the nurturing of the school system that makes them hyper-controlling. Give anyone thirty-five adolescents and see if they don't come up with a rule or two.

Then later, when I tell Josh the water is cold, she corrects me and says in fact it isn't cold. As an educator, this drives me doubly mad. For starters, she was not part of the conversation, something teachers recognize as rude, unless it's them doing it. Then they recognize it as monitoring. And moreover, how water feels on my body is not something I can be wrong about. We can be objective about the temperature, but not about my relationship to it. I hope she loses a thousand dollars, and I don't care how. Could be gambling. But she could also lose her laptop down the sewer. I'm flexible. It's what makes me an adept teacher. I don't insist something has to be a certain way. Like that the water must not feel cold!

We are in bed by 2:00 a.m., which is not great because we have to be up in four hours to catch our next train. This is because Josh is a night owl and I am a peacekeeper, so I kept him company. I don't want to abandon my buddy and cause a rift. I will put less and less effort into this as the trip goes on.

I will get even less than four hours of sleep. I can't shake the retired teacher's instruction on how to enter a pool, and her public correction to my subjective interpretation. Is this gaslighting? It sucks. If it's perhaps possible that I am incorrect about how to operate and interpret my own body in nature, what other relationships to the outside world might I be wrong about? Are all my perceived "warm" relationships actually cold? Am I not a graceful swimmer in the sea of community, but a dead corpse bumping up against the legs of cooler surfers? Or am I just sensitive to someone telling me how to interpret the world, when it's that very thing I'm trying to do. I'm unsure how I relate to the world at this point, who I am in it, but at least I thought I knew temperatures. Does everyone know more than me? Or maybe she was just lonely and wanted to start a conversation, and questions are more vulnerable than statements because questions start from a place of unknowing, and statements start from a place of certainty, and Western culture values certainty, even to our detriment, which is why kids have to be taught that saying, "I don't know," actually opens up an opportunity to learn, making us more intellectually fit than insisting we know something when we don't, robbing us of the opportunity to experience, and then...fuck. I stayed up all night ruminating on a retired teacher's prompt. Cool. She gave me homework.

"The experienced educator elicited expletives and existential evaluations."

DAY 3: TRAIN

Passengers: dying alone, traveling with kids, breakfast companions, and Alpine, TX

Catching the train is not for me. Although, maybe that's not accurate. It's 4:00 a.m., and at that hour, nothing is for me, outside of dreaming and an occasional late night trip to the fridge.

Our train leaves in forty-five minutes. I pre-scheduled a Lyft, and we are in a rush to take showers and catch our ride because at four in the morning, you are always in a rush. Otherwise, you wouldn't be up.

Showers are extremely important today because we are riding for twenty-five hours and forty-six minutes, the longest train ride of the trip. Our Lyft driver waits patiently for us, even though Josh and I are well past the five-minute courtesy window. I make it to the Lyft first and sit in the car with our driver, whose name I don't catch, but whose story I do. He tells me he moved to Maricopa to take care of someone in his family. He is vague about it, but I am able to infer that he made the move out of obligation, not opportunity. He looks to be in his late forties, and I bet, as a child, when he drew a picture in school of what he wanted to be as an adult, it wasn't living in Maricopa, Arizona, driving around tardy podcasters and taking care of his partner's parents. But maybe being married and finding love was. Sometimes there isn't enough construction paper to include all of life.

No kid ever draws themselves as an actor for twenty years, and then draws themselves moving back home to install tile floors for their successful friend's tile company, or waiting tables at the local pizza joint as they care for their aging parents. There are no drawings of living in the shadow of your parents until they die. In fact, death is rarely drawn in schools, and when it is, it warrants a call home, which is an overreaction. Although, you can't take chances with youth and death. But knowing death is coming is not morbid. It's practical. Considering it's the one guarantee in life, we expend a lot of energy putting it outside our mind. It shouldn't be required, but I don't see anything wrong with encouraging kids to draw themselves on their deathbed. *Who is there? What are you thinking back on? Are you alone?* Good for you. I think dying alone is the selfless thing to do.

When I talk about not having kids, people often offer up the proposition that it will be sad to grow old alone, and to die alone. And they are likely right, but it will be sad for one person. Me. And then I'll be dead, and a nurse, if I'm lucky, or a fellow vagrant, if I'm unlikely, will toss my remains in a body bag, if I'm lucky, a garbage bag if I'm not, and that'll be that. But if I have a family, they'll all be there when I go, again if I'm lucky, or they'll Skype in, if I'm not, and then I'll pass and they will weep, and work will be hard to go back to, and the space I occupied will still feel warm but empty, and they'll cling to nostalgia for a holiday when I was around, and it will hurt for a lot of people. But if it's just me, the world goes on. And I get to haunt the cruise ship I died on, if I'm lucky, or *Arby's*, if I'm really lucky.

We make the train, and I immediately go back to sleep. But this only lasts an hour because in Tucson, we pick up a mother and her two daughters, who together, fight like three sisters. The mom whines to her daughter that she doesn't want to sit next to her other daughter because the daughter is sick. It occurs to me that being a lousy dad is part of what I'm afraid of, but maybe accepting that it's inevitable will bring me closer to coming around to the idea. I'm not saying this woman is a bad mom. I think good parenting comes in many forms. But at this moment, she is at least being a selfish adult, which is a stone's throw away from faulty role model, which is the house next to inadequate child rearing. Welcome to the neighborhood. There is no curfew.

I will never understand traveling with kids. And just so we're clear, I am not judging the mom. I wouldn't want to sit next to a sick kid for twenty hours either. But that's where this woman and I differ. I think about that all the time. She might not have considered it until she got on this train, which is why she seems so indignant. It just hit her. Or she did think about it, and she's a good person who still elected to have kids, and she's just exhausted from working hard to raise them. In either case, she's breaking some eggs to make an omelet, and I'm in the splash zone. So I elect to go eat breakfast because I get low blood sugar, and although I haven't seen a doctor about it, you don't need to go to medical school to know the noise pollution of other people doesn't go well with an empty stomach.

Josh and I have our first meal in the dining car, and it's cafeteria-style seating, which means there are tables of four, and if you are a party of one, two, or three, you can expect to be sat with any combination of parties of three, two, or one.

I'm telling you this because the firm tone the host uses to tell us suggests many people, in fact, do *not* expect to be sat with strangers.

The dining car is, as you might imagine, stretched red vinyl over steel booths with placemats that make the dining feel equally cheap and fine. We get two parties of one sitting across from us—a gentleman from El Paso and a young student from Hong Kong. The man from El Paso looks to be in his fifties, and he hates living in El Paso. So far, it does not seem that many people in the Southwest like where they live. He recently received an inheritance, and so he is using it to take train trips. This trip is a trial run to see how he likes the sleeping car. He tells us, "When I was a kid, all great movies took place on a train, and they romanticized it as the greatest thing ever. Now that I'm finally doing it, it isn't that great, but it's still nice." That's a pretty good review, or mission statement, for most things in America—trains, baseball, politics. Actually, politics are never nice. Chicken fingers in a diner are nice.

The young man from Hong Kong has been in the United States for two weeks and has already traveled by train from San Francisco to LA, and now he's on this train en route to Houston. Then he will go to New Orleans, and finally Florida, where he will take an internship at Disney. One man, a native, is coming to terms with the limitations of what train travel can do to improve your life, and the other, an immigrant, is traveling by train to dramatically improve his life. Maybe America is what you make of it. Or maybe all roads lead to Disney. And those that don't aren't worth traveling down.

I heard a rumor that there's a great burrito at the El Paso Amtrak, so when we stop, I make my way off the train in search of such burrito. I see people exiting the train, people waiting to board, a few stragglers, and a vendor with a cooler in tow, peddling water bottles, but no burrito stand. Not even a person with a burrito. So I reboard the train as burrito-less as before. I suppose I'll have to wait till I get back to LA for a good burrito.

Speaking of LA, when I get back on the train, I learn that the woman sitting across from us is from Echo Park and actually sells hummus to Josh at the Farmers Market. Here is where I would write, "Small world," except I'm trying to purge that phrase from my system. It means nothing except that the world is so small there isn't anything new to say. I will not loathe much on this trip, or in these pages, but my own use of trite phrases makes my blood boil. Shit, there I used another one. I just don't see the point in saying the same wheelbarrow full of sayings my entire life. I should never say the same thing twice, or eat at the same place twice. Life is too grand and vast to revisit. On the other hand, I will spend a considerable amount of these pages talking about the joy that comes from revisiting action movies over and over again. So what does that say? I suppose it says, "Experience words and language and food, because there is so much to say and so many ways to say it. But with movies, don't waste your time looking for a new way to tell an old story when the best version is right there in front of you."

We stop in Alpine, Texas, and we rush off in search of a drink and a bite to eat. We've been eating bad train food mostly, and we're all out of booze. At least, booze we smuggled on. You're not allowed to bring personal hooch on the train, and this is for good reason. Before this trip, the only train I took was a semi-regular three-hour run to San Diego, and I'd say one in three trips had someone intoxicated on something that made their disposition rowdy and the other passengers uneasy. Once, a man repeatedly said to seemingly no one in particular, "I'm dating Hilary Duff, and if you see her on Insta with some other dude, tell him I've got nunchucks and I'll fucking beat his ass!"

I have nothing beyond anecdotal evidence, but there seems to be a correlation between unstable people in public and the frequency of their use of the word *nunchucks*. I am always hyper-aware of how someone breaking a social contract—such as resisting the temptation to shout irrationally in a public space—can make me, and I assume most people, feel immediately trapped. Despite all the distinct characters, upbringings, family dynamics, and cultural relativism, the mood and attitude the nation has settled on is mostly subdued and quiet. Anything that falls outside the range of sitting quietly, and perhaps exchanging a few pleasantries to a stranger, registers as atypical. Unless you're at a live sporting event. Then, by all means, go HAM. If you shout, or just start asking a stranger questions, people take notice. It goes the other way, too. If you sleep somewhere in public, people keep an eye on you. I wonder what established the range that we all accept. I suspect it's movies. Movies surround the main actors with quiet extras so we can hear the stars talking. And they make sure no one is sleeping in the background, because that would suggest boring dialogue. I guess, even though we all assume we're the stars of the movies of our lives, we all identify with the background.

Recently, in an airport, I turned to my friend and asked if he thought airports and other common areas for public transportation had gradually gotten quieter over the years as more people got music and smartphones and tablets. Everyone could sort of tune out the outside world and just hush up and binge *Breaking Bad*. My friend suspected I might be right. But the stranger sitting next to us said I was wrong. She was a slightly older woman, and I only mention this because her age gave her experiences that pre-dated mobile technology.

"People have always been like this. Before smartphones, it was newspapers, magazines, and books. People don't talk to each other," she said, bitterly, almost as if she'd spent her entire life trying to connect with strangers out in public, only to be continuously thwarted, first by black print on white, and then by Walter on White.

We are still in Alpine, Texas, a town so small I feel like I can see every store, house, and resident, entirely from the train platform. And not because all three are contained in one building. This town is *small*. It looks like fake towns on movie sets, just enough to fit in the frame of a camera lens. Towns like this fascinate me. In part because I grew up in one, and it was never fascinating. Small towns are like cereal boxes with mazes or word puzzles printed on the back. They only hold your interest the first time you lay your eyes on them. But seeing it every morning just reminds you that you know it front to back, which ironically doesn't guarantee there's a way out. And the prize inside gets increasingly underwhelming with age. So when I see a small town, I think of the people in it and wonder if what keeps them there is the feeling of having mastered the maze, or the fear of entering a bigger one.

The bar we enter is vast and empty, which might seem contradictory to the town I just described. But that's the thing about small towns. Every business is built to accommodate everyone, but everyone is never in the same place at the same time, except for the Fourth of July, so every building always feels like a dilapidated storefront in a mall that people no longer visit. I get the sense this bar depends on the stopping of the train.

Josh and I order mini-pizzas, and we have a beer while we wait. The bartender, probably in his late twenties, wearing a snapback hat and a sleeveless T-shirt, asks where we're headed, and I give him the podcast tour log line. He seems genuinely interested in the trip, but not at all interested in the podcast. People envy travelers. Steinbeck mentions this often in *Travels with Charley*, a book detailing his own cross-country affair.

Strangers would see his truck and immediately respond with want. With a train, there are more questions. I suppose a road trip is easier to comprehend. A train gives people pause. Or perhaps it's been romanticized to the point of exoticism. Not quite forbidden, but maybe a little kinky, or a little fatal.

We were delayed in Alpine because there was a medical emergency and one of the passengers was carried off on a stretcher. I saw the woman wandering the train by herself earlier, and I suspect she was traveling alone. I don't know what happened to her, but I hope whatever happened, she wasn't alone, and if she was, that train was her cruise ship, and the town of Alpine was her Arby's.

DAY 4: AUSTIN (1/2)

Population: roaming old white dudes and culture-savvy generations

I am talking to myself in a broken train bathroom. To be clear, the bathroom is broken. The train rolls on. This trip overlaps with *We're Gross*, so for the first time in three years, I will be missing our show. As a result, I pitched a segment where I send in a video diary. I do this because I think it will be funny, and because I am worried that the show will go great without me and no one will notice my absence, and it will be the night executives from Adult Swim are in the audience, and they will sign the show for six seasons, and I'll never be a part of it. My ability to go apocalyptic is both my superpower and my kryptonite. The perceived catastrophe motivates me to act, but it also weakens my ability to just be.

Overloaded with everything else around me, I forget to take video footage for the first two legs of the trip, and so I am scrambling at 2:00 a.m. in this bathroom to get some usable footage. The toilets are broken, or at least in need of respite, as the place smells like shit. But I need to brush my teeth, and so

I make a disoriented video about it, escalating the risk that I drop my toothbrush, or phone, or both on the bathroom floor. I don't, but something tells me not dropping the phone doesn't mean I avoided contaminating it.

We pull into Austin, shaken and exhausted as if we arrived on horseback. Austin glows. The entire time we're there, it never feels like my eyes are straining. Never so bright that it hurts my eyes, not too dark to see. It's like a Himalayan salt lamp or lava lamp—a light fixture someone cool would have. Which makes sense because I have heard from Josh, and just about everybody, that Austin is the town other towns try to emulate when they do cool things like have outdoor concerts or serve booze at the movies. It's fitting that Austin is really the only city with a name that could easily be your friend's older brother who doesn't have plans for the future, but he can surf and always has enough cash to buy you a coke and a pizza.

Although you wouldn't know it by looking at me, I am excited. My enthusiasm looks awfully similar to my unenthusiasm, which shows a shocking resemblance to my apathy, my anxiety, my rage, and my arousal. This has not always been the case, but rather the chemical compound of mixing overly emotional with non-confrontational for thirty years, and heating it over lukewarm concern.

Chalk it up to introversion, if you like, but I've been slightly deflated with how my feelings have been received by others. I try not to kick up dust, because I don't like things dusty, so whenever I did, I expected people to receive it as handle-with-care. After all, that's how I try to operate. If you share something as personal as how you're feeling, if you give something so intimate over to me, then let me hold it with care.

But inevitably, a trust fall with no catch felt worse than not falling. I didn't like letting someone else have control over my feelings, so I wrangled them all up. I elected to be even-keeled. I would have liked to just be excited and unflappable, but I couldn't quite control the lows and let the highs run wild. As a result, I have been described in my later years as having a "quiet cool," and also "cold and devoid of feeling." Which makes sense, even though I've never felt cool, and I feel a lot. But I've quieted it all down and hidden my feelings under the floorboards as if they were being hunted. I would let my relationships speak for me. "I'm fun," I declare. I cite having friends. "I'm loving, as you can see by the relationship I'm in." "Of course I have feelings; I'm close with my family." But as those have drifted and dissipated, it's looking like I might have to call up how I'm feeling. And right now, I'm calling up excited. It's just been a minute since anyone has used the phone line, so it might be a minute.

Our Lyft driver from the train station to our Airbnb is an old white man who tells us his son owns a bar called UnBARable. I try and imagine living in the same town as my dad, me owning a small business, and him collecting fares for driving drunks and visitors around. It is not hard to imagine, as my dad and I have been much closer, in literal proximity and familial bonding, in my adult age than when I was a child.

After their divorce, my parents had joint custody over me, opting to have me ping pong back and forth midweek. I would often get confused and end up at my dad's bus stop with no one to pick me up, or surprising my mom when she would get home from work to find me on the couch. But when I turned thirteen, they said I could decide for myself. I spent most of my time at my mom's because she lived within walking distance of my school, whereas my dad lived an hour-long bus ride away. And because my mom just seemed more interested in my life. My dad and I couldn't seem to connect. He would get me bird feeders for my birthday, and I could never really get into sports. We never fought, but we weren't especially close either.

He moved to Oregon when I went off to college, but returned to Colorado before I graduated, and actually moved to my college town, once his college town, of Fort Collins. He lived up in a cabin rental forty minutes away, which made for an hour-long school bus ride from me once again. I'd visit occasionally and sometimes bring some friends. Once, he bootlegged some rice wine for us. It seemed cool to have this mountain man dad moonshining up the hill.

On a side note, at the same time my dad was illegally home-brewing, my mom got arrested in DC for protesting George W. Bush's war. I felt (then and now) extremely proud of my defiant parents.

More often my dad would come down and join me at bars where my friend's band was playing. Or he'd dress up for Halloween parties. And at my graduation, he got more sauced and stoned than I did. I can be a little uptight about relationship roles—if you couldn't already tell by the eighty thousand words I'm spending obsessing over it—so I never really leaned into this dynamic, but I always liked that he seemed to be having a good time, even if he wasn't fitting the father figure mold I'd been given by *Growing Pains* and *Home Improvement*.

When I moved to California in the fall of 2007, my dad helped me organize and run a yard sale, bringing some of his own possessions to donate to the cause of me starting a new chapter of my life. He showed up with his pickup truck packed with boxes full of rocks, sticks, and seashells.

"What the hell is this?" I asked.

"Figured I'd sell some of these seashells I collected from the coast, sticks from hiking trails, and rocks I've collected over my lifetime," my dad replied.

As he set up a folding table and meticulously laid out his collection of earthly souvenirs, I thought that not only were we not going to make much money—as I only had a collection of

CDs, a TV, and a chair—but we were also going to look like backwoods idiots.

And I was right. Sort of. We didn't make much money because my CDs didn't sell, and the TV and chair were bargained down. But my dad *sold out* of his fucking sticks and stones! People lined up for them and cleaned him out. I even overheard one woman say, "I live in California, what am I even doing," as she purchased twenty-dollars-worth of seashells. My dad has always marched to the beat of his own drum, but today he found a band to accompany him. Despite my incredulity, he was still kind enough to give me his profits for my move. What he lacked in interest, he made up for in support.

Fast forward to 2008. I had just signed a year lease in the Inland Empire, fifty miles east of LA, to live alone for the first time in my life. In retrospect, I suppose being twenty-four and not having lived alone wasn't that rare, but it felt exotic to me. That was until I became lonely living in the desert and resorted to buying a used PlayStation 2 and…nope. That was about it. So when my dad's living situation fell through in Colorado, I suggested he come out to stay with me.

It was nice at first. He helped me get a bed, and we'd go out to eat or visit my grandpa, and he looked after my cat when I went to India. But then he rearranged my furniture. Strike one. It wasn't more than a couch and a TV, but it felt like a violation of my independence. Then we were watching all of *Deadwood* together, and he couldn't help himself and finished the series while I was at work. Strike two. That felt like a disregard for my feelings, even if I was actually being petty. And he complained a lot. Strike three, four, five…no-hitter. He complained about his dad, about warm beer, about society at large, even about the complex's hot tub. I finally had enough when we got into a fight over who was closer to my sisters—he who had raised them as their stepdad through their teenage years; or me, who was their brother. He probably was, but it wasn't that he was closer that upset me. It was that we were having the argument. I wanted a dad, not a roommate, not a competitive friend. I'm sensitive about roles, dammit.

I told him he needed to leave. And he did. With no place to go. On the whole, I consider myself a better-than-average grandson, and a suitable son, but this will always be a large blemish on my record. To this day, I feel shitty about the decision, but I couldn't live with someone who I wasn't in agreement with over the relationship we had.

When I think of my relationship to my dad, I always think about *Terminator 2: Judgement Day*. I actually just always think about that movie. But I think about it specifically with relation to my dad, not because we watched it together, but because it always symbolized for me the perceived role an adult male, or the technological equivalent, plays in a young boy's life.

Terminator 2: Judgment Day is the sequel to *Terminator*. Both movies are about time-traveling robots hunting someone with the last name Connor. The original film was a small movie about a man, Kyle Reese, played by Michael Biden, protecting a woman, Sarah Connor, played by Linda Hamilton, from another man, who is a robot played by Arnold Schwarzenegger. But because the budget was small, he's just a beefy man for 90 percent of the movie, and then at the end, there's a robot. The sequel is about a different man, a liquid robot played by Robert Patrick, hunting Sarah Connor's son, John, played by Edward Furlong, and now Arnold is the good guy protecting Sarah and John. It's a sci-fi action blockbuster, but it's also about how a son needs a mom and a dad.

At one point, John makes the Terminator swear not to kill anyone. First, he has to explain what *swearing* is. Then, when the robot shoots the guard in the knees, the terminator reassures John that "he'll live," meaning the gunshot was not fatal to the victim. But the Terminator, while not especially loving or warm, listens to John. He asks him questions and puts John's needs ahead of his own. The Terminator was a robot from the future, programmed to murder and disguised as human. But the command he carried out the most successfully was the program of dad.

In another scene in the movie, Sarah narrates as she watches her son teach the Terminator how to high-five. She says the Terminator, a machine, *"would never leave him (John), and it would never hurt him, never shout at him, or get drunk and hit him, or say it was too busy to spend time with him. It would always be there....of all the would-be fathers who came and went over the years, this thing, this machine, was the only one who measured up."*

That's a pretty fucking grim outlook there, James Cameron. And perhaps one a twelve-year-old with separated parents didn't need to hear over and over and over. But there was the slightest sliver of a point. Minus the lack of personality, this tin can seems to make a satisfactory senior to his junior. And is no personality really a bad thing? It's not like the term "dad joke" is high praise.

I think most dads are just men with kids, and mine has been no exception for most of my life. He introduced me to the world, but it was the world he was interested in. He did what he wanted. It just so happened I was there. We had a motor-cycle/side-car relationship. We would go camping together, or watch *A Few Good Men* together. But if I had an interest in playing video games or going to a water park, I would have to find the means on my time. And if a movie wasn't made explic-itly for adults, like *Rookie of the Year, then I would have to ask my mom if I wanted to see it.* There's a chance my dad has never heard the phrase, "Funky butt loving," let alone paid to hear it. And if he has, it wasn't in this movie, and that worries me.

My dad's parenting was far from negligent or harmful. It's just not how you would program a dad. He didn't hang with me, inquire into what I liked, or let me pick what was for dinner. That's probably not completely true or fair. I'm sure he did, but as a kid, it's the averages and outliers that win out. For instance, I can recall a time he caved, and he took me to McDonald's. It was on the way to a campsite, and the fast food bags left in the car later attracted a bear who broke through the driver's side window in the middle of the night. In the cartoons, it seems cute when Yogi does it. But in real life, it makes your four-hour drive home smell like gravy turds. I felt bad and he didn't make an effort to see that. He was just pissed. Rightfully so, as his car now stunk, but I felt alone in the car with him. On the plus side, when I locked the keys in the car months later, Yogi had made it easy enough to break back in.

As he's gotten older, my dad's gotten much more interested in my life. And maybe that's because I'm an adult, and kids just don't have opinions you can give the same weight to. But kids don't know that. Kids don't understand they have less of a say because they're less experienced and educated. Of course they want their way, but I also think being heard validates their significance. And when they're not, they can internalize it as being a being with less to offer. Which is why it's important to hear kids out. Not because they have something important to say, but because you want them to grow up knowing what they have to say is important.

Joking around is another facet of father-son dynamics that we—he and me—skimmed over. In *T2*, John Connor, the punk teen, teaches his mechanical surrogate father how to say "Chill out, dickwad." It's not exactly a gut-buster, but it sharpens the metal mouth. Terminator never laughs, but he's open to trying out some material, and his dryness works rather effectively.

I can only recall making my dad laugh one time, and it almost killed him. We were staying at a motel, and he was swimming in the pool, and as he tells it, I was "screwing around on the ledge." He laughed and breathed in a quart of chlorinated pool water, igniting a choking and coughing fit. It was at that moment that I decided never to try to make him laugh, or he decided never to laugh. It's one of those chicken or the egg situations where the chicken isn't concerned with fostering his egg's sense of humor.

It's hard to talk about dads without seeming pitiful or self-indulgent. I think it's because dads on the whole just don't get a lot right. They're too machine when they need to be human, and too human when they need to be machine. And I suspect that's why my grandpa once told me: "Never forget your mother. You can forget your father, but never forget your mother." He wasn't being mean. He was mostly being funny. But he was also saying it's okay to forget some stuff dads do. Because in the end, it's the Sarah Connors of the world who will save it.

Time travel back to Austin, and I'm looking at this dad driving for Lyft, and I'm wondering why he's doing it. If not out of financial necessity, is he bored? Just in search of variety? I think he must be an anomaly, but it will turn out he is the first of many old white men who will drive us around. In Maricopa, we had our young Audi test-driving friend, and then the man who moved to Maricopa to take care of an ailing family member—one not old, the other not white. Them, plus a fascinating woman in New Orleans, will conclude the diversity of ride-share drivers. What I will come to learn over the course of this trip is that those younger drivers that are so common in LA are an anomaly in the rest of the country.

In LA, everyone without a sufficiently profitable skill set drives for Lyft or Uber, or is a drone for some other app

(Postmates, Saucy, Wag, a laundry one). In other states, everyone with a profitable skill set drives for Lyft or Uber to make some extra money, or maybe just to keep busy. That is the sense I get from all these old white men. Many of them report that they do it to get out of the house, or because they retired and they're bored. But they also do it because they're men. It's a luxury, even if it doesn't feel like one. I imagine, for a woman, being in a confined space with a strange man is a nightmare, whether or not you're behind the wheel. I suspect women who are bored or retired opt for Postmates or something less creep inviting.

Ironically, states without idyllic weather and beaches have people who would have time to use them because the cost of living is manageable. But people living in those sunny, sandy states can't take advantage of the idyllic environment because they have to work to afford to live there.

Back home, I routinely go hiking up behind my apartment. And when I say *hiking*, I mean walking up an inclined paved road. I admire all the marvelous houses I can't afford. The houses sit there empty because the people who own them are working to afford them. I see young people walking dogs as a part-time job. I know this because the dog wears a bandana with the logo of the business app. I'm struck by the notion that the people with the marvelous houses and neighborhoods and dogs have to pay other people to walk their dogs and enjoy their neighborhoods. I will likely never have one of those houses, but I do get to enjoy them. Or at least, pet the dog that lives in them.

Thinking about the worlds we build for ourselves and the roles we play to live in those worlds, I wonder if it's possible to have the role and the world I want. Or will I be an old man driving for Lyft either way. So I can afford to live in Los Angeles but not enjoy it, or I can kill some time and save up for spring training tickets. In both scenarios, I suppose I'll just be waiting out the clock until they've replaced me with a driverless car. I will be forced out of a role I was never invested in, by a robot who is even less invested but somehow more efficient. And then I wonder if this is all just a metaphor for fatherhood. *Dun-dun, dun-dun* (*T2* score).

Josh and I check-in to our Airbnb. Actually, we don't check-in, because it's not technically available. They're still cleaning it, but we're allowed to leave our bags inside. It's a sparse and modern apartment with lots of animation art on the walls, and at least two remotes that suggest the TVs are not your ordinary fare, but something far more smart. It's a soft attempt at a home. Imagine the living quarters from some dystopian movie like *Bladerunner*. Except where those living quarters were sparse because actual things were expensive and everyone lived in virtual simulations, this dwelling is likely sparse because the host doesn't live here. It's set up for someone more interested in what's outside than what's inside. It's like those faux set-ups at IKEA or appliance stores. They always leave me feeling empty because they have an ulterior motive, usually commerce, sometimes science, if you're part of a sleep study. You can't fake a home, because a home wants nothing out of its inhabitants. While I'm at ease because there's not much to break, I'm also wondering if I'm being observed for my masturbation habits. Any time a residence or residence-adjacent is used for anything other than living, I feel like a test subject, someone once-removed from life.

We walk and get coffee at a place called Buzz Saw, a woodsy coffee shop where the coffee is strong and the pastries are rich and under a glass dome on the counter. It felt as if we were all dressed as lumberjacks—blue jeans, red flannels, and big boots—even if there wasn't a thread of plaid in the whole place. A place that makes you feel like someone else is a magic trick and a strong case for small businesses. No one feels like any-thing but a full jerk at an Applebee's.

We stroll through a green park and over a stone bridge. It's a breezy and sunny day meant to illicit peaceful introspection. However, we are on a mission for breakfast tacos, so fuck a view. Walking over the bridge, I get a call from Em. I tell her I would like to go to the zoo with her when I get back, because I am an infant who does not understand separation, but she says that will be too hard. I say I understand, even though I don't. There should be some upshot to a mutual breakup. Hearts were broken, but not by intent, or mistrust, or selfishness. We found out that we have different ideas of a shared future, but that doesn't change the way we feel about each other.

My mom and her first husband, Mike, remained great friends, even though they didn't stay married. There are so few people in this world that I really connect with and don't want to divorce from. One of them simply because we can't raise a family and grow old together. Maybe I'm trying to rush mend-ing what I don't think is broken. Or maybe I just don't want to let go. And since I don't know, I defer to Em because I suspect her judgment is more sound. This suspicion is immediately confirmed, as my next feeling is forfeit. Why even talk, then? I'm overcome with the urge to disconnect completely. I can't have my way and I'm feeling an emotional tantrum coming on, and I look over the bridge and consider throwing my phone into the river and running away and starting a fresh life as a Lyft driver is Austin. But I don't. Because I can't. I haven't had breakfast.

One of the things I'm noticing on this trip is a strong pull to find some place that helps define me. I often question whether LA is right for me, or if I would be happier in another city. And it's not that I'm unhappy. I'm just slightly more melancholic than I ever pictured myself being. And I think it would be easy to point to my geography and go, "There is the source of this somberness," but it would only be easy. I don't think it would be accurate. I'm no more affected by my city of residence than I am defined by it. People in Austin aren't defined by the city. The city is defined by them.

After breakfast, we get another Lyft from another old person who talks about moving to Austin for the scene, and how she lost her job, so she's been doing Lyft to kill some time. The rest of the country truly sees ride-share jobs as free, easy money. In LA, it's a war zone.

We arrive at one of those cool independent record stores that every cool town has because they are part of what makes a cool town cool. It's your *High Fidelity*, your *Empire Records*, your older cousin's basement aesthetic. Even the stuff you know is not cool becomes cool in there. A Smashmouth tour T-shirt? Hell yeah, I guess.

I don't buy any music at the record store because I have no way to play it. There are a lot of technological advancements interwoven into this trip that make me wonder how it would have worked ten, or even five, years ago. Without my iPhone, or at the very least an iPod, I would have had to bring CDs and a Discman. At most, I could make a reasonable case to bring ten CDs. Anything more than that and I'm just wasting space.

I suppose I could have burned a bunch of CDs onto a very big laptop and listened to the music from my laptop. And thinking about my laptop makes me think about the daily job we have of editing the podcast. Ten years ago, I can't imagine how that would work, or even checking my email. I've had a cell phone since I was fourteen, so unless I was taking this trip as a boxcar kid, I guess I'd always be able to make and receive calls, with spotty coverage, to be sure. It would be almost entirely hotels with reservations made before we left, or in person, like some '80s family comedy.

John Candy would have had a tough time making a tough time out of today's modern travel. Forget ride-sharing back then. Everything would have been cabs, and I doubt there were readily available cabs in all of our destination cities. But I suppose we would have managed. People have been traveling across this continent in search of their destiny since there were people on this continent. I just get to do it with the luxury of bringing every album, TV show, book, and movie ever made.

We walk through downtown Austin on the way back to our Airbnb. It's quaint and yet feels like Gotham compared to Alpine. We stop to get a doughnut at Voodoo Doughnut, and Josh asks about the nightlife. I am growing irritable. *We have a motherfucking Voodoo Doughnut in LA,* I think. "We have recommendations for nightlife," I say. Otherwise, I do not make my feelings known out loud because I know my irritability is unreasonable. I'm just tired. I want to be alone with my thoughts. Or it's possible I hate myself a little for wanting to be alone with my thoughts so much it's distanced me from everyone in my life except for those that have evacuated my apartment, my life, this earth.

I order a Lyft, but our old white guy driver gets tangled up driving in circles and he can't find us, so he tells me to cancel and order the ride again and he'll grab us. This, of course, does not work, and we get a ride with another dude. The original guy does eventually pull up while we're waiting for our new driver, and he asks if we ordered a Lyft. I lie and say no because this is already more than I bargained for in an interaction with a stranger. Our new driver arrives.

He's a very big young man, older than me, but probably not old enough to have a son with a small business. When he hears about our trip, he says he wouldn't ride the train unless he had a private room with a female. He's adamant about this and reiterates it three times during our ten-minute ride. He talks about it as if those things were both within his ability to get. He seems to be the kind of person whose attitude is, *This is what I'm doing or I'm not doing anything*, and I get the sense this attitude has served him well. He is one of the more jovial drivers we will have. He is right that a room and a woman would make the train better, but when is that not the case? If those were my requirements, I'd never have left my hometown. I don't exactly have the means for those kinds of ends.

After a nap, we take a Lyft—one of the few without a chatty driver—to ColdTowne Theatre. We check-in and go about a block down to get more Tex-Mex. This time, a habañero pastor taco and a cold brew coffee at an outdoor patio. I'm up and my mouth is on fire.

We have a fun show as our guests tell us about nearly dying on a camping trip twice and hating a birthday party at Disneyland. The place seats sixty maybe, and our show is fairly well-attended despite us being nobodies. We get a taste of outsider glamour as a few folks stay after to say good show. Josh seems a little disappointed with the turnout. I don't have the heart to tell him that any interest feels monumental to me.

Meanwhile, back in LA, Em texts me she is sick. She's stressed out. I would be, too, without the distractions of this trip. It's given me a lot to occupy my mind. It can sometimes be a gift to have shit to worry about, so as not to worry about the stuff we can't control. I will routinely shift between money woes, disease, social leprosy. If one gets worked out, I'll take a moment to relax. And then, like clockwork, my brain will tick through every facet of my life, tapping on them with a rubber hammer like a doctor testing reflexes, and any hesitation in a rock-solid reflex will require a CT scan, MRI, and amputation. A lobotomy would fix it all, but my brain is the head physician and isn't the Dr. Kevorkian type.

After the show, we get drinks and compare notes on the improv scenes in Phoenix and Austin and San Antonio and New Orleans. LA feels so separated from the rest of the country. I wonder if there is slight tension because so many people leave their homes for LA. It becomes a city of abandoners, whether anyone consciously sees it that way, and so when anyone who left returns home to visit, the rest of the country is like, "You said you were going out for milk, and the next I hear from you is in some Verizon ad?! This is not your home anymore, Mister Hollywood."

I chat with a woman who is Latina and Algerian. She's able to pronounce my name, a more common skill the more I distance myself from Colorado. When I was growing up, no one could pronounce it. Outside of Evergreen, Colorado, people usually get it. Most people living there were Johnsons, Wilsons, and Christophers. Or another way to say it is *white*. Jabbour is Lebanese with a French spelling. I'm white by almost all measure, but just having a foreign name stood out. It never bothered me, the mispronunciation, but I noticed it. What privilege to have that be the only otherness. That, and lack of affluence. By Evergreen standards. By the rest of the world, I was Mr. Moneybags. This is the most basic revelation from someone coming from white privilege, but you really just don't know you don't know your own privilege until it's pointed out to you either directly or indirectly. It's no excuse. It just doesn't come naturally. It's what makes privilege such a bitch to combat. Part of having it is not knowing you have it. We all need CT scans for our privileges, but none of us have the emotional insurance to cover the cost and pay someone who didn't sign up to be our doctor.

We go to UnBARable, and it's a house converted into a bar. It's packed with college-aged drinkers. We drink there until last call. Josh is feverishly using a dating app as I wonder how long

I will go without dating, or if I will ever date again. When a relationship ends, I often wonder if that will be the last one for me. Same thing with sex. It always seems miraculous to me that it happens at all, so I'm acutely aware that every time could be my last time. This is not self-pity. This is just how it feels to me. I've never gone out to get laid or hookup or get a girlfriend, and done it. Every time it happens, I'm a little surprised. It's like I'm standing around at a fair, only to discover that I've actually been in line for a ride this whole time. But every time I look for an attraction, I'm always too short to ride.

We are asked to leave, as it is last call. For the first time on this trip, and what will also be the last, I have my own room, so I masturbate. I feel stupid-guilty about masturbating in an Airbnb. Even if this is a sterile future-pad, someone writes its address down as their home. I happily will pay the extra money for a hotel room no one calls home so that I can orgasm in peace.

I'm extra careful about the cleanup and take the trash out afterward. This is the kind of rock star I would make. Let me do the dishes we smashed against the wall.

DAY 5: AUSTIN DAY (2/2)

Population: BBQ-ers, bluegrass bathers, and back-patio conversationalists

There are few things I regret more than paying for a meal I didn't enjoy. And almost everyone who lives in, or has visited, Austin has an opinion on which BBQ restaurant is the "one" to eat at. This is helpful. To a point. After that point, too much information is the same as no information. We are told that one place is the best, but because everyone agrees on this, the wait is very long. So long, in fact, that the ratio of time to taste is unbalanced. So we go to Terry's BBQ, where we are assured that the food is equal to the wait, if not better. Plus, it has the added advantage of being close to Barton Springs, a local natural springs we were tipped off to by our Lyft driver.

We "hail" a Lyft, and our driver's primary language is Spanish. I dust off my high school Spanish that was taught to me by the German teacher because my district was poor, and when the demand wasn't there for German and the supply for Spanish wasn't there, Frau Cook became Señor Cook and we learned Spanish as best he could teach it. I tell our driver that I am Señor Siesta and Josh is Señor Fiesta. I use 90 percent of the Spanish I know to tell 100 percent of the truth.

The BBQ did not disappoint. Laid out in a barn-type establishment, the restaurant reads one part cafeteria, one part line dancing. Trays carry two mains, two sides, and some pickles, and each portion goes down easily. So easily, in fact, that we elect to walk the two miles to Barton Springs because we overate and are now full and fat and will be taking our shirts off in public soon.

On the walk, I get a call from my former supervisor at a school where I previously taught. She asks if I'm available to come back and teach the following fall. I am offered a teaching position every six months, despite often leaving schools midyear and vowing never to return. But like they teach you, if you've ever done fundraising: you'll have better luck with someone weak-willed enough to have contributed once before than you will with someone never foolish enough to start. I tell her I'll think about it because I am always flattered when someone offers to pay me for something I do. Much like relationships, I am worried every time will be my last time.

Barton Springs is a natural spring converted into a public pool. The water is naturally occurring, and the bottom is smooth from all the people's calloused heels polishing it. They put in concrete platforms along the side and cemented in dam installations to keep the water high—and installed a diving board! Imagine if hobbits built a pool, or Bob Ross painted one.

Walking toward the springs, we pass a group of teenage girls, and one of them sees Josh and confuses him with her mother. This might be the funniest thing I hear on a trip designed to make me laugh. I don't know Josh's self-image, but I bet it's not the mom of a teenage girl. The game of look-alikes is a game people only like to play when it's not their turn. When it's not your turn, you get to say, "You know who you look like..." or "I'm sorry, I thought you were...." And when it is your turn, you get to hear those words. The weight we give to this is disproportionate. I know people who beat themselves up or seethe at strangers who make an unfavorable comparison. To me—and this is maybe because I've never gotten a flattering one, so I've had to adjust my perspective for self-preservation—it could not matter less who someone thinks you look like. If your friend found someone attractive that you did not, it would not matter to you. So why would it matter if they see a resemblance you do not? And if they are a stranger, who the fuck cares? Strangers are not authorities in appearance or look-alikes, unless they are casting directors. In which case, who cares? You could be on TV as pool patron #4.

A brief list of people I've been told I look like:

Russell Crowe, by a McDonald's drive-through attendant, which could be flattering, but it wasn't during his *Gladiator* phase.

Gerard Butler, but they specified "not *300*" Gerard Butler.

One of the guys in System of a Down, but not the main guy.

The Undertaker's brother (who I later found out is a man named Kane, but they didn't say Kane, so it's possible I just look like I'm related to a fifty-year-old roided-out death dealer).

Some half-rat, half-human from a children's show.

Russell Crowe again, by a different McDonald's drive-through attendant.

Late Elvis.

The rat from *Ratatouille*.

And Russell Crowe, but just from some dude. No McDonalds affiliation.

It reads like Twelve Days of Christmas: three Russell Crowes, two anthropomorphic rats, and a late Elvis on the toilet.

Austin charges three dollars to enter Barton Springs if you're a resident, and seven dollars if you're a non-resident. They have automated kiosks similar to parking pay stations, and I am fully prepared to lie and push the button for *Austin Resident*, but the pay station is out of order. And we sort of need it because the other option is to pay at the window with a clerk, but they only take cash, and we technically don't have cash. I say *technically* because I have a folded-up hundred-dollar bill hidden in the case of my cell phone for emergencies, but this is not an emergency. Yet.

We walk to the other side of the springs and try those kiosks. They also don't work. I am starting to get really impatient because I like pools. I love pools. They're my favorite body of water. It goes pool, lake, hot tub, ocean. I don't particularly love swimming or water slides or diving boards, but I love floating in the water like an otter, or laying in the sun next to the water like a lizard. A body of water brings out the harmless animal in me. And the voyeur. I also enjoy people watching. And if I'm being honest, if those people are in swimsuits, all the better. This is slightly more true if those people are women, but only slightly. I may not be attracted to the very large and tanned man with gold chains, sloshing around in the water, in the same way I am by a woman in a two-piece, reading Tom Robbins, but I'll spend equal time thinking about both sets of nipples. It's probably the '90s fault. Bad guys in action movies were overly tan meatheads, and there was always one scantily clad woman. And music videos in the '90s were more of the same, but usually with more plot. It started to have this almost reverse VR effect. When I would go to a pool or beach, it felt like I was being transported inside my TV. This isn't a novel observation. In fact, I think it was the aim of the producers. But there was such a late-'80s emphasis on body image, and that bled over into the taboo of mature content for young adolescents in the '90s, coupled with the explosion of music videos. It's almost as if it never occurred to music video directors that a music video could be something other than women in cut-offs, dancing to the song. So that Barton Springs was also known for its topless tanning was adding to my frustration with these fucking kiosks.

Within the span of three minutes and four women wearing bikinis, my will power shatters, and I break into my piggy bank. Josh tells the cashier he is a resident, and I tell her I am not. He pays three dollars and I pay seven. He says I should feel like a sucker, and everyone we relay this tale to later will say the same thing. But I am a rule follower when it comes to dealing with people, and often companies. I, like a patriotic American(?), recognize corporations as people, and feel bad cheating them. That, I do feel like a sucker about. I have illegally downloaded movies and then felt guilty about it, and ended up buying them. I convince myself I am supporting the art, but I suspect I've just been brainwashed by commercialism. Or is it capitalism? Or corporatism? But in this instance, in the interest of Austin and it's public springs, I do not feel like a fool for paying the full price. Sometimes I think if we all just did what was expected of us, most of our problems would go away. That's what the fucking honor system is. It's the honorable thing to do! But we all try to cut corners or give ourselves the employee discount, and that's what makes the regular price of seven dollars so outrageous (but still pretty reasonable). But also, who cares? Because we are now at the pool. Sign me up for the extended warranty, America!

It is a clear and beautiful day with enough warmth in the air to make the transition in and out of the water brisk and refreshing. We jump off the diving board and use our phones to take videos of us in loops going off the board and going in reverse from the water and then back on the board. It's a lot of fun, despite no nipples. Or at least, no female nipples. We're up to our tits in male nipples.

After about two hours at the springs, we wash up and meet one of Josh's friends who works crew for film companies in Austin. He lives in an apartment, and there is a fourteen-year-old boy there, who I was probably informed was his son, but did not figure out until later. Josh's friend is my age, so that he has a teenage son is as earth-shattering to me as if he had been to the moon. You're qualified to do that? Based on what training? What do you mean, *I could do it?* Based on what training? His son is staying with him for the summer, and they have made a little makeshift room for him in the living room. I am very familiar with this style of living arrangement.

When I moved to San Diego, my sister Michelle was renting a house from my mom, but my mom still lived there, effectively making her the landlord and a free-loading occupant. This meant that although my mom was living there, the rules of the house were set by my sister, and that translated to soft anarchy. Michelle, my sister, is a saint—a perfectly cluttered saint. Her heart is so big and caring that she has little room for organization or tidiness. This bothers me. Not because she's messy, but because so am I. Compared to my sister, I am equal measure messy, half-measure altruistic. My motto has always been, *I'm trying, so cut me some slack*. With her it's, *I'm succeeding, so I've earned some slack*. Sometimes I think if we all were a little kinder, in lieu of being clean and organized, many of our problems would fall away. Like an overworked staff at the only diner in town. We're a mess, but we're sweet about it.

After receiving my diploma and watching my dad sell out of hiking debris, Michelle offered to let me live with her rent-free in San Diego. The catch was that she was out of rooms in the four-bedroom house, so I would have a spot in the den behind some curtains hung from the ceiling. I lived behind the curtains for a year, had zero sex, and masturbated quietly. Always a son, never a father. But that only lasted a year because I moved to the Inland Empire by myself and masturbated as loud as I liked. I would put up goose eggs in the sex column for another two years.

"San Diego, sans sex, for this sad sack."

Josh's friend is taking us to Blues on the Green, a large, free, outdoor music festival, walking distance from his apartment. I am not one for music festivals. I thought I might be at one point, when I drove from Colorado to Tennessee for Bonnaroo. But when the toilets overflowed, and we brought more beer than food, and all my friends got coked out, I decided I would just make it a one-time experience. I enjoy camping, but not with ten thousand people. I like live music, but not after two days without a shower or a hot meal. I dislike cocaine.

However, this festival is rather nice. I do not know any of these bands, and blues and bluegrass is not my genre of choice, but this festival is laid back, with free water and food stands. There are maybe fifteen hundred people here, and everyone is set up on blankets and lawn chairs, and I feel at home. Or at least, at comfort. I could live in Austin. Maybe. Or maybe I could live anywhere that isn't the place I call home, because it's not attached to all the current feelings and emotions I'm going through. Austin seems nice because it's not the city my girlfriend and I broke up in, or the city I was in when I found out my grandpa died. But it would have been if it was where I lived. It's not LA's fault. It was just a witness.

Josh and I leave for our show at The New Movement. The New Movement has its stage down a small set of stairs, and it has a lobby and merchandise. It feels more rock venue than theatre space. It's that Austin stamp of cool. This show is a one-off from our live podcast. We will just be doing a live, two-person, traditional improve set. No mics, no guests, and much to our surprise, no suggestion. One of the traditions in improv is to get a suggestion from the audience. This, as far as I can deduce, is done for two purposes. The first, and most unnecessary, is to demonstrate to the audience that the improvisation they are about to see is not some parlor trick. We have not rehearsed what they are going to see, and to prove it, we will take any word to begin. This is a little ridiculous because improv is rarely so good that people think it's been pre-written. And if it were, we could definitely construct the set so that whatever word we got could be seamlessly woven into the show. The second purpose, which is more interesting but also more pompous, is that the improvisers are trying to perform an artistic and comedic set that makes a "statement" about the word.

Del Close, an improv pioneer, rumored dickhead, and inventor of the Harold form, was apparently fond of using what was in the news or in the zeitgeist to generate information for the sets, so that someone watching could receive a collaborative and instantaneous take on an issue. But here at The New Movement, they distance themselves from that and just come out and start improvising. It weirdly highlights the necessity for something unnecessary. It's not that the sets were any less fun, but they did seem to be more of a passing scenery than a landmark. And you know, that's totally fine. But take our train travel for example: the boat shop and dock on the river with the hand-painted sign that read, "We're recording you and have notified the police," recalls more vividly than the hundred miles of lush swamp land. Sometimes you need something to stand out. But I suppose that's part of the beauty of improv. It doesn't stand erect for revisiting. It's not a landmark. It's a moment captured in time. And it usually involves pantomiming tossing pizza dough in the air and troublesome Italian accents.

For us, in our moment, we offer no pizza, and nothing to suggest we scripted anything. It's fine, but Josh and I are still finding our sea legs, or scene legs. In three shows, I have discovered I've been playing with the home-field advantage they talk about in sports that I never understood. It seems like your athletic ability could not be swayed by the number of people rooting for you, but it must be true. It's certainly true for comedy. People who know you think you're funny. Or people who think you're funny know you, and success in comedy is usually measured by how many laughs you get—the universal indicator of being funny.

So with eight-plus years of performing in LA, I have slowly garnished enough of a reputation to warrant laughter (albeit minor, even just chuckles) from my stage presence or the way I express shock with my pronunciation of, "What the hell?" But on the road, people don't know me from the passenger on the bus shouting, "What is happening!" when the scheduled stop takes longer than expected. And to get laughs in a foreign environment, there are certain formulas that have higher rates of success—timing, misdirects, self-deprecation, patterns, breaking of patterns, and being an asshole who fails, or an idiot who succeeds, which are really just specific examples of misdirects. But when you haven't played those notes in a minute, your melody is off. And our melody is off. We don't bomb, but that's because it's hard to bomb if you're sincere in your effort. Pity isn't great, but it's not loathing. So we take our pity and roll on to Mug Shots for drinks.

Mug Shots is a dive bar, and to get there, Josh and I—and a man named Brian, who seemingly appeared out of nowhere, and who I only met when he offered me shotgun—get a ride from a woman named Erica in her two-door Honda. Surprisingly, she has a lot of props and costumes in her car. I say *surprisingly* because I thought for sure that phenomenon would be more localized to Los Angeles, the home of backseats that are home to wigs and lab coats. I have performed comedy in New York only a handful of times, but I know from seasoned East Coast performers that a sketch show in New York is written so that all it requires is you, because *you* are all you're bringing on the subway, or walking fifteen blocks with. And so I wrongfully assumed Los Angeles, as is our want, was being needlessly extravagant. If comedy could be done with less, it probably was being done with less everywhere but LA. We are so consistently and unfavorably compared to New York that we pad our resumes any way we can, including putting up comedy shows requiring police uniforms, breakaway suits, and an anatomically correct werewolf costume. So to see this effort put forth in such an effortlessly cool city caught me off guard. I guess we're all trying to be better than New York, even in the #1 city on the list of cities people would live in, if not their current city.

When we arrive at Mug Shots, I quickly learn that the name of the bar is not just a clever play on words, but that it is also literal. There are hundreds of photos from a photo booth pinned up to the walls, and the ones behind the bar reveal a shockingly abundant amount of women's breasts, not affable fools. Although, they're up there, too. Move over Barton Springs. I take far too long to order my drink.

I go to the bathroom, and above the urinal is a poster advertising a podcast called *Was This Always Weird*, and it's got a knife stabbing a VHS tape and blood is pouring out. I take my phone out and search for the podcast, and I read that the hosts talk about old movies with a guest, and *Terminator 2: Judgement Day* is one of the movies, so I subscribe because, as I've established, I think about that movie a lot.

It probably has to do with the fact that I watched that movie a lot. Every day, after school, in fact. And I would always stop watching right before the Terminator self-immolated by lowering himself into hot magma, because if I watched that scene I would cry. Was it because I was watching a dad dismantle himself to preserve a safe future for his son? Or was it because I was just a sensitive kid? Jury is out. But I can tell you that I recently rewatched it in 3D at a special theatre screening, and I still wept. I am more than a little excited to listen to this podcast.

I join our tour guides on the patio, and we trade our stories of comedy and improv and its few successes, many promises, and countless disappointments. Anyone who does comedy for a living will love to tell you how hard it is. And this is both true and also not at all true. It's true because there are so many small failures. From jokes or lines falling flat in a show, to bad shows altogether, to rejections from theatres and festivals, to existential dread. But really, this all exists in the time we have devoted to our leisure, and if you have any leisure time at all, those struggles are relative.

Coincidentally, without nudging on my part, the conversation drifts to *Terminator 2,* and I come alive. I am an introvert, and while this cluster of eight non-jocks suits my preferences, I only know Josh, who is seated at the far end of the table, and this whole set-up is also foreign, so I'm feeling wordless. But once time-traveling killer robots are brought up, I have too much to say, mainly about the robot's genitals.

If you watch a movie enough, you think about the fringes. Some people notice the continuity errors. Or some people observe the art on the walls and the books on the shelves in the background. Me? I think about the scientist tasked with making the droid's dick. For starters, it's useless. The steel assassins don't need to drink or fuck—this isn't *Westworld*—so it's just for show. Perhaps it's because they travel through time without clothes, so they needed to fit in, but they materialize out of nothing, leave a crater in the earth, and then murder the first person they see to take their clothes. If they left a witness, it's unlikely the first thing they'd recount was the man's lack of penis.

Now, consider that some scientist in the future had to spend his working hours crafting a useless penis for a robot. He had to decide on size, and for whatever reason, he went big. We know this because not one but two women in the bar look at it and smile. It's a head scratcher. In the third installment, it's a female Terminator and she has boobs and a vagina. Which, I guess if you've started down the path of anatomically correct killing machines, it would be weird not to be consistent. But still, *why?* And if you think that's weird, ask yourself this—do the robots have buttholes? Either answer is bizarre.

When I pause for laughter or approving nods, Erica, the owner of the car and the props, informs me she was a guest on the podcast from the bathroom for the *T2* episode.

Now, I am currently going through a breakup, and as a result, I want nothing to do with anyone in a romantic capacity, and also I am terrified I will get exactly that forever, so I am grasping for any connection with anyone because I might be on a path toward celibacy and solitude. In other words, I'm a mess. Man, I wish I didn't open with the penis bit, so I compensate. I pivot hard, as if a woman in the comedy community, who went on a podcast about movies to talk about *T2*, has not heard every nerd's passionate long-winded diatribe about the film's brilliance. But I don't care, because I need to fucking connect with someone.

The monoculture is evaporating, and that makes connecting difficult. We no longer have appointment viewing. There is no *Seinfeld* finale to unite us. We yearn for moments where we can compare and find similarities in our experiences. It's primal. It's how we affirm we're a part of the pack, essential to its survival—or in the modern world, to its zeitgeist. Since my previous pack disbanded, I'm on the hunt. If I can find one person who acknowledges my point of view as having value or interest, or both, then I'm safe from starvation and extinction.

I thought having a take on the junk of the tin man might give me some value in this crew, but after the twist that my audience, or at least Erica, is well-versed in at least mocking *T2*, I need to offer some personal and passionate pleas. I drone on to this near stranger about how well *T2* holds up, and how it's portrayal of Los Angeles is one I didn't come to appreciate until I got older and moved there, and that I think it sub-consciously influenced my love for Los Angeles TV shows and my catastrophic nature. This woman listens, even though in my attempt to connect by offering insight into pop culture, I've probably just put on a red shirt and stood next to a brick wall stacked with self-deprecating, movie-obsessed white male comedians. I'm not different from the guy sitting on her right, except that I arrived here by train. In my attempt to create a unique relationship with someone, I panic that I just blended in. I should be mysterious, and in fact, my backstory might even be intriguing. I mean, I've broken my back, served in AmeriCorps, worked with juvenile offenders, worked for Teach For America, and taught in Inglewood, California. But I don't know how to talk about that stuff without feeling like I'm bragging. The only opening up I feel comfortable with is obsessing, because I'm not letting go of anything by saying what I like, and hopefully what I like is close to what I am like. But tonight, I am like a nerdy passing stranger, because I am a nerdy passing stranger. This journey has been overwhelming in a positive way—the scenery, the shows, the workshops, the people. But the discovery of myself has been underwhelming. Talking about what I like isn't a revelation.

I get pinged out of this mind fuck by a text from Josh saying he may meet me back at our Airbnb because he is going to try and ignite some sparks with another woman at the table. I watch with mild interest from a distance and don't see even the hint of smoke, let alone sparks. As we're leaving, he texts me again to tell me I should order a Lyft. It seems like, indeed, there were sparks. But when the Lyft arrives, Josh gets in with me. He tells me he proposed they go to her place and watch TV, but she said it was better if they didn't. So Josh and I go back to our Airbnb. I admire how Josh puts himself out there. I'm a slow burn, bordering on smoldering, when it comes to seeking out intimacy. This should come as no surprise to anyone who has read this far.

When we get back to our place, Josh and I chat about our respective loneliness. We both seem to wrestle with it, but for different reasons. Josh is looking to exorcise it, while I am looking to study it. A priest and a scholar. Although, you wouldn't know it, because Josh falls asleep drinking on the couch, and I film myself bottomless for the button to my train clip show for *We're Gross*. However, I'm too tired to edit, and definitely too morose to feel emboldened to make a permanent record of my swimsuit area.

How did the term *tortured artist* become a thing? I can't get shit done when I'm self-loathing.

DAY 6: SAN ANTONIO

Population: people with trust issues, sharks, and enthusiastic improvisers

Today I need to rent a car. I also need to get coffee, and get supplements from GNC. The car is for our drive to San Antonio. The coffee is for alertness and a bowel movement. And the supplements are to keep me (thinking I'm) healthy and fit. I use all the technology at my fingertips and deduce that it makes the most sense for me to Lyft to the rental car place, then drive to GNC, then get coffee for Josh and me. I am efficient, even without my caffeine and vitamins.

I open the door to my room and see a pile of dirty laundry in the hallway. I remember that I told Josh I would do laundry in the morning, and to leave me his if he wanted any done. I regret this now, but round up his stinky drawers and shirts, because he did a lot more work putting this trip together than I did, and I will feel guilty until I do what I calculate to be a comparable amount of work in the form of laundry, coffee runs, room upgrades, and whatever else I can think of. I'm not an organizer, but I am a work horse and deal-finding looter. Book me for your road trips and tours.

Renting a car is easy. GNC is not open, even though it says it should be, so I go get two coffees from Buzz Saw. I then go back to GNC. It's open, and I get some multivitamins and a fat-targeting sleep aid. It's mostly just melatonin, but the placebo effect it has on me allows me to eat twice as much BBQ and tacos with half the guilt.

I go back to the Airbnb, and we have to be out by noon. I emailed and asked for a late checkout, and that was the best our host could do because the cleaning crew is coming at noon. Unfortunately, our clothes are in the dryer and they will not be done until 12:30. I am a rule follower, so I pack everything up and make Josh meet me in the laundry room, which, after setting up my laptop and a cup of coffee, I declare my new office.

Before leaving Austin, Josh and I do two things: we go to Torchy's Tacos for breakfast tacos, and we go to the Alamo Drafthouse for a movie. We go to Torchy's because it was recommended to us no less than four times. One of the people who recommended it did so in a text message that went something like this (I am paraphrasing because I set my messages to delete after thirty days in an attempt to not linger on the past too much):

> *"You can try to eat at the famous one, or just go down the street and eat at the other BBQ joint. It's just as good. Here's a list of bars and a good place for tacos. Although take all this with a grain of salt, as I was getting loaded there and watching my life fall apart after my wife left me."*

In a single text message, my friend described a life I'm not sure I will ever know. I am aware of my obedience to rules and guidelines, and with that comes being a risk-avoider, and so my life, while full of events and experiences, never comes that close to anything one might call dramatic or intense. Any time a situation that might be harrowing rears its head, I just pick up and move. Sometimes physically, sometimes psychologically. Here is where I lay my head, until I don't. And home is where my heart is, until it isn't.

After excellent breakfast tacos, and a successful resistance to buying hot sauce or a T-shirt, we go to the Alamo Drafthouse. This is a stop Josh has been insisting we make since the inception of this trip. If you're not aware, as I wasn't, the Alamo Drafthouse is a movie theatre with, essentially, cocktail servers. We watched *Guardians of the Galaxy Vol. 2* while drinking a lemonade mojito and a pale ale. I had seen *Guardians* once before, and I can honestly say that access to booze did not amplify the movie. But I suppose I will remember this experience for its uniqueness. I am someone who enjoys not pushing it. My breakfasts could be better with Torch hot sauce, but if the server doesn't ask if there's anything else, I'll be fine with a mild meal.

We are on the road to San Antonio now, and we have a pit stop in mind. Rudy's for more BBQ. It's slightly out of the way, but when you're traveling four thousand miles and Texas BBQ is in the equation, *slightly out of the way* is a non-factor. At Rudy's—possibly inspired by my over-eagerness to connect with Erica, and Josh and I drunkenly opening up the night before—I breach the subject of my breakup with Josh. Up to this point, I haven't really said anything because I'm not sure I have the answers, or because I'm uncomfortable giving the answers to the questions I know he will ask.

I suppose in any breakup, people will always ask what happened, out of a sense of concern. When it's planned and mutual, people will ask out of a sense of curiosity. Curiosity is much harder to satisfy than concern. So I tell him I don't want to have kids, and he, like everyone else, almost refuses to accept this as a reason. My mom didn't accept it. My friends didn't accept it.

And so, in this BBQ restaurant in the middle of the country, thousands of miles from anyone else I may know, I tell Josh it comes down to trust. And this is maybe the most honest answer I've given to anyone. I can't say there is 100 percent trust in the relationship, and not necessarily absent in each other, but in ourselves. Or myself. I can't speak for her. I think a relationship requires complete trust in each other and in one's self, and that is something we don't have. It's never been said, but it's never not been said. The details are small enough to ignore, but large enough to matter. I can't do something with someone that requires them trusting me, if *I* don't trust me.

Even though Josh doesn't accept the reasoning, he kindly relates to the cost of any breakup. He talks to me about his own, and how it was hard to say goodbye to someone he felt so intertwined with, and the rapid fire of feelings of love, frustration, abandonment, pining, resentment, and regret. Here we were, two Pumbaas, sharing and listening, eating and drinking. Misery loves company, I guess. And BBQ. These ribs are worth the detour and the heartache.

We arrive in San Antonio and stay at the Wyndham Gardens. We only have one king-size bed, and this irritates Josh. They try to appease us with a beautiful view overlooking the river, but it doesn't work because we're train folk now. Beautiful views are a dime a dozen. But an individual bed is the stuff of legend.

I am trying to figure out how to drop the rental car off. I managed to rent from an establishment that is close to the theatre, and then I rented a room at the Wyndham Gardens because it is close to both. I thought I was being convenient and forward-thinking. I planned ahead and organized—something I'm not known to do.

I get done just about everything I set out to do, but my pedagogy is not predictable. In job interviews, I always confess to poor organization. But I clarify that I don't lose things, which is true. I rarely lose anything. Statistically, my losses are on par, if not under par. But when you're disorganized, people love to point out when you lose something. But when an organized person loses something, they get a pass, even though the same fucking damage is done. The thing is lost. Who cares how much time was spent trying to prevent it? In fact, it's the asshole who wasted all that time and still lost the thing that we should stone. I wasted no time at all losing something.

But this time I planned and prepped, and so I want a ribbon (at least the results) I was promised for organizing. But I do not get what I want. That stop for BBQ set us back just long enough that the rental car place is closed and they don't take key drop-offs, and so now I have to take the rental car to the airport, and Lyft back. But that comes later. First, we have two shows. Man, planning is for the birds. Who migrate South in the winter. I'll just hibernate in my own filth.

We meet Tina and Dan, the owners and proprietors of Bexar Stage. Dan and Tina just opened up this new theatre at Bexar Stage, and the community is pumped for it. Members of the improv team show up hours before the show just to hang out. In LA, performing teams often show up after their call time. These are the same people who picked up their lives and moved across the country to pay $450 a class to learn how to professionally play make-believe. And now they can't be bothered to leave their house on time to drive two miles to do exactly what they trained for. Give people enough of what they want, and they will take it for granted.

Everyone is hanging out before the show, and I leave to go to the hotel to shower and shit because I haven't yet today, and I'm not interested in sitting around and making small chat. Small chat makes me nervous. Give me an hour of unplanned stage time to perform, and I'll drive across the country for it. Give me thirty minutes of networking, and I'll find a bathroom to hide in.

When I get back to the theatre, there is a man dressed in a head-to-toe shark costume, sitting in the audience. San Antonio is all right by me. I learn nothing about this man, and that is exactly how I want it.

We do two shows. One with the house team, and then we do our podcast. And it will prove to be one of our best shows of the tour. The energy in San Antonio is infectious, and for an hour, we are all electric with improv. Improv is so much about doing something spontaneous well and on demand. It's hard, but not impossible, and that makes it addictive.

Tonight, we catch lightning in a bottle. The jokes land, the stories impress, the players find group mind (a term for when all the players on a team are in sync. They're speaking in the same coded language. If you've ever played Charades or Pictionary and been smoked by the other team because they're just flying through the cards, that's group mind). It feels incredible.

After the show, our hosts and the house team want to go out for drinks. Unfortunately, but not really, I have to return the rental car. I'm actually now thankful I have this errand to run, because it buys me some time to myself and I can go right to bed afterward. This is how I celebrate.

The exits to the airport are closed for some fucking reason, and now I am not thankful. I am fucking furious and want to drive this rental car into the fucking river. Perhaps this will prove to be an adventure I can talk about later. It's not. It's mostly just inconvenient.

I loop around and finally get to the rental office, and then I get a Lyft back to the hotel. It takes an hour. The Lyft driver is...you guessed it, an elderly white man, this time with mints and a charging cord in his car. I tip him because there is a tip jar. I think it's weird that he has one in his car, and I actually prefer the rides where they don't, but this guy gets my money because he asks. I'm a pushover, but I also think anyone in any type of service industry is entitled to a tip. Those jobs rarely pay what they should. Serving people can suck. It doesn't always, but because it can, and can it will, often with no warning, it seems appropriate that money should be thrown at those willing to wield the serve.

I fall asleep alone in a hotel room with a beautiful view I do not take in. I sleep poorly. I think I am becoming accustomed to the train.

DAY 7: SAN ANTONIO, HOUSTON, AND NEW ORLEANS

Population: metal heads, kind souls and chicken fingers, stick-up survivors, and randy bunkmates

"Give me fuel, give me fire, give me that which I desire." Heavy metal lyrics, like Van Damme movies, make kids and teenagers feel like adults. Since they were made by adults, the logic for the kid is, *These are adult things that I understand, so I must not be a kid anymore.* But then when they arrive at adulthood, they realize they had it backward. They weren't relating to adult things. Throwing stars, shotguns, and guitar shredding are what adults do to feel like kids.

It is five o'clock in the morning, and I am sitting in an idling car, waiting for Josh and listening to Metallica. I'm not so much listening to it, as I am being assaulted by it. Our Lyft driver informs me that Metallica is going to play a concert in San Antonio, so he is apparently getting pumped up for it before most of the city has had coffee. I tell him I like "St. Anger."

"Their new stuff still rocks pretty hard," he tells me. It occurs to me that "St. Anger" is probably no longer their new stuff, as I remember that album coming out in high school. There was a period in high school when I listened to a lot of heavy metal. I have always listened to rap, but there are perforations in my adolescence where I explored Pantera, Sepultura, Soulfly, and Hatebreed. This was also a period where I was working out a lot and getting laid a little. I don't tell my Lyft driver any of this. "This song kicks," he says, before turning it up. Josh eventually joins us in the car, and we head for the train depot.

We're back on the train, and I go to sleep hard. If you are reading this and worried that I will sleep through all the travel on the actual train and you will not get to hear about this country, you are half-correct. But you are halfway through the trip portion of the book, so really it can't be all bad. But it should be said that I was not asleep for the entire ride, and you are not missing much from LA to San Antonio. The desert can look beautiful at sunrise and sunset, and there remains some vintage human architecture on the trail, but by and by, the landscape is void of people as a result of the mostly void landscape. An Ansel Adams photograph will do far more justice than my prose. If a picture is worth a thousand words, google "desert" and save us both 999 words.

I wake up just as we are pulling into Houston. Houston is massive and unpredictable in its mood. I can see large buildings in the near distance, but there isn't much in the way of style. When I would visit Los Angeles before I moved there, I always felt weirdly at home driving on the 101 and seeing murals painted on the concrete embankments, billboards for movies, and, of course, the Hollywood sign. LA looks entertaining. My hometown of Denver has its Coors Field and Broncos stadium, once called Invesco, now called Empower. Observing the mountains on the horizon, you feel a team spirit and an appreciation for physical prowess. But in Houston, from what I saw, I couldn't tell you if it was menacing or sleepy. Inviting or standoffish. It's like the new kid at school who is bigger than everyone else but doesn't make a declaration, so no one knows how to interact. I might have left Houston with no real sense of its attitude, if not for Josh.

We are stopped for an hour, and Josh finds a restaurant on the Internet called Paper Co. Cafe that appears within walking distance, but it also appears to be a church. As we cross over to the other side of the tracks and make our way around a warehouse, we find that Paper Co. is a converted warehouse. It is both a cafe and a church, and today there is some sort of teachers convention going on, as many of the patrons have badges and carry three-ring binders and an assortment of colored pens.

I order the chicken fingers and a coffee, and both are fucking good. There is an expectation that fried chicken is good in the South, and the South knows this, and they live up to it. I suppose fried chicken is not that hard to screw up, but it's also incredibly hard to do very well. I've had perfectly prepared seafood inland, and top-notch Mexican food outside of Mexico, but I don't think I've ever had Southern fried chicken as good as the chicken fried in the South. It crackles in my mouth and has enough heat to awaken my taste buds but not assault them.

This cafe seems to be donating money to the church. Or perhaps the employees are at-risk or displaced individuals. There is a specific vibe here. There are small, literal signs everywhere that emphasize gratitude, and it makes me think that profit takes a backseat to some sort of social priority. It's shitty that just a slight uptick in generosity suggests that people aren't in it for the money. It's too bad we can't have both. But it does make the chicken taste extra good.

I love to support the underdog. And that's not to say social services or philanthropy are underdogs, but hell, who am I kidding? Of course they are. The most powerful people in the world rarely run nonprofits. Bill Gates dabbles in philanthropy as a hobby. And by the way, I think he's bad at it. Like he keeps making more money than he can give away. Needless to say, I leave Houston with a full belly, a spicy tongue, and a little reinforcement that people are trying their best and to do some good as well.

Josh and I hop back on the Amtrak to complete our third leg on the train, our second longest commute. Compared to twenty-five hours, fifteen is a breeze, and I could do it with my eyes closed. Because I sleep a lot.

We are one week in on this trip, and unsurprisingly, the contrast between LA and the rest of the country stands out more than any individual community's uniqueness. It's like the sum of the parts of the country do not equal the whole of LA's distinction. We have trouble booking workshops because the train schedule has us arriving in towns during the middle of the week, and we are met with reminders by the locals that "people have jobs during the day."

I observe people talking about their in-laws, watching the kids, and using the weekend to go see a superhero movie. Out the train window, I see farmers tilling the land, people driving to work on empty roads, and couples waiting. Of course, these motions are not absent in LA, but the farms are markets on closed streets of Echo Park, the roads are never empty before 10:00 p.m., and working Monday through Friday is no more common than working three overnight shifts, or collecting unemployment, or doing one commercial a year. The rest of the country seems to be connected, and we, the people who have left for LA, try to connect through our standup and screenplays and TV pitches by telling stories of the places we ran away from. We look to use our art to remain connected to communities we couldn't wait to separate from. I suspect this is because once we leave our hometowns, we find ourselves to be just another fish in the sea of eager entertainers and aspiring artists desperate to stand out. The thing that used to define us, the thing that separated us from everyone in our high school and local grocery store—our pursuit to be unique through self-expression—became what made us blend in our improv class and new grocery store. And ultimately, it's not about the thing. It's about what the thing represents, and that is uniqueness. So we *all* stand in line at Starbucks, or eat handrolls at a sushi bar, or hike up Runyon Canyon and look around and go, "Wait a second, I'm just like everyone else. That can't be. My story is unique." So we dig our claws into that former community to chase that individuality that we were originally chasing. "I come from Idaho Springs, Colorado, and my graduating class was sixty-four people, and I broke my back my senior year of high school, and at least three of my friends' parents committed suicide." Moving to LA didn't validate my sense that I am unique, but maybe where I came from will.

The truth is, it doesn't matter. Sameness, uniqueness, none of that equates to value. This is something I'm beginning to see on this trip. My generation was raised to believe we were special. *Star Wars* told us that we needed to be special to make a difference. And not just *Star Wars*, but most storytelling and parenting pedagogies following the Greatest Generation went to great lengths to put personal over patriot. But we don't need to be special to make a difference. Making a difference is what's so special about people. And regardless of the difference we do or do not make, value is inherent in all of us simply because we are here, living and existing.

And that's what I take notice of outside the window of the train. People existing. Their entire lives in a snapshot. It's every beautifully shot episode of *True Detective, Sharp Objects, Treme,* or any other expensively produced HBO show designed to show you your backyard through an auteur's lens. Minus the violence and vice, of course. Every shot from the frame of the train window is distinct yet repetitive. Neither grand nor insignificant, but simply a glance at a slice of life. And that's just it. A glance. A red Acura stuck at a train crossing, a cook and a server smoking on their break after the dinner rush, balloons and a BBQ pit in a backyard. If you're not on a train, the people you see in passing are doing exactly what you're doing—grocery shopping, walking for exercise, sitting in traffic, or riding on a plane. But on a train, they're living their distinct lives, and you're just passing through. I'm channel surfing. With TV, I can go from cooking eggplant parmesan, to an overtime basketball game, to Jim and Pam, to breaking out of Shawshank. All with or without pants. The train is like that, but in 3D. It is the inspiration, and often the roots, from which HBO writers cast their yarns. And Cinemax. But Cinemax will often show more nudity than people find in their daily routines.

It's becoming apparent that I don't know this country. I thought this was going to be a cultural exercise in revealing how little I actually know, but it's turning out to be CrossFit with apple boxes and that thing where you whip the big rope up and down. As is often the case with meaningful experiences, I didn't stretch properly. I set out on this trip with the hope that I would figure out who I am, apart from who I am in relation to anything. But so far, I've only gotten as far as what I am not. I am not working forty hours a week, Monday through Friday, with a house and kids and in-laws, and a local bar, and rec basketball league, and a backyard. In the middle of the country, I am its void. If it's uniqueness I'm craving, then I've found it.

But it isn't making me feel better. I don't feel like I know myself any better, but I do feel like I'm getting to know other selves better.

I spend fifteen hours on the train today from San Antonio to New Orleans, and it is an embarrassment of riches. Luxury views in excess. This is the part of the country I had envisioned when we set out. I point my camera out the window, trying to get a snapshot of the countryside, and for every one I snap, I miss a thousand. In a flash, both figuratively and literally, I witness a smoker puffing out BBQ clouds, children running shoeless on the porch, the chef slicing brisket, grandma in the rocking chair. Three generations of a family tree in three seconds. In the next flash, there is a haunting warehouse that appears to manufacture, or at least store, cement tombs. Even in writing this, I miss crossing a massive river with a rust and white-painted steel bridge in the distance.

Traveling by train is simultaneously the opposite of *blink and you'll miss it*, and the essence of that very sentiment. I have to assume I'm missing lots when I'm not paying attention, but I somehow feel like I'm missing even more when I am paying attention. It evokes a feeling I had when I entered social services. It's easier to not look for poverty, because once you start, you're aware of how much of it you really aren't seeing. It's Plato's *Allegory of the Amtrak window*. I was less enlightened, but also less frustrated, just letting the shadows of a thousand timelines pass over my iPad.

We arrive at the Amtrak station, and I order a coffee from a machine. It tastes like the machine wasn't built to make coffee but was instead repurposed to do so. "Don't throw out the garbage disposal; we can use it for coffee at the train station," I imagine some innovative Louisianan saying.

I worry about technology taking over because until robots can have opinions, they will always provide services based on programming. Essentially experience by proxy. And experience by proxy is why Dick Cheney couldn't be sympathetic to homosexuality until he had a direct encounter with it. It takes incredible empathy to consider anything you haven't had direct exposure to. Which is why my coffee sucks. This coffee maker has never enjoyed a cup of coffee.

We get to the hostel. It has tapestries donning peace signs, a mishmash of chairs on the patio, and every inch of the inside has the fingerprints of all the precious guests—a guestbook; photos taped to the walls; a refrigerator with magnets and stickers, and inside, a bunch of plates and Tupperware with names written on them in marker. Josh made the reservation, so we have our own bathroom, and two beds! They are, however, bunk beds. Josh gives me the bottom bunk because it is larger and he's being nice.

At a hostel with people from all over the world, we meet two people from Austin, and share a Lyft with them to Frenchman Street—the "new" Bourbon Street, meaning it is what the old Bourbon Street was. It's supposed to be the place where locals go. But if what I've heard about it after being at the hostel for only ten minutes is true, I can't imagine it's that far off the grid.

Our Lyft driver, a young woman, tells us a story about being held up outside a Popeye's Chicken. She casually shows us pepper spray on her key ring and a taser in her middle console. She tells the story with such disregard for its gravity, you can tell she either tells it a lot (probably), or she is one of those people who experiences life without pausing to let it intimidate them (more likely). Do you know the kind of person I'm talking about? They lock on to their interests and goals, and their drive becomes unflappable. So they will be a Lyft driver with no qualms or opinions about it because it's a means to an end, and they will talk about an armed robbery as if it were the same as misplacing their keys. Part of what makes me think this woman is this type of person is that she was able to soothe the robber by offering him her Popeye's.

"I didn't have any money, so I just offered up my chicken." This is a maneuver only accessible to someone who is able to access their executive functioning. This means she was able to turn off her fight-or-flight and see beyond the threat of the gun pointed at her because it didn't factor into her plan. She would make an excellent general.

Frenchman Street looks indistinguishable from Bourbon Street. One long stretch of people pouring out onto the road from bars and saloons, with loud music both live and digital. The only difference, I suppose, is everyone seems a tad bit more put together. Sure, they're all drunk, but it's not a classically buffoon drunk; it's more of a measured inebriation. This isn't their vacation, after all. They've got to show their faces around these parts again.

We get sandwiches, a beer, and a shot at a small hole in the wall. After eating and drinking, I go home. I am not for that party life. Josh stays out much later, and I awake to him and a woman climbing into the top bunk. It suddenly occurs to me while writing this that there is a not-too-outlandish possibility that you are wishing Josh wrote this book because his life seems more exciting. Sometimes I wish that, too. But that book unfortunately would not tell me as much about me. So instead, I offer this: a college flashback.

During my freshman year of college at Colorado State University, my roommate, Adam, fucked someone in my room, and our beds were both pushed up against the heater, so when they thrust on his bed, I would feel it on mine. I remember part of his sales technique: "If you let me fuck you, I will rock your world." I was trying to sleep, but even with my eyes closed, I managed to roll them. But it worked. It actually worked. She said okay. This was early in college, and I remember thinking I would not have much sex if it took talk like that.

Adam lost his erection mid coitus. No judgment. We've all been there or will get there. But what's of interest is how I came to know this fact. After the woman left almost immediately, turning down a ride home, Adam *woke me up*! He fucked a woman with his roommate in the room and, to his knowledge, did it without disturbing me. So how does he celebrate this achievement? By waking me up to complain he went soft. He asked me to go outside and smoke a cigarette with him so he could talk about it. I did it because I'm a Beta male, and Alpha males can sense this, and generally without me trying, they take me under their wing, even if their wing is the stairs to the dorms, and being under it means listening to a jock talk about his ED. I didn't like Adam. He was an asshole and probably still is. But for a moment, we shared a fear about not being up to the task of being a "man." He that night, and me every other night.

Adam dropped out after a semester and left me his office chair, which was more expensive than my computer.

Cut back to New Orleans 2017, and here I am preparing myself for the déjà vu of faking sleep while a woman does not enjoy herself. Instead, I hear some heavy breathing, followed by snoring. They are asleep. And I am left to wonder if the amount of times I've had to lay witness to another couple hooking up is above average, average, or below average.

In the middle of the night, I awake to Josh's legs dangling over the edge of the bed. He then leaps off the bed, lands on his feet, and cries out in pain. The leap was done asleep, and the landing woke him up. He walks into the bathroom, does not shut the door, and from my vantage point on the bed, I get the glamorous view of him pulling his pants down and sitting on the toilet. Cue the heavy breathing, followed by snoring, and he is asleep. This, I'm sure, is above average.

I wake up sometime later to the woman climbing down the bed and gathering her belongings before quietly leaving. I see Josh is still sleep-shitting on the toilet. *Oh God,* I think, *I hope I don't have an Elvis on my hands.* What a sad end to this trip that would be. But it would probably really boost our listenership.

Podcaster Perils on the Pot.

"Josh, Josh, are you okay? You're not dead, are you?" This wakes Josh from his crap nap, and he climbs back into bed.

Never fear, Adam from Colorado State University. You still hold the record for worst sexual encounter...that I witnessed. As for worst ever, that belongs to me.

Again, in college, now 2005, I was having sex with my college girlfriend—from behind because we're sexually liberal, to a point—and I feel the sudden tension and release you get from pulling a rubber band until it snaps. I take a step back and look down to see slight dark coloration spreading across my erect penis. I ask if my girlfriend is okay, and before she can fully grasp what is happening that would necessitate that question, I feel the tip of the condom swell and sag like a water balloon on a faucet, just as I become light-headed.

I run to the bathroom and remove the condom. Blood pulses out from under the head of my penis, covering my white sink and streaming onto the floor. I grab the towel rack and flash to my dead raisin body being identified by my parents: *That's our son, all right. At least he died doing what he loved—worrying about disappointing his parents.*

I bring myself to examine my member, and I can see I have torn the foreskin at the point where it meets the shaft, and my erection is signaling to my body that it needs blood, because that's how boners work. Thankfully, the sight of all the blood immediately diffuses my arousal, and I, like Josh in 2017, manage to find respite on the toilet. Unlike Josh, I do not pass out. Also, presumably unlike Josh, my penis hurts.

My penis was out of working order for five weeks. I still have a scar. And there's one on my penis, too. College is a harrowing experience for the privileged.

DAY 8: NEW ORLEANS

Population: oyster lovers, backyard improvisers, and flirty divorcees

Gentrification sucks. A statement so obvious, they should just roll "sucks" right up into the definition of what gentrification is. Still, that's what I think, even as I slurp up some of the best oysters I've had in what was once a fish market, but is now a sort of artisanal fresh food court. It is my self-congratulatory reward for doing a good job teaching improv not less than an hour ago. Josh is teaching now, and I have wandered from The New Movement improv theatre across the street to St. Roch Market. It's indoors but feels like it was outdoors and then they just threw up some columns and windows. Which they probably did. The ceiling is so simple and unobtrusive, it feels as if I'm in the open air. I have sidled up to an oyster bar with a marble countertop, and am thinking about the local generic liquor store I passed on the way here. I could have gone in there and gotten potato chips and a soda, but instead I am spending three times that to suck down saltwater bivalves. I would eat oysters every day if I could, but I think that would give me mercury poisoning and an unconquerable erection. Who am I kidding? My erections are weak and easily injured. As you all know now.

St. Roch Market appears to be a relatively new landmark in this neighborhood. It is a rash—the first sign of an infection. Before long it will spread, and the liquor store owned by a local and the barber shop run by a family will be replaced with a corporate Philz coffeehouse and a franchise barbershop, a Floyd. And sure, it will ring familiar to me, and I will feel more comfortable, but comfort shouldn't trump culture. In fact, being uncomfortable is good for us. If I prioritized comfort, I would never have discovered I love oysters or improv.

I've spent a decade working with disenfranchised, underserved youth, and I've spent a decade playing make-believe with entitled, affluent college-educated people—almost exclusively white. Those two decades don't directly overlap, but there was a six-year span where I spent the workday being the only white person in a room, surrounded by young people of color who qualified for free and reduced lunch. And then I would spend the evenings in a room where there was only one person of color, and most of us were fortunate enough not to have to rely on the government for sustenance. Government reliance doesn't make you less than, but I have been told it makes you anxious always. It could not have been a clearer lesson. Affluence and privilege not only afford opportunities and education, they have the ability to transform life from being about necessity, to luxury. Having the money to spend on make-believe is a fortune so easily obtained for some, and so unbelievable to others.

Josh teaches improv for money, and I spend my money on oysters, and afterward, we take our privileged asses back to the hostel. I ask him about his evening, and sure enough, he has no recollection of jumping down off the bunk, posting up on the pot, or returning to bed. Looks like this book will be light on ribald adventure, no matter who writes it.

We have plans to meet Josh's sister for dinner, but she cancels. We are not deterred. We go to Jacques-Imo's, a restaurant that was on Josh's "must-do" list. It's in a house with tables tucked into every room and corner. We each get a different kind of fish, and we get alligator cheesecake. It is a delicious meal that I enjoy alone because Josh is on his phone Tinder-ing. Normally, I would not mind, but my phone has no service. So I can either read a book on my Kindle app or just stare at Josh. I feel like *Home Improvement's* Jill Taylor in the episode where her husband, Tim "The Tool Man," is trying to listen to the Detroit Lions game on a transistor radio while they're at dinner. What a terrible show that mostly was.

Fun fact, *Last Man Standing* is basically the same show, but Tim has daughters this time. It has also run for close to the same number of seasons but has something like half the number of viewers as *Home Improvement.* Here's another weird fact. Jonathan Taylor Thomas guest-starred on the show as Tim's daughter's boss, and he comes to pick her up to take her to work for some reason (to shoehorn this guest star without it being a weird date). At one point, JTT comes to pick the daughter up, and Tim comments on the souped up car Jonathan is driving. Jonathan says his dad is into cars, and Tim does a Tim Taylor grunt.

I find this fucking mind-blowing. This suggests that Tim from *Last Man Standing* and Tim Taylor live in the same universe. But Tim Taylor is somehow older than Tim from *Last Man Standing,* because Tim Taylor was raising teenage boys in the 90s, and Tim in *LMS* is raising teenage girls twenty years later. Part of this is unquestionably because of sexist standards in TV entertainment/life, but I do like to see the seams and borders of fictional landscapes as they bump into one another.

Another example is HBO. Larry David plays himself on *Curb Your Enthusiasm,* but he also plays himself on *Entourage.* So that means both shows exist in the same TV universe. And we know *The Sopranos* exists in this universe, because Larry loses one of the DVDs and Turtle dates Jamie Lynn Sigler. But *Entourage* and *Curb* couldn't be on HBO, because they are the reality in the universe. So what comedies does HBO have during the early 2000s? Furthermore, in season five of *The Sopranos,* Junior watches an episode of *Curb.* So then, what DVD does Larry lose on *Curb* in *The Sopranos* universe?

After dinner, we go back to the hostel to change, and then head to the theatre for our show. The New Movement improv theatre is the coolest theatre I have ever been to. During the day, it seems just like a two-story house with bedrooms, converted into classrooms. Because it is. But at night, Christmas lights hang in the backyard, a bar opens up in the basement that serves inside to the theatre and outside to the patio. Perhaps it's the Christmas lights—a decoration that says let's celebrate with company—or the ample benches apart from the theatre seats, or maybe that it's packed, but the whole space rings of an invitation to come in, stay a while, and enjoy. It's really what every comedy community should strive to be.

In a city like Los Angeles, where improv is prevalent and people are more hungry to perform than to watch, it's rare to feel outright welcomed. This is not meant to bash on Los Angeles, and the more I write about the differences between LA and the rest of the country, the more acutely aware I become of how tricky it can be to compare and contrast without somehow putting the specimens on a scale of better or worse. What I simply want to point out is that here in New Orleans, the purpose of the improv theatre is to entertain, like many of the cities we visit, while the purpose of the improv theatres in Los Angeles is to create. And on the surface, these two acts look almost identical. But when you zoom in, you see that creating is often for the creator, and entertaining is often for the entertained. With so many theatres and creators, the duty to entertain is broken up between many, and thus, attention can turn towards creation which breeds inspiration and innovation, and that's why cities like Los Angeles and New York generally offer more finely tuned, nuanced, and avant-garde live theatre. The creators are bouncing off each other, picking up where the last left off, zigging where the other zagged or zipping where the other zopped, if you're an improv nerd. Whereas, in a city like New Orleans and at a theatre like The New Movement, the duty to entertain through improvisation falls squarely on their shoulders, so they pour their energy into a scene that invites, comforts, soothes, and delights the spectator. I imagine the reverse is true for the jazz scene. Walk into any jazz bar in New Orleans, and you might be surprised to find they're not advertising and they don't care that you're there, but the music coming from inside is like nothing you've ever heard. Travel back to the West Coast, though, and it's "Jazz Night! Hear all the popular hits and enjoy 2-for-1 cocktails."

We do our show to a fairly decent audience, and one of our guests is on a house team at the theatre, and the other one opened the theatre both here and in Austin. He says he hasn't paid his student loans back, and he gives his social security number out on the mic. He's reckless and one of those people who makes success for himself but probably burns a lot of bridges. I am a rule follower, and so I don't have a lot of success, but most of my bridges are still intact.

The show goes okay. Josh and I are still finding our rhythm as hosts and guests. One thing I am noticing is that the Voice Of Reason, or Straight Man, is a role not often chosen by our scene partners from across this great land, and I suspect it has something to do with the creating versus entertaining theory

I mentioned above. When you're investing in an art form for the purposes of entertaining, it's often more fun to play away from your everyday existence than to remind the audience of an everyday existence, which is the primary but not sole role of the VoR. (This may be unnecessary, but moving forward I will only use the term Voice of Reason, or VoR, because I think it's more appropriate). I defined it earlier, but allow me to go into a little more detail. Sorry if you thought the lessons were over. I'm an educator. What can I say? Just be glad I haven't told you that you aren't really cold, while you go to grab another blanket as you curl up to read.

In an improv scene, you are searching for something or someone that reflects an unusual idea or point of view. That unusualness is then highlighted, explored, and heightened for comedic effect. However, since everything in the scene is being made up and imagined, the "world" is not an inherently established reality until you build one. The analogy I liken it to is setting the table for a dinner party. If we are throwing a camping dinner party, then I may set the table with a tent, a fire, scary stories, and so forth. The moment someone sets, say, a conch shell on the table, I go, *Wait, that's an unusual thing to bring camping*, so I inquire about it. My scene partner may say they are planning for, or anticipating, a *Lord of the Flies* type of situation. This is unusual behavior. Because I called it out, the audience knows, or has their suspicions confirmed, that it is indeed weird to bring a conch shell camping. I am the person telling the audience, my scene partner, and my team that a conch shell is unreasonable. But if I do not flag the conch shell as unusual to bring camping, then the audience goes, *I guess that's not unusual. I'll keep waiting for the weird thing.* Until the rules of the world are established, the improvisers and, more importantly, the audience, does not know what is unusual, and therefore, unexpected or comedic.

This is not the only way to relay the reality of the scene to the audience, but it is the most common. When a VoR does not exist, you may get a conch shell, a volleyball with a handprint, and a *Godfather* reference. For this dinner party, it's hard to say what doesn't belong, because it's not a dinner party that I or the audience recognizes. This isn't necessarily bad, but it makes identifying or framing what is unusual more challenging because the dinner party is not one we recognize, so we either accept it all as the norm, or we have trouble investing because it's too far removed from our understanding, and we tune out and instead pull out our phones and go on Twitter where the rules are clear: shame, and shame often.

People tend to default away from the VoR for a few reasons. One, the VoR is seen as less fun. It's seen as the David Spade to the Chris Farley, or the wife to Jim Belushi, Tim Allen, Homer Simpson, or any woman married to an unattractive male marrying way outside his league for sexist casting purposes. It can quickly be the uptight role. And if we're improvising to let loose and entertain, why would we ever want to play with a stick up our butt?

This is a false assessment of the VoR, but a widely held one, particularly because of TV and movies mismanaging or broadening the roles. A VoR can be extremely fun to play because you get to play the disbelief, exhaustion, and outrage, as well as connect with the audience. It's a great role when given space and autonomy.

Jim from *The Office* is the VoR. As is Fraiser's dad, Morty; Ann from *Parks and Rec*; Jason Bateman in just about anything he does; and so on. They're not the quoted roles, and in TV, there are usually episodes where their quirks are highlighted, but in general, and certainly in the pilot, they're the backbone of any great comedy. And often the biggest laughs come from them stepping outside the VoR role, or when the unusual character plays the VoR. But in general, it's seen as a thankless and unfun role, so people don't play them. Especially people who are looking more for an outlet to entertain than to create. So if you're not investing forty-plus hours a week into improv, like the privileged few from Hollywood, then looking for ways to subtly shift or subvert the role of the audience surrogate is likely not all that attractive. You are providing comedy entertainment in a city where there isn't much. The audience doesn't need reminding of a base reality because it's all around them. Whereas, in the city of showbiz, the base reality is hanging on by a thread.

In a single day, I shot a docuseries of animated erotic fan fiction, coached adults in my living room about how to heighten bee stings on butts, painted my genitals to look like Gonzo, gave a PSA on social etiquette, and then ate chicken wings ten feet from Quentin Tarantino. In a world like that, it's not only necessary but can be a relief to have someone go "What the hell is going on?" And that is a beautiful thing for me. I can utter that sentiment all day to roars of laughter.

For the record, this show does not elicit roars of laughter, as my VoR characters don't hit the jackpot with their astounded catchphrase. It makes sense. The audience knows this is all absurd. It's why they came.

After the show, we start talking to three women, who tell us they are all divorced moms. I know I am getting older because these attractive women are my age and have kids. I saw them in the audience and thought they were attractive women who were both my age and in college. Not to say women my age can't be in college, or that college students can't be parents. It's just atypical. I am reminded of that every year as it becomes less likely that someone is my age *and* in college. Doing improv for a living will really fuck with your acceptance of aging.

The conversation starts because I am wearing a sweater—one of two sweaters I own—and it is extremely humid in New Orleans. With a little encouragement from Josh, they immediately take to teasing me for wearing a sweater in this weather. I take it off and put it around my shoulders. I think this looks more absurd, but I am told that it is not. One of the moms, Christy—or Kristy (the spelling I did not get, nor was I able to figure it out through some light investigative work on the Internet)—is very attractive and we seem to be connecting. My humility and self-awareness can be charming. I know this because I have been told this, and so I emphasize it. I am aloof, not an idiot. I suspect it comes off self-assured, but I'm just being upfront about my insecurities. I am mostly a buffoon who takes my cues from anyone who will give them to me. Hence, the sweater around my shoulders.

Kristy, like me, is also an educator, so she is privy to an abridged diatribe that Josh stops short by handing me another drink. In addition to being physically attractive and having an interest in me, Kristy is also appealing because of her marital and parental status. This is, perhaps, surprising, as I am not interested in marriage and do not want kids. But I have always admired someone who has been forged in the fires of life's unpleasantries—divorce, custody, pink slips, death. You have to know more on the other side of that, and that adds incredible value to you.

As for the children situation, it is true I do not want kids of my own, but I am a quality uncle (my nieces, and nephews' opinions of me range from acceptable to adored), and so I think I could make a pretty good stepdad, or at least a decent "Mom's boyfriend, Jake." I am mostly set up to succeed in low expectation situations or undesirable vocations. I was an excellent busboy, and I frequently do well on the phone with customer service. I excel in roles no one expects much from.

For the first time on the trip, I feel out from under a cloud of self-loathing and self-inflicted romantic isolation. I miss Em. I still love her, but I also miss the activeness of that love. In the immediacy of a breakup, I feel the intention to let go of love for one another. It is not deliberate or malicious, but an undercurrent of necessity I suspect we all go through. And that process feels dark and sad and sharp. Some people immediately find someone else to connect with so that they can disconnect more quickly. I think of people as having ports for connection, and when they connect with someone, they fill that port, and when their ports are filled, they stop looking to connect, and when they disconnect with someone, that port is open and exposed. Introverts have only a few ports, and extroverts can have endless ports. I have somewhere around seven ports. Two for friends, three for family, one for a partner, and an extra port for the co-worker, partner of my friend, or Lyft driver. I currently have an open port, but it was running hot for so long, it seems unwise to upload with someone immediately. In fact, sometimes I'll purge all the ports and just put my operating system to sleep.

But a woman shows interest in me, laughs at my jokes and teases me, and suddenly I'm blowing the dust out of the port like a NES cartridge for *Battle Toads*. On my list of turn-ons, somewhere near the top is *attraction to me*. I've dated a few women who I otherwise was not initially interested in, simply because they were interested in me. It's nice to be wanted, to receive validation that you are in fact desirable, regardless of the source. Perhaps not. The source has to be kind and respectful. Once, a woman tracked me down at my parents' home after college, and that was not a nice feeling. Give people space. I mean it. It's respectful, and you can't connect with someone you don't respect.

The women decide to leave for a dance club, and they suggest we meet them. I am not sure if this is them trying to kindly exit the situation or subtly advance the situation. It has been, and continues to be, my interpretation that it is always the former, even when it is the latter. I give Kristy my Instagram handle, which is like saying, "Want to get to know me through a disguise I put on for strangers?" It's like Bruce Wayne going on a date as Batman. Which actually makes sense because Batman is cooler than a billionaire. When you think about it, no one would like Batman if they knew he was a billionaire. The idea of the mega-rich saving people sucks because if they really wanted to help, they'd stop being mega rich. It's just another luxury possession. I have $2 billion, a vacation home in Malibu, a private jet, and I save poor people by wearing a cape and punching criminals.

And briefly, while I'm here, does Superman need his job at *The Daily Planet?* He does, right? Being Superman doesn't pay, and he wouldn't steal the money or obtain it by any illegal means, but he does have an apartment. I don't know what the rent is in Metropolis, but it's at least got to be New York competitive. So Superman needs to work as a journalist, and he needs to pay his landlord by the first of the month, pay ATM fees. And he can't just fly to work every day, right? That would just increase the risk of being seen if he's popping in and out of phone booths every morning and evening. He has to take public transportation to work, and he's probably not getting paid enough to ride-share or take cabs, so a man who can fly has to sit on the subway! Even as Superman, the dude is probably lower-middle class, at best. He really should date as Superman. And cook dinner at the fortress of solitude, because going out to eat ain't cheap.

After an agonizing thirty minutes of me waffling, I convince Josh to go to the club to find the divorced divas. It takes

us ten minutes to walk there, and that, combined with my
indecisiveness, is too long. The club is closing down. They're
packing up the amps, for fuck's sake. The women are nowhere
in sight. I am immediately filled with a sense of missed opportunity. I was not playing coy, and I wasn't not pursuing because
of lack of interest. I was unsure about the social contracts laid
out on the table, and I spent too long looking them over. The
other party literally left the building. It would be seen as tough
negotiating if I had an outcome in mind. Would someone else
have known what to do there? I really didn't have a clue, but
I felt pretty sure every choice I made was wrong. It would not
surprise me if they said anything from "We were just being
nice," to "We were very clearly signaling for him to tutor our
kids." Of course. How could I be so dense?

Josh and I head back to our hostel. Our Lyft driver tells
us a wiki page worth of information on alcohol laws in New
Orleans—what they used to be, what they are now, how to
drink and drive more or less legally. I had enough vodka and
blood oranges to not remember a single fact except something
about "open bottle," meaning literally *that*. So a cup with a
cover is okay. It's hard not to find this amount of information
unsettling. Knowledge is power, and I'm hoping that's all our
driver is drunk on. But I'm tossed, so I mostly just hope, crash
or cruise, I keep my oysters down.

When we get back to our hostel around one in the morning, Josh ventures back out to meet up with a woman from
Tinder. I spend the next hour trying to find the divorcees on
the Internet, but because all I have to go on is their names,
Lyndsey and Kristy, and because those names are not as singu-
larly spelled as Jake, I come up empty. This is fucking pathetic.
Two weeks ago, I was at a wedding with a woman I love, and
because I feel strongly that I do not want to have kids, I am
now unsuccessfully investigating a woman's digital fingerprint.

I feel like a washed up private eye who lost his partner and is doomed to a life of chasing imaginary dames. It feels lousy, and it has a tinge of permanence. If I'm right about not wanting kids, I don't think I'll be any happier than if I'm wrong. This existence can't be better than one with kids, can it? I think my privilege as a white American male has given me the impression that life is about maximizing happiness, but my general anxiety has driven me to focus on minimizing pain. So no kids seems less painful, not more pleasant. The whole thing leaves me confident in coming up short, and content knowing it could be worse.

DAY 9: NEW ORLEANS (3/3)

Population: runaways,
funeral directors, and dads

I am floating in an outdoor pool with a wood deck completely surrounding it. It's one of the perks of this hostel. In the pool, I am chatting with a woman, early twenties I'd guess, although if she said thirty, I wouldn't be surprised. She is from South America and is lounging in a big pink inner tube, with shades on. This hostel provides a surprisingly affordable rock-star atmosphere. She tells me about the clubs she and her friends went to the night before, and the drugs they took. I tell her about the comedy show I did. We both do our best to impress the other, but we make the assumption that what impresses the other is what would impress us. This would prove true that old adage about how when you assume something, you make an ass out of you and me. But how was she to know I'm not a fan of drugs? I mean, I am staying at a hostel in New Orleans and floating in a pool with shades on. And how could I possibly know she would not be into long-form improvisational comedy? I mean, she is a human being with eyes and ears, after all. We float away from each other.

Josh and I have to be out of the hostel at 11:00 a.m., but our train doesn't depart until 2:00 p.m., so we head downtown for breakfast with the entirety of our belongings in tow. Josh has a spring in his step. I am happy for him. Because of our luggage, and perhaps because of Josh's satisfied gait—a gait specific to getting action in a town you're only in for one night—we are mistaken for a rock band when we enter the cafe. This is almost as funny to me as Josh being mistaken for a teenager's mom. While there are a surprising number of rock-star components to this trip, the only rocking I'm doing is in a chair to nod off.

Both our Lyft drivers from the hostel to downtown, and from downtown to the train station, tell us roughly the same general story. They both left New Orleans but then came back. When I tell the second driver, a male—either a young-looking forty or an old-looking thirty—that the first driver told us something similar, he says, "Everyone tries to leave New Orleans, but no one does." Even though the sample size for this is two men who work ride-share, I take it as fact because of what the guy says next: "Shit, everywhere is fucked. Might as well be in New Orleans." This I know to be at least half-true. He then says of New Orleans, "The good is really good, and the bad is really bad." I trust people who can be both complimentary and critical. When someone's point of view is an extreme, I usually get the feeling I'm being pitched to. Solicitors in front of grocery stores never tell you their organization could use some improvement. They start the conversation by asking how you're doing, or if you care about some disenfranchised group, but they don't really care. Like a magician asking you to pick a card—your contribution isn't about you.

Conversation for me has always been about learning through connecting. If there's a motivation to persuade, it can dilute the entire enterprise. As a teacher, I would find the most success in asking students questions about what they were thinking or feeling. And when I say success, I don't mean subtly nudging someone toward the path that ended at my agenda. I mean success in the sense that they were thinking for themselves and striving to come to some conclusion on their own. I mean, it's possible they processed the themes of *Catch-22*. I wouldn't know. I only read the CliffsNotes, so I could help them. Real connection, I learned, happens over interests and passions, and not presentations and bills of sales.

As a teacher, few things irked me more than professional development because it was always a sales pitch masked as a conversation. Professional development meetings, or PD meetings, would take place after school or on certain days, when the school was closed. They would have titles like "Investment and Engagement," or "Data Matters." They would all be run the same. Some outside hire, or one of our administrators who went to an off-campus hire, would stand at the front of the room and ask us a question or give us a prompt. After we shared, they'd then use our answers to pivot us toward their method, often "scientifically proven." It was always meant to feel like they were listening to us and providing a tailored solution, but what they were usually doing was giving us time to *feel* heard before telling us what to do. It was meant to get us to buy-in, but it always made me feel patronized. If they had only spoken with passion, or invited us to observe them, or came around and observed us, asked us what they could do to help, I would have been so much more receptive to their expertise. Although they present themselves similarly, the intention between talking to me about what you like, versus what you want me to like, is palatable. One is about wanting me to know you better, which means you value me. And the other is about wanting me to think like you, which makes my value negotiable. I have no time for the latter. As for the former, you can have my ear for as long as you like. Or at least eight hours of golf.

Something remarkable happened in 2008, when a forty-four-year-old golfer with a soul patch by the name of Rocco went toe-to-toe with Tiger Woods. Rocco tied Woods in the regular tournament, then again in the 18-hole playoff, before finally coming in second after losing in sudden death. And then the remarkable thing happened.

I know about this event not because I'm a golf enthusiast, or because I happened across it on Wikipedia (although, I referenced the online encyclopedia to check my memory), but because it was the first and only golf tournament I've watched.

I was living at my sister's house in Imperial Beach because I was a poor AmeriCorps member, and she is a good person. Her father, Mike, was in town visiting. Mike is not my dad. He married my mom and had two children with her almost twenty years before I was born. A lifetime before I was old enough to understand that my parents had lives—and in this case, families and spouses—before I came into existence. Mike was introduced to me as Uncle Mike. I can't recall when I became privy to the truth, but at some point, Mike lost the uncle identifier and became my sister's dad. I would see him at Christmas and Thanksgiving, as he and my mom were still sympathetic friends. When my sister Nicola couldn't go on a trip to China, Mike took her spot. Mike and I were bunkmates for the ten-day international trip, and we got along well. Not as father and son, because I didn't see him that way, but as dorm mates or friends of friends. There wasn't a lot of bonding. However, we went out for a shot of whiskey at a bar one night, and he and I climbed a section of stairs at the Great Wall. It seemed inconsequential. But now, as time has distanced me from that trip, I recall that experience with great fondness. He's the only person I shared that specific milestone on that historic landmark with. Whether I go back to the Wall is uncertain. Whether I go without Mike is. Since that trip, Mike was diagnosed with Parkinson's, and then later opted for physician-assisted suicide. That time on the Wall with him was once in a lifetime.

But that was thousands of miles and many years from this lazy weekend of golf watching. I don't care for sports. They don't interest me, especially something as slow as golf. My grandpa loved golf, and I attempted to get into it, but like any sport, it requires physical ability, coordination, and a twitch of competition. None of which I was born with, nor could I seem to work toward, barter, or buy. And while I'm not competitive, I'm still not crazy about doing something I'm bad at. But as Mike watched and talked about what was happening—the extraordinary way Rocco was playing, that we were watching a real-life David and Goliath—I found myself drawn in more and more. First, by the event. Then by his interest in the event. And then by him. Mike wasn't trying to sell me on golf so he had a viewing partner. He was expressing his enthusiasm, the organic version of an endorsement. Mike's passion for the sport was infectious. Passion works like osmosis, permeating the surface of whoever it comes in constant contact with.

I've known many married couples to adopt each other's proclivities. I have married friends who see every *Atmosphere* concert together. Another couple roots for the Portland Trailblazers, and a third fly fishes. They didn't bond over their shared passion. Their bond supported sharing the passion. But this was slightly different. A man I knew from a distance, whose life didn't routinely impact mine, nor mine his, spoke with such joy over this golf game, that I grew a fondness for him and the stakes of the tournament. Sell me on *you*, and I'll buy anything else. But try to sell me anything else, and I won't buy *it* or *you*.

So I like this man from New Orleans because he speaks with passion but fondly and critically of himself and his city. He's not painting with broad strokes to build his identity. He's offering a picture that has some detail, some blemishes, and some personal touches. In the quest to find what colors best reflect me, I'm drawn to others who seem clear in their self-portraits. Or another way to think about it: How could anyone who knows themselves not possibly be wrestling with imposter syndrome? And if you've got it, why hide it? Wouldn't that be the most authentic thing you could do? Admit you're not sure if you're supposed to be where you are?

My feet settle back into their new home on the footrest beneath the seat in front of me. My bag is under my legs, and my headphones are on. I'm back on the train, giving my attention over to the scenery whipping past the window. Josh and I ride the train from 1:30 p.m. to 9:30 a.m. the next day. Josh takes up conversation with a funeral director, the first person we've talked to over thirty years old since this leg of the trip began. I admire Josh's effortless friendliness. I look over occasionally but am not interested in talking with someone for an undetermined amount of time. But then Josh steps outside during a pit stop, and this man likes to chat, so he tells me about the state capital building of Mississippi, presumably because it is just outside our train window. "Of all the state capitol buildings, it looks most like the nation's capital," he tells me. This man is not from Mississippi, and so I ask how he knows this. "I look up a lot of stuff."

So do I, I think. But it's quickly forgotten, or not something I'd tell a stranger on a train. "Did you know that in an early season of *Entourage*, Dana Gordon had a husband and kids, but then they dropped that so they could write the love storyline between her and Ari? Where are you going? I've got some interesting facts about the filming of *Mission: Impossible–Rogue Nation.*"

We pass by a water tower, and I seize my opportunity. Any time I take a road trip, I pass by a water tower and I'm reminded I have no idea how they work or what they work for. I've looked it up, but like I said, I forget. So I see a big ol' tower, and based on what this guy has taught me so far, I know I can ask him about this and he will be excited to tell me, and I will be excited to not have to think about making a normal impression. He explains that the water tower has a well underneath it, and the water is pumped up. I am satisfied with this answer, and the man is satisfied with the question. I am making all sorts of friends today.

When we talk about his occupation, he says, "I never say sorry for people's loss because it's disingenuous." This resonates with me. I know people don't mean to be disingenuous when they say it, but you can feel it. When my grandpa died, lots of well-intentioned people said they were sorry, and I'm sure they were. But you can't be sorry for everyone who loses someone, and have that sentiment carry much weight. It's similar to asking how someone is doing. The question is more of a formality than an authentic check-in. There's simply not the time. It would be a full-time job. But I'm fine not being checked-in with. I get it. You don't have to ask to see my vacation photos. Someone will, and one is all I need. And I get it with death, too. But when people say sorry, it can sometimes feel like the experience was not unique, and of course it's not. But my grandpa was, and I didn't want losing him to be compared to anyone else's loss, as awful as that sounds. Because it somehow felt like it was normalizing who he was. A grandparent, as opposed to *my grandpa.* Losing him was a terrible feeling specific to me.

Grief is the one sub-category of misery that doesn't always enjoy company. It changes the person. Their life is altered.

Every experience after it is different than the ones previous. Sometimes in small ways, such as fewer phone calls. And sometimes in big ways—there is one fewer person in this world who has known me my whole life. I don't want the profound change to be summed up in a "Sorry." It feels like trying to put a bow on a badger. You can't wrap up loss. Sometimes it's too big, or takes on an awkward shape, or it bleeds through. It sucks.

Everyone loses people they love. How can we possibly have the time and energy to be there for all of them with precise packaging and attention to detail? We can't. But maybe we can acknowledge that we can't. We can leave that box unchecked because it's not something on a to-do list. It's on a live-with list. So I immediately feel compelled to adopt this funeral director's principle. He so succinctly described my feeling. And I mean, who would be more of an expert on condolences and grief than an actual death dealer. Moving forward, I will now search for other ways to convey my sympathy when someone is in the fog of loss. I don't know what it will look like, and I suspect I'll often stumble or miss the mark in providing sympathy and comfort, but that has to be part of it. Not having something prepared, a willingness to stumble through it and offer the effort, even if it means failing a little, because an effortful failure shows that it matters. And we all know it matters. That's why we offer "Sorry." It's the safest way to acknowledge that someone experienced something we wish they hadn't. And I've spent a great deal of my life trying not to rock the boat, but maybe when somebody goes overboard, it's okay to sway the ship in sympathy.

This funeral director, this passenger on a train, changed my life in a small but significant way. We return to our respective books, occasionally looking out the window together.

Later, the man gets a call from his wife, who updates him on the "parking lot fiasco." He tells Josh and I that his funeral home is across the street from two businesses—a craft store and a dentistry—and that they share a parking lot. There is an obvious disagreement about how the parking spaces should be arranged, as one morning, there are lines painted diagonally, and the next morning, someone else is out there painting them vertically. He tells us that, for weeks, the two businesses have been going back and forth. The crafts people will stay late and paint the lines the way they want, and then in the morning, the dentist will arrive early and paint the lines back the way he wants. I'm stunned. I cannot comprehend caring about anything that much. The only thing I am that passionate about is not doing work. I would stay as late as I had to if it meant doing nothing. Everything else is abandonable.

I call my dad because it's Father's Day. On the ever-growing list of conversations between us, this one ranks in the top three for all-time pleasantness. Normally, talking with my dad is hard. This is because he does not talk to many people, but he has things to say, and these things build up like a dam. They sit in his head until he can open the floodgates, and I am like Noah, trying to preserve two-by-two my little thoughts and feelings before they are drowned in a sea of radical opinions on capitalism, TV show pitches, his third self-published novel, and his newfound support for Donald Trump. But this conversation sidesteps all of that because my grandpa is dead and we are both starving for a connection with someone who has known us our whole lives, and the small collection of people that includes just got significantly smaller. On the scale of loss, losing my grandpa weighs in at a metric ton, and it sits upon my back, held there by a frayed strap connected to my heart, and with every step, I feel it pulling, leaning, teetering on the edge, a whisker away from slipping off and crushing me.

When I talk to my dad, I can hear in his voice that he carries the same weight, although I'm sure it's shape and density differs. I do not tell him that I am sorry for his loss or for mine. I tell him that I love him and that I am grateful we can be here for each other as we experience for the first time in both our lifetimes a Father's Day without Nicholas Jabbour.

When we were cleaning out my grandpa's apartment, I claimed his answering machine because his outgoing message was him singing, and I wanted to preserve it, perhaps repurpose it as my own. When I hit play, there recorded on the machine was a message from me wishing him a Happy Father's Day, unaware that he was in the hospital at the time, and even more unaware that he would be dead in four months.

Father's Day and Mother's Day do as much to make me think about all the people without parents as they do to make me think about appreciating my own. At some point, everyone stops calling their parents on the corresponding holiday. You can choose to call your mom and dad year after year, until one year you don't get to choose. This was the year the choice was made for my dad. And that must be unspeakably hard. I used to make calls to three men, and then two, and now just one. And one day, I won't make any. And unless I have a profound change in life philosophy, the phone will never ring for me.

I have been relatively fortunate in my life with regard to loss. Mine came all at once, and it was relatively tame. My roommate of eight years moved out. It was somewhat short notice, but to be fair, after eight years, no amount of heads-up seems enough. Far from devastating, but still I stood fixed while my friend disappeared into the distance. Then my grandpa died. This eviscerated me, leaving the parts of my identity that had felt the safest vulnerable and exposed to the elements. Lastly, my girlfriend and I broke up because I can't stand the thought of creating the potential for more loss. I can't understand how anyone gets through life without abandonment issues. But they must, right? Otherwise, abandonment issues wouldn't be a thing. It would just be part of the package. It's not like some people have thirst issues. We all feel thirsty. But we don't all feel left.

This Father's Day etches itself in my brain one window pane of scenery at a time, until it is too dark to see outside. It's night now, and it's interesting that everyone sleeps on the train at night. Even though that makes total sense, there's still a little nonsense in it. Of all the things we do differently, we pretty much all go to sleep when the sun goes down. Even bad guys, assholes, basketball stars, and brilliant scientists usually go to bed when it's dark out. Sure, we all pull all-nighters sometimes, and there are some night owls. But on the train, when the sun sets, the train policy is it's quiet, and when it's quiet and the lights are off, people sleep. I know it's biological, but that becomes less and less of a reason to do things these days. I think in this case, it's more social contract than natural tendency.

But I don't sleep. I can't right now. While others sleep, I leave. The train allows me to perpetually leave. I am a fugitive. Abandonment is the US Marshall, my Tommy Lee Jones, and he is after me so that he can catch me, lock me up, throw away the key and leave me in a hole. But if I flee, I'm safe. If I'm on the lam, then there's no me around to be left? I'm leaving the capital of Mississippi, and the swamps of Louisiana, and vinyls in Austin, and airports in San Antonio, and swollen eyes in Phoenix. But I can't seem to leave this grief. It's hanging on for (my) dear life. And it's claws are buried deep in me, keeping me up while the rest of the train sleeps. It's broken the skin, and I cry, looking out the window, thinking about how much my grandpa would want to hear about this trip, and how I will never get to tell him about it. And how loved I felt knowing there was someone out there interested in my life and thinking of me. And how now, there is one less person out there like that.

And I guess that's maybe why calling my dad was so nice. He, for the first time that I can appreciate (I'm sure he did it plenty times before), was just on the phone asking me questions and pouring his heart into supporting me, and that filled me with the kind of love I know only a good dad can provide. You see, I don't think being a dad would be the hard part. I think being a dad and being something else would be the challenge. To be a dad and a good employee, or good boss, or good teacher, or good stranger, or good friend, that would be hard, on top of what it takes to be a good dad. I know people who do it, and I am in awe of them, but it doesn't mean I could. I will likely never know. And so I'm going to bed. Goodnight, dads. You're doing a lot of work—not always to a high standard, but that's not all on you. We live in a time where the demand is more than one person can provide. So you're doing your best, and I appreciate it. Happy Father's Day.

You must put in the effort to be fatherly. You can screw up, sure. But accept the role; think about it and reflect and grow from it and be better. That's a dad. A man with a child is not, by definition, a dad. They can just be an asshole with a kid, if they don't put in the effort.

Taking a page from my grandpa once again, it's more important to me to recognize the effort put in to being a dad, not the achievement of contributing to the creation of life. Dads who do their best, this round is on me.

DAY 10: CHICAGO (1/2)

Population: bigots, wanderers, and world builders

I wake up an hour before we get into Chicago, and I race to the observation car. The view of the buildings crammed together, one overlapping the other and others soaring above the rest, looks like a comic book panel. It's possible I've been influenced because Chicago was used as Gotham for *The Dark Knight*, but Chicago truly looks like it was drawn for aesthetic purposes. It's balanced but not too clean, but it doesn't look like a living organism the way New York does, or even a movie exterior the way Los Angeles does. Chicago looks like it was turned out over a long night by a comic book artist on absinthe. It looks like a city should look, but with an edge about it. If New York is for business and Los Angeles is for pleasure, then Chicago is for action. I take a picture. I'm very proud of the pictures I get, and I post one to Instagram for validation. That pic got a lot of likes, and I took immense satisfaction in pointing at a machine I didn't build, in a city I had no hand in planning, at a time of day determined by the train schedule. I am an artist because I was there. So says the Internet.

We get out at union station, and we have trouble connecting with our Lyft driver. He calls me, and I hate talking on the phone. He asks if we can come around to the other side of the street. I say no problem. This is the second time this compromising pickup has happened with a Lyft driver. Considering how many we've taken, it's probably a reasonable percentage. But navigating a landmark with a stranger over the phone will always be one time too many.

Unlike the encounter with our previous lost driver in Austin, we pursue this confused laborer because we're downtown and it seems like securing another driver would be challenging. I have no sense of direction as we emerge from the station, and I feel as if we are in a crowded octagon with our driver saying, "Go to the upper corner." Hindsight will show us we were wrong. Our driver picks us up and explains that he doesn't normally drive this side of town, but he was here for something. He's an older white guy, and the more he talks, the more he comes off as bitter and angry, and he makes a couple disparaging remarks about people from the Middle East. He's a construction worker who got pushed out essentially because of his age and health. The risk and cost to his health wasn't worth the money he was making. He's clearly bitter at the world and frustrated with his new position in life. He gets lost a lot.

When we get out, Josh tells me to give the guy zero stars, and especially no tip. I nod, but know I am lying. I give him two stars and one dollar. I do not tell Josh this, and, in fact, if Josh reads this, it will be the first he hears of this. I cannot see how making this guy's day worse will teach him anything. In fact, it seems like his bad days have made him this way. So I compromise and give him less than I've ever given anyone. I think the thing to do would have been to try and have a discussion with him and then tip him well, but he was already pretty pissed, and when people are angry, their executive functioning gets compromised, and they are not able to listen and learn effectively, and since he was still in charge of getting us to our destination, and in effect, in charge of our lives, I thought it best to just reassure him we weren't in a rush, and then give him as bad a tip as I've ever given. Also, I am a coward. So instead of doing the assertive thing, or the spiteful thing, I will do what I always do in these situations—look for an out I deem equal, if not greater in measure, that requires no confrontation or hurt feelings. It is my belief that scolding, shaming, and shouting do more to soothe the ego of the one wielding the righteousness than they do to educate or enlighten the recipient. It rarely solves anything, but sometimes it's all we have.

Our education system has told us that if we are incorrect, we fail; thus, we are a failure. This makes people dig their heels in when they are called out, especially if they are called out in front of others. No one wants to be a failure—effortless, effort-full, or otherwise. So if you want to change someone's mind, you are best to do it in private. Private reminders and public praise are the methods used by progressive educators. And I would go one step further and say that the mind is hard to change, but easy to nurture. So while I may not be able to do much for our close-minded, prejudiced, old Chicagoan, I may be able to nudge the next youth, with years to marinate, to think of others first, and to realize and appreciate that kindness costs them nothing. Perhaps it is cynical to say it is too late for that old man. Or perhaps it's just a coward's way of avoiding a conflict and investing in the notion that progress comes from focusing on how to be better, not on how to be right.

The hotel lets us check in early, which is great, but they only have a king bed available, which is bad, but it's a suite, so there's a couch, which is good, but there is construction that keeps Josh up, which is bad. I go right to sleep, which is good. But I'm not Josh, which is good for me, bad for him. Josh stays awake and makes an Instagram story to vent his frustrations about the sound. This is neither good nor bad. I never check, but I bet my picture got more attention. This pettiness is certainly bad, but feels good.

When I wake up, I am feeling particularly anxious, so I decide to take my dirty clothes to a laundromat. I offer to take Josh's, too, since he is in a bad mood. I suddenly relate to countless spouses who avoid their angry partner by doing chores. It gives me chills.

This errand is not successful in one sense, and extremely successful in another. It fails to be efficient. I can't find a laundromat. I try three dry-cleaning apps, but none of them will be done by the time we leave the hotel tomorrow at 11:00 a.m. I pick up lunch at a sandwich chain and take it back to the hotel, head back out, and this time I take a Lyft to a laundromat. This is the unsuccessful part of the errand.

The successful part is that I get to relieve my anxiety through putting my feet to the pavement. I have been carrying a lot of anxiety. I always do. But eventually, if I don't let some of it go, my body, usually without my consciousness, sends me on a walkabout.

Before this trip, I went with my sister Nicola to visit her dad, Mike, up in San Jose, as he had recently been diagnosed with Parkinson's and his condition was rapidly declining. I went for moral support and because I love the hell out of Mike. My mom and Mike met in high school and got pregnant with my sister Michelle; then they got married and got pregnant with my sister Nicola. That was their life, with no anticipation that things might change, and that sixteen years later, I would come along, the product of my mom's love for someone else. Mike and my mom didn't stay married, but they stayed very close, my mom cherishing their relationship as it evolved out of partnership and into friendship. Mike spent many holidays and birthdays with our family, even becoming friends with my dad for a period. There's an infamous story of my dad and Mike staying up to make my sister Michelle a birthday cake when she was a kid. They would mixed the batter, put it in the oven, did cocaine, and then forgot about the cake, leaving it to burn. They then remade the batter, put it in the oven, and did more cocaine, repeating the process with the same result. By the end of the night, they had made extra trips to 7-Eleven, bought the convenience store out of cake mix, and made four inedible birthday desserts. I think about how self-assured my dad and Mike must have been to hang out together and not let jealousy or resentment dictate their relationship. Or maybe cocaine is just that powerful. In any case, I've always loved Mike and seen him as a sort of inverse stepdad. He never raised me, nor was he some deadbeat who walked out on my mom. But rather, he was this cool dude who served as friend and father figure during the holidays and family get-togethers.

In San Jose, I spent most of the three days quietly on the couch. Nicola, Mike, and I would watch TV or a movie, but I usually wound up finishing whatever we selected by myself because my sister would have doctors or therapists to talk to, and Mike would fall asleep. We went to a comedy show one night and shared in a round of cocktails. It wasn't eventful, but it wasn't supposed to be. It was supposed to be comforting and a little fun. It was both. But it was also anxiety producing. After all, a man we loved was dying. Before I knew what was happening, I found myself alone on a three-mile walk in flip-flops, in the hundred-degree heat, for a sandwich. I had blisters on my feet for weeks. The walk wore me and my anxieties out. As stressful as the trip was, I'm glad I went. Mike would elect to die eight months later.

This walk, like many before it, gets me centered, even if it takes me out to left (Wrigley?) field. This is my second time in Chicago. The first visit was in 2015, for a sketch show, and coincidently, I was also recently separated from Em during that trip. We started off as an open relationship, something I thought I could do, but will never do again. She wanted to stop seeing me after New Year's. But we spent the night together before I left for Chicago. And then I left, assuming we were done. That trip was weird, as I'd thought constantly about Em, certain she was not thinking about me. We got back together, so I must have been at least partially wrong. I often find myself thinking about people who I feel certain haven't given me a second thought. I'm doing it right now. I'm thinking about Carrie, a woman I had a crush on in first grade, who moved away, and then we ran into each other at a party eleven years later, and she immediately became attracted to me when I told her I had a crush on her in first grade, even though she didn't remember me at all. And now I'm thinking of this guy I used to work with at Walmart, who befriended me, and we would drive across the parking lot, flying kites out of the window of his car. And now I'm thinking of the mom of one of my students, who told me, in a conference with the principal, that her ex-boyfriend used to have mounds of cocaine on their coffee table that she'd needed to package while watching her son.

Thinking about people thinking or not thinking about me makes me feel powerful but inconsequential, like a hurricane that never touches down on land. Look at all these people and personalities and memories I can swirl together, but thinking about them, holding them in my mind doesn't do anything for the potential impact, or lack thereof, I may have had on them. And then I think about something Maya Angelou said: "…people will forget what you said, people will forget what you did, but people will never forget how you made them feel." As a teacher, I've been gifted that quote in some form or another (mug, card, plaque, etc.) no less than a half-dozen times. It's meant to serve as reassurance that even though you don't get paid well or respected very much, and a lot of your job is unfairly measured by test scores and quantitative numbers, you, a teacher, are making a difference. It's a sweet sentiment, and also, I suppose a little intimidating, but it did keep me going as an educator for far longer than I ever imagined. It served as reassurance and a reminder. It's important how we make each other feel. I've also thought about it on the receiving end of feedback. I've had many a mentor or guide who made me feel important, heard, and valued. And sadly, I've had some who made me feel small and burdensome.

I can't be certain any of those people have ever given me a second thought. I assume they haven't, because they haven't contacted me. But then again, I haven't contacted them. I can't tell if it's insecure to think no one thinks about me, or narcissistic to think I'm the only one capable of thinking about other people. I guess my reason for thinking about others is that, in some way, it comforts me. If I'm able to recall them in some light, then perhaps they can do the same. And as is becoming a theme of this book, seeing someone is valuing them, and it's my hope that if I can recall them, then I saw them, and if I saw them, then hopefully I valued them, and that's the feeling they remember. Then again, that could just be wishful thinking. Carrie, David, Ms. Smith, if you're reading this, please leave a review letting me know how often you think about me. My self-perception depends on it.

Here I am, two years later, back in Chicago, and back apart from Em. I feel certain Em is not thinking of me, but I am thinking of her, so I text her. I confide in her that I'm sad and depressed and anxious, and for the first time on this trip, and only the second time ever, I feel myself fading from her consciousness. Her response reads compassionate, but not concerned. The way you might offer condolences to a coworker. I am not mad at this. I accept it. I understand how a breakup works. But it guts me all the same. At one time, our mutual love for one another was racing neck and neck to grow, and now the race has slowed to a jog, and some days it feels like her pace has slowed exponentially, and other days it's mine. And pretty soon, we'll drop out of the race altogether, and we'll maybe pass each other as strangers walking in different directions.

Tonight, Josh and I have two shows, but first we have an interview with Charna Halpern. Charna is partially responsible for our modern interpretation of long-form improv. She worked with Del Close and sort of expanded the form and founded Improv Olympic. She is hard to get to agree to an interview. I know this because Josh tells me. I do not talk to her until we get in her office and sit down with her and her dogs for the interview. I could never be a journalist. I wonder how many journalists are extroverts. It seems like if someone else did the reaching out, an introvert would be a good journalist because they would be interested in deep conversations, if they could only get over the hurdle of asking for the interview.

When we sit down with Charna, she is gracious with her time and optimistic. She is a woman who taught and witnessed the rise of talents like Chris Farley, Tina Fey, Adam McKay, and Amy Poehler. She speaks of them fondly, takes some credit for putting them on the right track, and is as hopeful of the new generation as she is adoring of the older ones. It's a thoughtful conversation, and one you can hear for free on the Internet, if that interests you.

One anecdote she tells is of letting Adam McKay stay with her when he was broke and his parents' patience had been exhausted. She said she knew he was a genius, and that she'd believed in him. When I hear this, I think about how most people must identify with Adam McKay, or at least allow themselves to fantasize about mimicking his trajectory, especially when the chips are down, but that story takes two people. And I wonder how many people identify with Charna. I wonder if Charna identifies with Charna. Did she always see herself as the believer and supporting figure, or was there a time when she was the ambitious artist, the auteur? Is the nurturer ever anyone's first choice? Do people ever aspire to be Lorne Michaels first, and their backup career is stardom?

We meet up with Josh's parents and uncle and aunt for an Italian dinner, and Josh's dad encourages me to order three meatballs with my spaghetti. He is a good man, and I will remember him for the rest of my life. I do like a family dinner. Maybe more than a friends dinner, or a group dinner. Parents ask questions and we answer them. But it's not the center of attention aspect that I think I take comfort in. It's the defined roles. It's the podcast parameters all over again. I equally enjoy being the uncle asking my nieces and nephews about their lives. So long as I understand the direction of the current, I can go with the flow. Wave pools and parties are what make me feel like I'm drowning. Whose leg is touching mine? Whose responsibility is it to inquire into the employment of the other? I haven't asked my uncle about his work for twenty years. But I always ask my nephew Tony about his week.

Josh and I leave early for the iO show. We set up in iO's brand-new facility, complete with a bar and food service. It's quite a venue, and we have a fun, but short, show. We have time for a quick beer with Josh's old friend, and then we race over to The Annoyance Theatre for a show with Susan Messing, a Chicago legend, and Emily Fightmaster, someone we have not met, but who a mutual friend suggested we invite on.

This show is not exactly a hit. There are very few people in the audience, and if you exclude Josh's friend, and my friend

Maddy and her boyfriend, there are closer to zero people than there are to five.

After the show, I meet up with Maddy and her boyfriend. This is the Maddy of Em-and-Jake-meet-and-send-photos-to-Maddy fame. Maddy is one of the brightest souls I have ever met. Any good qualities I see in other people inevitably remind me of her. It's almost as if she has a patent on charm, and if anyone else exhibits it, I have to send her mental residuals. I met Maddy in San Diego, and we became fast friends. We would often eat our weight in quesadillas on many an evening after she crushed karaoke and I crushed Jägerbombs, only one of us looking back on the night humiliated by our choices. And when I came out to Chicago for my sketch show, I asked her to be in it because one of our actors (sensibly) thought it did not make financial sense to fly across the country to play an idiot cop. Maddy did an exceptional job, and I will remain grateful for it. It is hard to count on people, so when you find one, let them know. Maddy, you rule.

When I came out to Chicago the last time, and Em and I were not seeing each other, I looked to Maddy for some comfort. Maddy wished me well, but never said a bad word about Em, even when I was probing for one. I was desperate for any hint that the person who didn't want to be with me might not be all that great. It's much harder to be rejected by a wonderful person. I never got that respite. That took integrity, and I admire Maddy for it.

I ask Maddy about a story that's been rolling around in my head: "Did your sister get arrested for not returning a rental car?"

Through surprised eyes and laughter, she says, "Oh my god, yes." Her sister got into an accident and was given a rental car by the insurance company, and she just never returned the car—until she was pulled over and arrested for grand theft auto.

The reason that story rolls around in my head is that I traverse from point A to point B with so much general anxiety, that the thought of traveling between those two points in a car I inadvertently stole because I didn't go to the trouble of returning it would paralyze me with so much fear that I would probably never get out of the driveway to get pulled over. Recalling other people's brushes with jail and death and divorce often helps me face the day. I suppose they could serve as cautionary tales, but I see them as a dark reminder that it could get worse, and that I should count myself lucky. But also, hey, if it gets worse, there's plenty of evidence in other people's journeys to suggest I get through it and be able to laugh about it later. It's yet another perk of the podcast. Hearing other people's dances with despair are my fairy tales. It's sitting across from the knight who slayed the dragon. They're bedtime stories devoured to help me sleep better at night. Yes, there is evil in the woods, and yes, it can be defeated.

I say goodbye to Maddy and her boyfriend. Josh's friend takes me back to the hotel, and Josh and his friend go out late-night drinking. I am sitting alone in a hotel room, and I have this feeling of familiarity, and I can't place it because I'm alone in a hotel in a foreign city. This is the opposite of familiarity. This should feel entirely new. After all, being alone in a new city is exactly that. New. Different. But it doesn't feel that way. It feels like…Baltimore.

Immediately following the 2016 election results, I bought a ticket to DC to participate in the Women's March. I did it so impulsively, I don't think I realized I had done it until I was on the phone with my mom saying she should come with me. And at first she was going to, as political trips have taken the place of baseball games for time spent with my mom. She once paid for me to go to DC with her during George W. Bush's presidency for a week-long training on grassroots organizing.

Fired up on democracy, we stayed up late making presentations on the power of grassroots politics that were to be evaluated by former campaign managers and political idealists. It was fun but also ridiculous. My mom and I, sweating the aesthetics of a poster board as if we were going to get a bad grade and it would prevent us from voting in the next election. What can I say, my mom and I are students of academia.

Anyway, my mom couldn't swing it that time, so I decided that if the world was going to shit, and I felt helpless against it, I'd at least incur some debt to march around in solidarity to the novel idea that women should be treated with equality and respect. Hard to believe that needs to be said. Or maybe it's not hard to believe. Just heartbreaking. I met a friend out there, and we shared a room for the first two nights. And in between those two nights, I underwent a life-affirming transcendental metamorphosis.

That probably seems hyperbolic. And I admit that it might be. But being surrounded by a million-plus people for an entire day, all exerting at least some portion of their mind and body to the well-being of women, changes you. I was raised by women, so I thought I had a fair understanding, or at least acceptance, in how different men and women were treated, and how unfair that was. My mom was the first person to correct me when I used the word *chicks*. She told me that we shouldn't be "teaching tolerance"—the common term of the time to address sexism, racism, and prejudice—but we should be "teaching acceptance." She also explained how, as a female teacher, she had to change the tenor of her voice, overemphasize the rules, and essentially work harder to garner the same respect as her male cohorts. She had a conversation with me about consent so causally that I assumed it was as commonly understood as stoplights.

Additionally, there was simply a lack of male influence in my life. I wasn't around my dad enough, nor did I have older brothers who might have persuaded me to think or behave in more archaic and chauvinistic ways. My point is I wasn't born with an innate understanding of respect and equality. I just had the luxury of growing up with my mom and my sisters, who were putting into practice and conversation the necessity for effortful consideration.

When I got to college I gravitated toward making female friends. I found social situations populated by solely dudes uncomfortable at the least, and at the worst, repulsive. And still, I was naive. Patting myself on the back throughout two college degrees and multiple careers working with youth from diverse backgrounds, where the role of women can be shocking, I thought I had a solid understanding of the intense disparity and struggle women faced. But I did not. I do not. The Women's March was proof of that. The subway was so packed with passionate souls that it literally took my breath away. In part because of the cramped conditions, and in part because that number of people surrounding me gave me anxiety. And I know I wasn't the only one. My feet hurt from over ten miles of walking. My bank account was emptied because of expensive plane tickets, hotel rooms, transportation, and food. And I know I wasn't the only one. My voice was gone from shouting, and I know I wasn't the only one. And my mom, a woman I love and would do anything for, wasn't there. Neither were my sisters, my nieces, or my girlfriend. I was marching for someone who wasn't there, and I know I wasn't the only one.

It took a lifetime of learning and a considerable amount of effort to get to put my feet down on the National Mall that day. And as far as my eyes could see, there were other people doing the exact same thing. And if I was there with only a fraction of the understanding and experience of the injustice, then what must everyone here have seen, heard, and experienced? Everyone there was marching for someone who wasn't there. On a single day, I was hit with the physical impact of hundreds of millions of people who were not afforded the respect and equality all human beings deserve. You don't know until you know. You know? And what do I know? I know enough to know that even after that, I still know nothing. And I hope I never stop looking back at my life and recognizing I was naive. It's the clearest way to know you're learning.

I don't think I'll ever experience anything like that day again in my life. Or if I do, I'm worried that it will be during a zombie apocalypse and we'll all be looking around grateful that at least the zombies aren't racist, homophobic misogynists running for office. They just want to eat our brains.

My friends left the day after the march, and I had an additional day because that was when the cheaper flight was, so I got a hotel room in Baltimore and spent the day wandering around an exhausted city, eating oysters and fried chicken, and getting into a fight with Em over the phone. I can't even remember what it was about now, but I remember wondering if I should just change my number, disconnect from the Internet, and disappear into the streets of Baltimore. This is my go-to, as you can tell. Go-to that I don't go to. I sometimes have this feeling when I feel overly exhausted or agitated. It's a freeing feeling. If I give up everything I hold dearly, if I'm able to do that, then nothing can be taken from me, nothing can hurt me. It's a sentiment stolen from the movie *Heat*. Robert DeNiro's character says there shouldn't be anything in your life that you couldn't walk away from if you feel the heat around the corner. The irony of this is that he does find someone he can't walk away from, and then of course the heat comes. I'm not a mastermind thief, or even a dumb one, but that movie romanticized the idea of having your whole life in your control by not having much in it. But that's not a rich life. Everything about my life that I love comes from the connections and attachments I've made. But those relationships are also where the pain comes from.

I'm fortunate that, even though my back is broken and I don't have the coordination to jump rope, I'm able-bodied. I grew up poor-ish, but I'm a white male, so that helped immeasurably. I haven't struggled with substance abuse or intense mental health issues. So when something in my life hurts, it usually stems from relationships—either from them not being what I want them to be, or obstacles coming between them, or being complicated by obligation or lack of insight. So I fantasize a purge, not because I could, but because the act of being able to do it would mean I was able to sever my ties to everything I cherish and wipe out any previous, present, or future heartache. It would give me the control over every loss in my life, and somehow by controlling it, it would hurt less.

Mike made a similar but much more severe choice when weighing the options of living with Parkinson's. He opted to receive medical support to end his own life, rather than wait for the disease to take it. Now, my situation pales in comparison to his. I won't even pretend to say they belong in the same category. I'm bitching about a breakup, a change in living situation, and the death of a grandparent. None of which living with would ever categorize me as strong or courageous, the way people saw Mike. However, regardless of the situation, owning loss feels less painful somehow. I guess if I could move myself to make the choice, then perhaps I'd have accepted the separation a little easier. It's the resistance that hurts the most. The friction caused by the unwanted loss. But there are pastures of gray between accepting loss and inviting it. And the point, if there is one, is not to avoid pain altogether, but to learn from it and let it tell me who I am. Not just when things are going my way, or when I'm in control, but who I am when I'm alone, frustrated, grieving, reflecting, sharing, engaging, loving, losing, succeeding, and, of course, failing.

Running away in an effort to cast aside any one of those will teach me nothing. And that's what writing this book and traveling the country by train is about. To wax poetic about all the times I've hurt my penis, about the grief of losing a loved one, recording make-believe scenes with strangers where adult men who break their legs are sent out to pasture and castrated, *and* achieving life affirming self-actualization. Plus, I have a cat I love too much. She wouldn't understand or care. She'd just move on to the next person who feeds her, and that would really break my heart. My purpose whited-out with the ease of opening a can of wet food.

I put on shorts and curl up on the couch in my suite. The bed remains empty and preserved for Josh. What a strangely isolated way to spend a night in Chicago. I toss and turn with both the guilt of not telling our Lyft driver off, and the guilt of tipping him only one dollar.

DAY 11: CHICAGO (2/2)

Population: abandoned dump trucks, isolated back breakers, and conservative dinner company

It's a gorgeous Chicago morning. The kind of morning where the sun is out but the air is crisp and cold. It's like those Sprite commercials where the athlete is sweating and they twist open a Sprite and ice crystals form around them. But it's also bright and yellow, like a SunnyD commercial. You could drink today from a cup. It's a climate I've felt before in Denver. The kind of climate that reminds you why millions of people would willingly live in an area that gets bombarded with snow, freezes ice to your windshield, and makes walking anywhere a slog. It's for these kinds of mornings that you can't get anywhere else. Humans have manufactured hot tubs, saunas, sweat lodges, tanning booths, and iceboxes, all designed to mimic a specific and extreme climate, but we've yet to crack the code on the bright and brisk morning. You can see farther than you'd think, your hands are cold, but the jacket or sweater you have is enough to keep you toasty, so long as you don't catch the wrong side of a gust of wind.

I am picking up my laundry. I put on Kanye West, as he is a Chicago native and it brings me joy to listen to music made by a man who maybe once stood where I am standing. I am having a glorious morning.

Addendum: This was long before Kanye West's latest barrage of outbursts, and so I didn't write about that because it hadn't happened yet. It's getting harder to write about anything because culture doesn't crawl along decade by decade at an easy-to-document pace. It soars tweet by tweet. When Kanye radically steps into the spotlight, I will think back on this day and how Kanye probably walked the streets of Chicago imagining, hoping, maybe even knowing he would become a star. But this emotional turmoil in the public eye? That had to be a surprise to even him. Still, I bet he wouldn't do it differently. I bet the cost is high, but the rewards are worth it. But I bet there's no going back, and that's got to be tough. I hope he takes a walk. I hope he finds peace.

Because I walked far and am tired, I call a Lyft to take me and our clothes to the hotel. My driver tells me he works as a long-term parking lot attendant. I ask him if anyone ever leaves a car and doesn't come back for it.

"Oh yeah," he says. "Earlier this year, a man died on vacation and his children had to come pick up his car. You could tell it shook them up by having to do it."

He tells me that another time someone parked a dump truck in their parking garage and it sat there for three years before they had it towed and sold. I find this fascinating and ask him what he thought happened. He says he has no idea. Neither do I. But I suspect it had to do with organized crime. The long-term effects of growing up on action movies are plentiful and mild, one example being everything unexplained is usually the result of some nefarious man or enterprise.

Unbeknownst to my driver, he's triggered one of my favorite mental pastimes: thinking about property that sits while we live our lives. That's it. It's simple, requires no calculation or creativity, yet I do it a lot. When I return home after a long day of teaching or being stuck in Los Angeles traffic, I will pass by the Batman action figure my friend John gave me for my birthday, gathering dust on my bookshelf, and feel comfort. If I'm stressed during an IEP meeting, or feeling a particular sense of rejection, I will visualize the laminated VIP pass for Rock the Bells 2008, and remind myself that this, too, shall pass because it's an experience, not an object. The biggest event is more temporary than the smallest ticket stub.

In the face of all I experience are the things that remain unchanged if not interfered with. In a way, it's their permanence that reminds me that everything else is impermanent. True, Batman and Rock the Bells have emotional significance, but it also works with items I'm unattached to. As frustrating as a flat tire can be, or as humiliating as rejection can feel, they can't affect the permanence of the Case-Mate full of burned CDs in my closet, or the longboard under my bed. I suppose a fire or earthquake could affect those things, but even then, there would be something—a tiny dictionary, stashed away in my car, or a pair of headphones tangled in the bottom of my backpack—to remind me that even the devastation of a disaster will sink into the past. I need not cherish the totems for them to have significance for me; I just need them to remain permanent.

I often look at the Jose Canseco book given to me by a woman nearly a decade ago, still unread, or the little photos and cards I have pinned up on my cork board, and think how they all sat there when I got accepted into TFA, overwhelmed with excitement, and that they were still there when I quit with exhaustion. They remained stoic as I excitedly flirted through texts and cried through a breakup. Whatever I go through won't be earth-shattering. It can't even shake my cork board and loosen a pushpin. From the Lincoln Memorial to a bench at the botanical gardens that reads "In loving memory of Sam," monuments are erected to remind us of some person or event or thing, so that no matter what happens, we will remember what Lincoln did for the country, or that Sam sure loved walks through the azaleas. But for me, these trinkets are lighthouses, physical landmarks that weather the darkest storms and the calmest waves, casting out their light in reassurance that this, too, shall pass. On the smallest of scales, they are the monuments erected to my little life, and a testament that it will go on.

I tell my driver about my podcast. He asks where it's available, and when I say, "any podcast app," he says I should put it on YouTube. It's where he goes for everything. He makes a good point. I'm peddling my content out on podcast apps, the digital equivalent of a mom-and-pop shop, when YouTube, the Walmart of content, will carry it for free. Why wouldn't I take the additional step to have them carry my goods? It will stay on the shelves forever. To gather dust, or to be picked up by the most recent reader of this book. Go see for yourself. Have I finally uploaded my podcast to YouTube?

The hotel has turned our water off. I complain to the app we booked from, the ever-exceptional Hotel Tonight. They give us a discount, and the hotel gives us a key to another room so we can use the shower. It is not uncommon for me to use a hotel bed but not a shower. This will be the first, and I presume only, time I will use the shower and not the bed. It's strange. They give us drink tickets we never use.

For the first time on the trip, I pick the restaurant we eat at. I enjoy that Josh has places he wants to go. It takes the pressure off and avoids having to compromise, both thing I don't like. I'd prefer one person gets what they want, and the other person settles. Why should we both not get exactly what we want? If I will agree not to get my favorite, then why shouldn't you get yours? No sense in both of us picking our runner-up. And that is my working philosophy nine times out of ten, provided I do get the tenth. This is that tenth. Josh doesn't say it, but I can tell he's not thrilled I'm picking. There's a sluggishness to his moving, micro-stalls on our way to fill our bellies. I'm not sure why. Perhaps because he's been to Chicago, so he's got an idea of a meal he'd like to revisit, and if my choice isn't compara-ble to the nostalgic idea he's been fostering (a near impossible task), then I'm the dream wrecker.

Our Lyft driver to the restaurant informs us he used to snow-board semi-professionally before breaking his back. "Wow," I say. "I also broke my back. Do you have residual pain? What vertebrate was it?" He doesn't answer my questions, nor does he show the slightest bit of interest in learning about a similar rare injury. Instead, he talks about getting drunk in bars in Chicago. There goes my attempt at connecting with a stranger. Look, dude, I understand tiring of telling the same story over and over, but we have a unique, shared life experience. Aren't you the slightest bit interested in comparing notes? That would be like if John Glen didn't want to talk to Buzz Aldrin about what the Earth looks like from the moon. You will not find a ton of other people who can relate, you know? Is your prob-lem that I'm comparing a broken back to space travel? Well, fuck you then, and fuck trying to connect with strangers. This always happens.

Once, I was visiting a friend at their apartment pool, and the pool had a metal fence around it. I left the pool to use the

bathroom inside my friend's apartment, and the gate was at
the opposite end of the pool that my friends were at. When I
returned, the gate was locked and there was a guy on his phone
less than five feet from the latch. A total stranger who I normally would not have interacted with because he was a total
stranger, but I didn't want to yell across the pool for help, so I
said, "Excuse me, sir, do you think you could help me out and
let me in?"

"Nope," he responded, without looking up.

"Oh, what?" I chuckled with humiliation.

"I'm in the middle of a game on my phone, and I can't
pause it." Still not looking up.

I had to yell across the pool for help. He literally reinforced
my—until now, I assumed—irrational fear of not reaching out
to strangers because they will be cold and dismissive. And now
I got this bro with a broken back, talking about a bar with shot
glasses made of ice. We're both stonecutters, asshole. Now do
the handshake.

We arrive at Au Cheval, a bar-restaurant with an open
speakeasy vibe, and eat burgers. The burger would give all of
LA a run for its money. It bleeds with cheese and an egg, and
the knife is almost not long enough to cut through the tower
of beef and bread. Then we get a flight of beers at a brewery
next door. Every city has a brewery now, and it makes me think
we must not have a water shortage. Or it makes me think that
looking back, it will seem absurd that at the cusp of exhausting
our world's carrying capacity, we were using our most valued
resource to make peanut butter stout.

We meet up with Josh's friend at his apartment, which
has floor-to-ceiling windows and a rooftop with a pool and
a gym. We meet him on the fifth floor. It is a combination
lounge-library-cafe. I am aroused. If this place has a coffee
machine, I could orgasm. And I'm sure if I did, some Roomba

would mop it up. I have modest taste, but I definitely think I would be happier living in this luxury apartment than my two-bedroom dwelling.

Josh gets a kick out of me jaw-dropping all over the place. After nearly two weeks of me picking slant-luxury hotels, Josh has come to see and appreciate my predilection for a comfy palace. I'm not a freak. Everyone would enjoy a glamorous roof over their head, but I'm the rare breed who will spend the money I don't have to sleep under one because it feels like fantasy. Much like improv, it's playing make-believe with a life that is not my own. It's safe to say I will never be able to afford this kind of living. Actually. Fuck that. If I'm not sure who I am, who is to say I'm not built for riches and fame? This book will make me the kind of money to maybe not live floor-to-ceiling glass, but at least I'll live in a downtown apartment with a pool. Or at least I'll be able to afford a Roomba that cleans up my spills. As God, or Carrie from first grade, or whoever is reading this, as my witness, I will purchase a vacuum robot.

Our visit goes long as Josh and his friend catch up, and I gawk at a building probably owned by Donald Trump. So big, so grand, so unnecessary. We then race across town to the train station. I'm getting anxious because we have to make this train. The rest of the trip depends on it. I'm racing through the station, and Josh is behind me telling me to relax, and this only succeeds in filling me with uncharacteristic rage. In the history of people freaking out, has the command "Relax," ever brought someone down? Maybe it used to be effective until movies took it over, and now we can't help but hear it as condescending.

We make the train, and Josh says something to the effect of "See, we're fine," and I want to ditch him in the caboose and disconnect the car. I was racing because I thought we would miss it. So either we make it and I'm wrong for thinking we wouldn't, or I'm right and we miss it. Either I will feel foolish or not get what I want. I eat a candy bar and, no exaggeration, feel a thousand times better.

There are some Pennsylvania Dutch people on this train. That is, at least, what Josh and I have determined after snapping a pic and sending it to a friend who grew up in Ohio. I would have said Amish, and I would have been wrong. It's funny how little I know about my immediate surroundings, and yet I'm still quick to make assumptions. I wonder how one stops that. *Self-awareness?* I think, while writing a self-indulgent book. I suppose I could ask, but I've never cracked how to respectfully inquire about someone without seeming rude. And it would appear neither has the woman who sits across from us at dinner.

This is our last overnight on a train, and so Josh and I splurge and have dinner in the dining car with a Trump supporter. What a treat! We, of course, didn't know this at the time because they don't allow hats—even MAGA hats—in the dining car. But this woman's politics would soon be revealed to us. If you're getting antsy reading this, I don't blame you. I would assume a meal where you learn your dining partner is a fan of Trump would be a meal in which someone gets wine thrown in their face or smashed into a cake that reads "Universal Health Care!" But that is not the case here. This is an anti-climactic tale about recognizing my eternal need to define myself in relation to others, and the missed opportunities for self-discovery that come with that.

The train staff seats us across from a mother and daughter. I estimate the mother to be in her mid-fifties, and the daughter her mid-twenties. They were seated before us, and when we sit down, they have drinks and a basket of bread already. They share their bread with us. The mom is retired, and the daughter is a bartender. They use an Amtrak credit card to rack up points and then take a trip. They're headed to New York to see some Broadway shows. Josh and I, as a sort of ice breaker, do a round of our tongue twisters, filling them in on the running joke.

"My bumbling bopper bounced his boost on the beach."

Our dinner guests don't appear to appreciate our tongue twisters. At one point, the Pennsylvania Dutch family sits down across from us at another table, and the mom with all the absence of tact I've ever seen just straight up interrupts this family's dinner to ask, "What are you?" I bet people unlock pool gates for this woman. Meanwhile, I can't muster up the courage to ask the server what the soup of the day is. What if his dad drowned in a soup factory?

The family politely and simply responds, "Dutch." The succinctness of this response informs me they must get that question a lot. If I got that question, I'd stammer, "Afraid. White. Poor. College-educated. Debt-ridden. Pampered. Privileged. Guilty. Lost. Uneasy. Existential. Two days from a shower. Sleepy. Horny. Ambitious. Delusional."

The mom gets a piece of chocolate cake to-go and retires to her personal car.

Remarkably, I sat and enjoyed dinner with a Trump supporter who wasn't my dad, and it didn't end in bloodshed, or even tear-shed. We enjoyed each other's company over a meal. This was an important moment, and it made me feel foolish. Before knowing this woman's politics, she was another passenger on the train, just like me. She represented the group I was currently identifying with: train travelers. I didn't know her politics—that of a group I adamantly disagree with—and as such, I didn't see her as an other. In fact, I enjoyed our meal together and found her to be, at most, harmlessly quirky. I could learn a lot from this exchange and apply it to exchanges with my dad. Perhaps we'd talk more, and I could learn from him if I just waited until after the phone call to remind myself he voted for Trump. Sometimes the hardest thing to do with someone you disagree with is to see how much you're alike. And those are moments of self-discovery and change. Or at least, moments of potential. Which is why change doesn't happen often enough or enough-enough.

Let me introduce a hypothetical wherein the host of the dining cars gave me the option of going to a dining car with a Trump section or a dining car with a non-Trump section. "Oh my god, what a thoughtful consideration. Trump detesters, please," I'd say. Once there, the host then offers tables for Bernie supporters or Hillary supporters. I make my choice and then find out I can choose between a secular booth or a seat at the atheist bar. I'm given a couple more sorting options, and soon enough I'm eating alone, feeling isolated on a train filled with people whose only commonality is the direction we're headed. I've now defined myself so specifically that I have no one around to share my point of view with except those with the very same point of view. And since I'm so sure that my position is correct, what I'd really like to do is have the opportunity to debate, and eventually influence, those who disagree with me, but now I don't have the opportunity. And while political discourse never took place between myself and the train-adoring Trump supporter, we did get the chance to literally break bread, the first step in listening, conversing, and hopefully seeking to understand, which is a step further than we would have gotten if the host had given me the choice to sit in the non-Trump section.

Now, the step is the first of a long journey, longer than Josh and I have on this train, but it's the step toward genuine change and enlightenment. Instead, we want to bend others to our will or force their hand, because it's easier, but it's not as effective. I think about the mini-series *Show Me A Hero*. It was created by David Simon and was based on the nonfiction book by Lisa Belkin, of the same name, which tells the story of public housing desegregation in Yonkers, New York, in the late '80s and early '90s. A federal judge rules that the city must build public housing in an effort to desegregate. Not surprisingly, the white middle class resists this, going so far as to incur federal fines for noncompliance. Eventually, they give in because of cost. Another subplot is of a middle-aged white woman played by Catherine Keener, who is unambiguously racist. She is tasked with being part of a neighborhood committee to brainstorm solutions. She must regularly meet with and work alongside non-white people, and over the course of these meetings, she becomes exposed to another way of life and begins to change. The journalist David Wiegand wrote about her performance: "...she constructs an ordinary woman whose values and beliefs are largely unexamined and derive from a lack of exposure to alternative ways of thinking. At heart, she is not an evil person, just fearful of what she doesn't know."

I think about that description a lot. Especially when I'm confronted with the belief systems of "others," that I may label as wrong or evil. It's easy to give the woman on the train the benefit of the doubt that she is not evil when I don't know her politics. It's much harder when I do.

I didn't achieve enlightenment from having dinner with this mother and daughter. They didn't give us life advice or ensnare us in an Agatha Christie-esque train mystery. We had idle chitchat, and had it not been for her obtuse inquiry into the Pennsylvania Dutch family, I might have forgotten all about the exchange. But when I learned of the mother's political affiliation, I was jarred and ashamed of my knee-jerk response. *She wasn't so bad for a Trump supporter*, I thought. What kind of attitude is that? Here I am, on a train, trying to figure out who I am, and while I haven't had any epiphanies yet, I don't expect the big reveal to be that my identity is democrat or progressive. Those identifiers include belief systems and government expectations, but they are also categories of relationships. Identifying as a democrat is no more precise or finite than being a roommate, boyfriend, or grandson. They are hats I wear. Blue ones that read "I'm with her," but still just hats. I am learning that I am more than that. As much as I want to be the things I like or the groups I belong to, I am a part greater than the sum. I exist independent of who I live with, who I love, and who I vote for. And so, at the very least, I should grant that same understanding for this woman, who shared her food with me and couldn't have been more polite to me. I can assume she wouldn't have been so kind or friendly if I hadn't been a white male, or if I had suggested we all pool our money together to pay for the medical bills of the woman who was carted off the train in Alpine. But that's an assumption rooted in a narrow definition of a relationship.

So while no wisdom or venom was exchanged across that dinner table, and I left with no clearer understanding of who I am, I did sit with a full stomach and think about who I want to be. That would be somebody who gave everybody, even the people I disagreed with most, the opportunity to express themselves beyond my labeled presumptions. I want to give everyone the same opportunity to claim their identity that I'm working to give myself.

DAY 12: DC

Population: movers, shakers, bathroom guests, and friendly fiancés

Hands down, one of the best things about the train is waking up on it, looking out the window, and taking in a completely new and interesting landscape. In this instance, Virginia. It's almost like waking up is when the dreaming starts. Instead of closing your eyes and drifting off and becoming conscious in some dreamscape, you open your eyes and find yourself transported to a whole new world, one that eats up your entire viewfinder with red-brick fire departments, rotted wooden bridges, parking lot basketball courts, and the occasional Applebee's. Lots of people dream of being rich, but the rich cannot dream up this universally acceptable viewfinder. To have it, they'd have to slum it with the rest of us.

I have always wanted to live on the beach, or the Venice canals, or a house at the top of a mountain for the very obvious reason of waking up to a spectacular view. To be greeted by the natural world from the comfort and safety of your home is the only luxury I truly envy the wealthy for. But for a fraction of the price, and considerably less accommodating sleeping arrangements, o a train you can have a view of the entire city, state, or country, depending on the length of your journey. The rich may have one glorious view, but they are limited by the immobility of their home. Only the maniacal villain from Wild Wild West has both wealth and a moving mansion. He traveled by train, and by a giant robot spider, if you forgot.

Virginia is beautiful country. It's green like something out of a fairytale, and rustic like something out of a folktale; a setting fit for Paul Bunyan to retrieve the ring from hobbits. It makes editing a podcast and eating a protein bar for brunch epically transcendent. I love this country, and in this moment, I am convinced that a train trip by every American would bring us all closer to the middle. I feel the same way about a two-year teaching commitment, David Foster Wallace's commencement speech at Kenyon University, and Jay-Z's *4:44*.

The teaching commitment goes without further explanation beyond the perspective it gives you that you are probably at a point of privilege in your life, and that our education system needs serious attention. The commencement speech is by the author of *Infinite Jest*, but far more accessible and on half as many bookshelves. David Foster Wallace is a flawed person, but his speech to soon-to-be contributing members of society proposes we all assume that the person next to us could benefit from our patience.

4:44 is the thirteenth studio album from Shawn Carter, and the first one in recorded memory where he admits fault and apologizes for something other than his success. The album is an apology to his wife, Beyoncé, for his adultery. It's been criticized as a commercial tactic to drum up attention, but whatever the reason, it's a recorded testimony of a successful artist admitting he was wrong and asking for forgiveness.

You don't get a lot of admissions and apologies these days from anyone, let alone billionaires. But the beauty in it is, in a music genre known for exaggerating, glorifying, and hyperbole in service to hyping its listeners up, the legendary Hova rhymes that he is sorry. Is he posturing, as his genre has always encouraged? Perhaps. But if his apology inspires just a tenth of the people who went out and bought a Brooklyn Nets hat because Jay-Z said to to take responsibility and apologize, that will still be thousands more than before. If music moves us and Jay-Z got everyone to "get that dirt off their shoulder," imagine people being a little less protective of getting that dirt on their knee to show reflection or remorse.

These are but a few—even if a few is all we have—examples of concentrated doses of living a life distinctly different from the comfortable one we know. Without having to reinvent ourselves, and still altering our role in our own life and the lives of others. We can never really know how it feels to live as someone else lives. Even if we try every day. Which no one does. But especially if we never try. And that gap between trying and not trying is where sympathy lies. Empathy comes from recognizing ourselves in someone else's situation. Sympathy comes from trying even when we can't. And sympathy can go a long way to better understanding, communicating, and co-existing.

We arrive in DC, where Josh has planned for us to stay with a fellow improv enthusiast by the name of Pete. Introductions were made over the Internet, and so our first in-person meeting is when Pete greets us at the train station. He reminds me of a high school football coach. But not the old, out-of-touch kind. The football coach at my high school once challenged two of my friends, who were repeatedly screwing around, to fight him outside behind the gym. Now that I've been a teacher, I totally empathize with that level of frustration but am totally appalled he acted on it. Pete would never. He embodies the intense, dialed-in, and vigorous type of coach. He takes us through the "fun part of town." I'm surprised by this description because, while I find DC extraordinary for its political heartbeat and historical significance, I never think of it as fun. It's mid-afternoon, so it's hard to get a sense of the fun Pete is referring to. Still, the independent coffee shops and record stores with their stencil font on the windows and wooden chairs set outside seem to suggest a friendly spirit.

Pete is the guy who gets shit done. He wills it. He seems to be almost single-handedly not only keeping improv in DC alive but also raising an army of improvisers. He tends bar, but sees to improv with more intensity than I do with just about anything. He has knowledge about improvisers in LA, programs multiple shows of improv a week, and teaches workshops to teenagers. It's easy to admire someone like Pete because, as anyone who has pursued art knows, the journey comes with its fair share of disappointment, and so being resilient is key.

Pete puts us up in his apartment. It's on the second floor, quaint and welcoming, with wood floors and a furniture layout that feels thoughtfully considered. My apartment is basically a place to put stuff down, so I'm always a little taken back when I go to someone's place and I see that there is an end table next to the front door, with a bowl for keys, and a coffee table centered in the living room, equidistant from all the couches and chair so people can utilize the table but also don't have to squeeze around it. And what is this? A coat rack? But then, what are the backs of your kitchen chairs for? Oh, this art hanging makes the walk down the hall aesthetically pleasing. It's almost like you want to feel comfortable in your dwelling by stylizing it to your tastes.

By god, this is your home.

Both my parents moved out of their respective homes when I left for college. My mom moving to Denver, Colorado, and my Dad, Lincoln City, Oregon. The rooms I grew up in no longer exist, and the new dwellings my parents moved into didn't have a room for me because that would be impractical, as I didn't live with them anymore, and they didn't have money for an extra room for their phantom son. Both of them moved every few years for a while, and so when visiting for the holidays, I would sleep on the couch in an unfamiliar living room. I didn't have an attachment to my "home for the holidays."

Meanwhile, back in Los Angeles, I moved into a two-bedroom apartment and never looked back. I've been there for close to a decade. It is now the closest thing to a home that I have, but my family doesn't live there or visit, so it doesn't feel like a home either. I've never even spent a Christmas or Thanksgiving there. As a result, I'm in this living limbo where my apartment doesn't have a homey feeling, and going "home" feels like renting an Airbnb. Having not decorated or taken any thought into how my place makes me feel certainly can't help this quest to find myself. So when I see Pete's place, I can't help but define myself in contrast. His place has a personality and a style, and as it is foreign to me, he is my "other." So do I then have no style or personality, or is my style a lack of personality? This again is the danger in defining oneself by comparison to others. This home underlines me not having me figured out yet. Which is why I like hotels.

I prefer hotels to being a guest in a home. And not just a fancy hotel; I'll take a Motel 6. I like the vacancy of a rented room. No one lives there. It makes little sense to compare my living situation to that of room 401. Yes, hotel rooms have a style, but the style is for the comfort of the guest, not the owner. Plus, I can be a pig if I choose. Or, as is often the case, not choose. I have a friend who orders hot wings and eats them in the second bed and uses the sheets to wipe her hands. I never go that far. Mostly, I just leave the towels on the ground and poop with the door open. My biggest messes are always unintentional, and often sparked by the pressure of being in someone's carefully curated home.

I am an agreeable guest. A quiet, unobtrusive guest. But still, I have the visiting coordination of a baby. I always do something buffoonish in someone else's house. In theory, I strive to be Mary Poppins, helpful and delightful. But in actuality, I am Mr. Bean, a murmuring wrecking ball.

Pete introduces us to his wife, and now I know I'm doomed to drop a dozen eggs or get my pants sucked into their oscillating fan. If Pete were a bachelor, then the havoc I will inevitably wreck is at least confined to the host who invited me in. But for someone with a partner or a roommate, the fallout could be astronomical. I'm in hot water. Literally. I use their bathroom to shower because I spent the night sleeping on public transportation. It's like camping on the floor of a 7-Eleven. It seems strange that one would smell worse as they get older, but I think that's the case. The teenage years are designed to be a trial by fire. As young adolescents, we smell awful and have no self-awareness about it. Then we're thrown into a classroom with hyperaware, insecure peers who are looking for any weakness they can exploit to mask their own insecurities. Enter deodorant or cologne, or whatever the hell Axe is. This is all to prepare for adulthood when, I guess, your body begins dying, and you smell worse faster. And judging by my smell, I'm due to be buried at dusk.

I get into the shower—a standalone, claw-footed tub. I turn the water on and it comes out of the faucet, so I bend down to pull the knob that directs the water up to the showerhead, and the water comes rushing out of the nozzle and splashes off my back, soaking the window and blinds in these fine people's home. *How did he get water on the top of our drapes? What kind of Neanderthal isn't familiar with indoor plumbing?* I imagine them saying. Still, on the scale of bathroom calamities, this ranks mild.

"Rub one out?" My friend Pat asked when we were sixteen. I had disappeared upstairs for a substantial amount of time during a sleepover, and if a teenage boy is out of sight for a second longer than two minutes, his friends must accuse him of masturbating, or he may then accuse them of masturbating while he was gone. Why masturbation requires accusations in the first place was never made clear to me. Making yourself orgasm in private seems like something one should be proud of. But teenagers are insecure, so I guess anything that might bring them joy is immediately seen as vulnerable, and therefore worthy of being mocked for. But I was not masturbating. Boy, how I wish I was.

I left Pat's room in the basement to go number two, and then clogged his toilet and flooded his bathroom. Pat didn't yet know this, so he and my friend John teased me when I returned downstairs, defeated by the massive clog.

"Uh, Pat...I, uh, clogged your toilet, and I can't get it to stop. Water is everywhere," I confess.

"What the fuck are you saying? What?" Pat asked.

"Ha-ha, you're so fucked," said John, who was usually not this redundant.

"Please, just help me, assholes," I say.

John and Pat exit the room, and we hear the drip of water hitting the basement floor with increased frequency. It was leaking through the house.

We rush upstairs and Pat turns the main line to the water off. It's funny. I know that's the first step with an overflow, but I panicked. Pat threatens to wake his parents up. I plead with him not to. Too late.

Pat's dad, Darryl, fills the doorway to the bathroom, observing the destruction of his house in nothing but his white briefs.

"What the fuck have y'all done?"

"Apparently, Jake took the world's biggest shit," Pat says, laying my head and sphincter under the wheel of the bus.

Darryl instructs us to step aside, and he grabs the plunger. It does nothing. He goes for the snake—a coiled piece of metal designed to, as its name suggests, *snake* its way down the pipe, pushing any turd or sock out of the way.

"Fuck, it's fucking stuck," Darryl says.

The snake was now stuck, and Darryl had to put one leg up on the rim of the toilet bowl to get the leverage to pull it out.

"Did you flush my cat down the toilet?" Pat asks.

And I think, *no*, though sort of wishing I had. Being a psychopath seemed better than a toilet destroyer.

Pat says, "We should wake mom up," with a twinkle in his eye.

"No!" shout I, John, and Darryl.

Pat's mom was not to be trifled with. She ran a daycare out of her house, so she demanded respect and had to be thrifty with her patience. She wasn't keen on you asking for a snack at three in the afternoon, so we could all see the writing on the wall if we woke her in the middle of the night to a flood and a burrowing turd.

Darryl eventually got the toilet unclogged through force of will and elbow grease. He was even kind enough to suggest a toddler at daycare may have flushed a block down the toilet. Even if that were the case, teenagers weren't exactly prone to accepting a solid defense theory when it was much easier to show up at school on Monday and say, "Jake's giant asshole nearly drowned Pat's parents."

My poopy plugged Pat's porcelain.

Fortunately, teenagers have short attention spans and idiotic instincts, so it wouldn't be long before another kid passed out at a party with his testicles exposed, and for some reason was shamed for this. It seemed to just be the combination of loose shorts and big balls, but I wasn't about to step in to defend him. I basked in the respite. My doody debacle was now lost to the sands of time, only to resurface in an interview with Terry Gross about this very passage.

Josh and I go on a walk for coffee. Despite the thousands of miles we've traveled, it's these brief walks together where we cover the most land between us. With shows to recap, workshops to plan, and episodes to edit, Josh and I have plenty of business to discuss. But whether or not intentionally on his end, we don't. We check-in with each other. He asks how I'm holding up. I say, "Well enough," and express excitement for New York and settling down for a few days. Josh agrees and makes a joke about how he's surprised I'm not most excited for a cheesesteak. He knows me well, and on second thought, he's right. That is what I'm most excited about.

After coffee, we each make a phone call to a woman in LA. What happens on Josh's phone call remains between them and the NSA. I express some version of faith through the phone. Not faith in it working out, but that it not working out will be okay. I have always felt a breakup to be a failure. After all, it's not what anyone starts a relationship for. To have it end. Right?

My mom has always said that a relationship ending is not a failure. It can be just as much a sign of growth, as one continuing. That the experience is not measured by the destination, but by the journey. For the first time in my life, I'm seeing that. I had always assumed that it was the divorce that tainted my idea of eternal love. Because I had so few Christmases with Mom and Dad, and with memories of family road trips fading, and not a shred of evidence of a date night, it was easy to believe love between two people belonged in the same cultural camp as Santa Claus and trickle-down economics. My parents never got remarried, and so I had no first-hand experience as to what a whole household looked like. I assumed it must be idyllic, or at least greater in joy than the pain caused by separation, and that staying together was a mark of success. But this experience with Em is proving that line of thinking to be inaccurate. My parents didn't throw in the towel. They succeeded in loving themselves and me. They put their happiness first, societal expectations and norms be damned. Staying together wasn't for them, and that takes incredible self-assurance to know that.

Marriage is painted as a milestone (packaged with tax breaks), so it's easy to see it as a goal. Anniversaries are winning streaks, and the participants, champions. But the truth, as I understand it now, is that milestones are merely watermarks in the depths of love and happiness. This misconception is what I get for using sports metaphors when I don't watch sports.

Over the entirety of existence, we will feel full, empty, and everything in between. But it doesn't change our ability to hold. We're a reservoir defined not by our levels, but by our capacity. Sometimes the source of water is marriage, but it doesn't make much sense to keep tapping it when it's run dry.

I was getting topped off from the relationships I had to my grandpa, my girlfriend, and my roommate. They made me feel brimming over, testing the strength of the dam. But when those sources dried up, I felt empty, unsure if I could still identify the same way. And if I was a reservoir that didn't hold water, wasn't I somehow defective? A failure. But what I'm experiencing here is not failure. It's sad and makes me feel Sandra-Bullock-in-*Gravity* levels of loneliness, but it doesn't make me feel like a failure. It makes me feel aware. I am a reservoir with a certain depth, admittedly shallow in some parts, cracks and soft soil where I leak. I have a sleepy embankment, and a dock to run off naked. Yes, I am a receptacle for the outpouring of others, something that makes me attractive to streams of friendships, downpours of disenfranchised youth, trickles of lovers, and the occasional stranger runoff. And I flood easily. Earlier, I said I had ports for connections, but maybe pipelines are more accurate. But wherever my sources come from, they don't create me. I'm not Legos. Whether I'm brimming over or bone dry, I am a reservoir. My nature is to rest easy and receive. I'm comforted by this revelation, as it's much of what I've been searching for, even when it comes packaged alongside the incompatibility with someone I love.

Em can't be my source, but that doesn't mean her absence changes who I am. So much of my life has been peering out a muddy windshield as I drive, or sometimes being locked in the fucking trunk, barreling toward some unknown destination. But this moment, while terrifying, at least shows signs of the lines on the road. For now, it's a deserted road. But at least I can see enough to avoid a head-on collision. Maybe I'm not a reservoir, but an above-ground pool. That would at least account for the lack of sturdiness and class, and the bursting around the seams. And for now, I'm being transported, so I'm empty. But wherever I end up, I'll still be an above-ground pool.

For a while, I was set up below Em's water slide. She wanted to invite some kids over to play, but I was worried they'd drown, and felt more comfortable just having an inflatable donut float about. In this analogy, kids are kids, and the inflatable donut is a donut. So we got packed up and sent in different directions. There's no failure in that. I'm grateful that we got to share some sunny days together. Just because we will not end up in the same backyard doesn't negate the summers we spent splashing around. We complemented each other, and we both got to have more fun, but we didn't define each other, and we're not any less of ourselves without the other one. She's still a slide, and I'm still an above-ground pool. I realize this is a lot of reassuring I'm doing here, but I'm feeling alone, and so I need to tell myself that being alone doesn't define me any more than being together does. Believing that is necessary if I'm to feel comfortable with slides, pool noodles, and spilled beer. Because while those things won't define me, they make the splish-splashing more memorable, more meaningful, more-more.

Take Josh for example—the spilled beer in my analogy. Without him, this trip would look much different. For starters, it wouldn't have happened. That Pumbaa worked his little tail off to make this happen. We had a pretty chill thing going for us in LA. We were doing what we wanted (improv), with whom we wanted (our friends), and how we wanted (breaking as we played horny idiots). We weren't making any money, but improv has never been about the money, because there isn't any. It's been about recapturing and preserving our childlike desire to pretend. It's an easy endeavor on paper, but a far more competitive and head-fucking one in actuality. But we were doing it, with almost no downside, minus the weekly hat-in-hand vulnerable invitations to other adults. "Any chance you're free to come over to my apartment and sit around the table and play make-believe?" People almost always said yes, but it still feels a little pathetic when so many of your peers are opening IRAs, making reservations at three-star restaurants, and researching car seats.

So it never occurred to me to make an active effort to inject a change. Change almost always comes with some discomfort, so it's usually in response to an even greater feeling of discomfort. I wouldn't have thought to illicit any change, because the podcast was comfortable for me. But to Josh's credit, he is always looking to inject some new stimulus. Perhaps he feels discomfort. Although, if he does, he hides it well. Don't get me wrong, the dude complains, but his creative spirit is always independent of his gripes, so he always appears pure and positive in his pursuits, which makes him incredibly attractive as a friend and partner.

When the trip finally started to materialize, I viewed it through the lens of a career opportunity—both for the podcast and for writing a book—and as a chance to fucking escape the deep abandonment I was feeling. That seems like a lot, right? Well, with Josh, it's been so much more. New towns aren't just work destinations, but opportunities for nights out with cocktails and unknown companions. Alone, I would know the possibility, but I would never chill with hostel-mates, venture out with the hosts, get drunk with moms, or try to hookup. Those interactions intimidate me. I'm afraid I will upset someone's equilibrium or find myself vulnerable in a context I can't control. And yes, it's true I have passed on most of Josh's gambits. But I've said yes to far more than I would have had I gone alone. And those negligible amounts of invitations I've accepted have heightened my experience. No Josh, no chat with the funeral director, no revelation about grief.

It is not a coincidence, and in fact, it makes all the sense in the world that my relationship to Josh and this tour are rooted in, and driven by, improv. The fundamental tenet of improv is *Yes, and.* Accept your scene partner's offer, and add to it so that the scene grows, becomes more interesting, more comedic, and perhaps even more memorable. Again, more-more. From my first improv class, to Josh's invitation to get breakfast burritos, to our most recent walk to get coffee, I am saying *yes* to a proposal, and adding *and* with my presence, opinions, and feelings. And just like in improv, it matters very much who your scene partner is. Your scene will look wildly different if your scene partner says "Yes, I'll bake a birthday cake with you, and let's get some ice cream to go with it," versus "Yes, I'll bake a birthday cake with you...and let's do some cocaine." I am the former kind of scene partner, whereas Mike and my dad are the later.

But what I'm learning is for Josh there's something about me bringing the ice cream that he values. I'm trying to figure out what the value is, how who I am shapes our scenes. But in the meantime, I'm thankful for the scene. I value that Josh wants to bake a cake with me, because it validates my presence, and I get to enjoy cake with someone instead of destroying a California Pizza Kitchen (CPK) butter cake alone at an airport bar.

Once, at LAX, while waiting for a flight, I sat at the bar of a CPK and ordered a personal pizza. After the pizza, I treated myself to a butter cake. When the cake came out, they served it on a plate with *four spoons*. Now keep in mind, the bartender had been serving me all night; she knew I wasn't keeping any company. I choose to believe the kitchen put the spoons on the plate, and the bartender was too busy to think to take them off and save me the embarrassment. Or maybe it was muscle memory when she grabbed the silverware. But regardless of how it happened, it happened. I, and everyone in proximity, was reminded that I alone was eating a dessert meant for a double date.

I share this anecdote partly because it's funny in a sad way, or sad in a funny way. But also because it was a scene by myself. And while I could speculate what it says about me or the waitstaff or the West Coast's pizza laboratories, it doesn't grow without a scene partner or an audience. It's just a hint of humiliation in my life. And without Josh on this trip, or Em by my side, or my grandpa watching my back, I'm alone with my experiences. No *yes...no, and*. My relationships aren't there to define my existence; I'm an above-ground pool either way. My relationships are there to enrich my experiences.

It's important that I write this down because it's easier said than done. Easier typed than believed. Even as I put the words down, I don't feel them. What I feel is drained. Evacuated with signs posting "Contamination," as a soggy turd smears at the bottom of my deep end. Self-examination is the active diarrhea of the soul. So I go to the snack bar.

Josh and I find a falafel house. I wait for my food and am transported to my deathbed looking back at this moment. The moment in my life where I eat a Middle Eastern dinner across from my best friend, in a city I have little familiarity with, before we do a live show for a podcast I'm trying to make significant, thinking about this moment as the moment I considered that I might be alone forever, accepting it, and somewhere on a future deathbed, surrounded by no one, confirming it. This falafel is the best I've ever eaten, and I know this because it keeps pulling me out of total existential dread. The opposite of Carl's Jr.

Our two shows at the DC Arts Center are well-attended, the largest crowds so far. It's a testament to the work Pete has put in. Even though he couldn't attend, Pete provided someone to work the tech booth and a photographer. Both shows go pretty well, but I honestly can't be certain of that. All that existential examination, distance from others, pool analogies, and delicious falafel has me detached from everything sensory. I feel like a balloon that slipped through a child's hand. I'm floating above it all, and I can't tell if it should worry me or liberate me. Which is probably how the balloon feels. This is the discomfort that comes from change. All I've ever known is that child's tiny, closed fist, and now it's no longer there to restrict me or protect me. I am no longer Em's boyfriend, or Nick's grandson, or Ryan's roommate. I'm free to be me. That's fucking terrifying. Especially since most of those balloons end up fried in a power line, or choking a bird to death. Few of them ever do book signings at Barnes & Noble.

After the show, we go out for pizza and beer with some improvisers and the woman who ran tech. She is both engaging and engaged. She tells me she identifies as having attention-deficit/hyperactivity-disorder-like behaviors. We talk for maybe an hour about our experiences with public education.

Disappointment in the education system is a universal language. Some people think sports are the great unifier, but they're not. Some people aren't interested in sports. And sports don't override political or religious beliefs. But education binds us. Even republicans and democrats agree our education system is broken. And they each use it to support their own agenda. Liberals argue more money for schools to improve them. Conservatives argue fewer resources should go into schools because they're bad. It's frightening how complacent we all are with the utter failure of the system. No one argues that it's bad. We all argue about making it better or letting it die. Or worse, we don't care what happens to it. It's fucking pathetic, and we should all be ashamed of ourselves. Humans are natural learners. We are eager to learn and grow, and yet we've often made it a torturous and deflating endeavor, one we couldn't imagine spending a second instilling in someone who isn't blood-related. A marvelous feat, to be honest.

Me and this woman exchange numbers in the event she comes to LA. This is easy for me to do because she is engaged, so any feelings of anxiousness or self-consciousness about reading into anything are muted by a hard-to-misinterpret social contract. "This ring means I have plans that don't involve you." Excellent. We should all wear rings, along with those opinion tags I pitched in Phoenix. Tags for conversations, and different rings for marriage, engagement, divorce, dating, broken-up, actively searching, isolation. That way, the conversations can be more direct for us less savvy elbow rubbers. Rings for relationship statuses, and badges for conversation availability.

I realize I'm pitching something out of a dystopian '80s novel or sci-fi movie, but I'd venture those stories were erected in the minds of introverts with low self-esteem. We fantasize about a system that would make us more comfortable, and then fear it would destroy society. I myself am rarely accurate when it comes to subtext versus intention. It's what makes me effective in professional settings (I overcompensate), and a buffoon in social ones (I second-guess what's certain and double down on what's not).

When I started my second teaching job, my supervisor said the IEP meetings would take over two hours on average. I got them down to sixty minutes. That's because I'm fairly good at comprehending someone's non-verbal communication and replying in kind. The first thing to remember is that our education system is severely under-resourced, so regardless of the effort of the teachers and staff, it's likely a parent, and especially a parent with a child with special needs, is feeling like their child's needs aren't being met to satisfaction, because they usually aren't. The next thing to do is to remember how it feels when someone tells you your feelings are inaccurate. This isn't the temperature of a casino pool; this is a parent protecting their child's well-being. Acknowledge that their feelings are valid and accurate. Let your guard down. Listen actively. Nod your head, repeat back what they say, give verbal affirmations, sit next to them and not across from them, accept, apologize, accommodate. Ninety-five percent of disputes can be solved through making it clear that the person is being heard, acknowledged, and valued.

I've helped families and schools across different socio-economic backgrounds, language barriers, domestic disputes, immigration statuses, and more, simply by nodding, assuming I know nothing, and wouldn't you know it, "Yes, and-ing." And I've also been involved in a lawsuit that cost a school over sixty grand because an administrator bruised the ego of a wealthy and insecure parent. The dispute was over a handful of homework assignments. A lot of kids lost a lot of resources because a couple of people assumed they knew enough to be right. I always operate from assuming I don't know enough to be wrong. It makes me a pretty good educator. But unfortunately, I'm training myself, not teaching myself.

In social situations, I always zig when I should zag, or zip when I should zop, if you're an improv head. I've been slapped for insensitively inquiring about a romantic situation, put a patient's gown on over my clothes at the hospital for fear it would upset the nurse to find me naked in one. I once alarmed my friend's conservative parents into thinking their son and I were romantically involved by saying how I thought we were soul mates. I intentionally mailed out an artistic nude photo of myself announcing my graduation from college as a joke, which really upset some people. And in a truly spectacular debacle, I reminded an entire family that I had hooked up with both their daughters when I crashed on their couch during one of the daughter's destination wedding. I always look before I leap, but I guess I don't know what the fuck I'm looking at.

The year was 2011, and I was invited to my college friend's wedding. We were excellent friends in college, and even dabbled in an occasional hookup. We quickly discovered we benefited more as friends than friends with benefits. I also had had a brief romantic tryst with her visiting sister. This makes me sound like a scumbag, either by the events themselves, or by recounting them, but hopefully you will cut me some slack when I tell you these individuals are two of the smartest and most spirited individuals I have ever met. I never felt so free and playful, and I was at their mercy. It goes without repeating that I am not a *Playboy*, or even a *Maxim*. I'm the *Sports Illustrated: Swimsuit Edition*—once a year, I get to see a woman in her skimpys.

Among the things we did together were ski trips, cliff jumping, drive-ins, road trips, cross-state scavenger hunts, indoor food fights, naked hula-hooping, and San Francisco Bay skinny-dipping. They had a key to my soul and could just wind me up. And still, when I got the invitation to the wedding, I was more than a little surprised. We had had an infamous falling-out, and not because I had kissed both of them. The details I can't disclose, but I played a rather significant role in my college friend's life being upended after I betrayed her confidence in a desperate attempt to help her. She was pissed at me for longer than I could bear, but she was also safe and happy—a hefty price I was willing to pay. If you have to choose between your friend and your friendship, choose your friend. Friendships can be mended.

Anyway, I figured if I'd been invited, then it was likely that many of our mutual friends had been invited. It was a destination wedding, so I figured I'd just share a room with a friend. By the time I reached out, too close to the wedding, I learned I was only one of two friends she had invited. Evidently, she had forgiven me and was at least partially as fond of me as I was of her. So I flew up to the small town, thinking I could book a room when I got there. I could not. The town was so small, and it was vacation season, so there was only one room available at $450 a night. My plane ticket back wasn't for three more nights. I couldn't exactly call my friend the night before her wedding and add another thing for her to think about. So I called her sister. Not the one I had a crush on years back (and maybe still did), but her other sister, who had, on more than one occasion, served as host to me and her sisters on college trips. She said I could stay with the family at the house they rented. And so I did. I slept on the couch of the parents whose daughters I had hooked up with. And the kicker is the parents knew, and they knew I knew. It could have been a *Meet-the-Parents*-level disaster, but they were beyond kind, including me in family game night, and setting a place for me at breakfast every morning.

I'll never know exactly why I was treated with such hospitality. Maybe they're just decent people. Or maybe they appreciated my difficult honesty so many years earlier. Or maybe my friend just had a big enough heart to give me a pass. Whatever the reason, I couldn't have been more grateful to witness my friend find love and to be welcomed with such compassion when I had been such a social weasel. I also did the dishes every morning, noon, and night, trying to earn my keep.

A fun sequel to this is that a few years later, I went to the other sister's destination wedding, was given a seat at the wedding party table for dinner, and even attended the bachelorette party. We got hammered. Four women and myself, donning plastic penises and drinking to love and matrimony—my own version of baking birthday cakes and doing coke with my lover's ex. Oh my god, I am my father's son.

Those sisters, my friends, are two of the best people to have a good time with, and I'm thankful they could look beyond my buffoonish nature and let me into their lives. When I relay this story to other people, they roll their eyes and say something to the effect of, "I'm surprised their husbands didn't knock your lights out." I am, too. But their husbands probably are more secure men than me and know how lucky they are, and couldn't be bothered by my social ineptitude. For a rule follower, it's astounding how much trouble I have pinning down the social ones.

With those events in my personal history, I'm reluctant to talk to this woman with a fiancé about meeting up in California some time. It's probably harmless enough, and maybe all the subtext is self-created. And since I'm trying to discover who I am, being open to connecting with someone over a shared passion for education could be potentially illuminating. So I say, "Let's keep in touch," and I hightail it for the door, never to hear from a potential friend again.

Before leaving, I make eye contact with Josh. He gestures that he's sticking around, so I slip on my ring of solitude and head to Pete's. I blow up the air mattress I've been lugging across the country. Over the course of the night, the mattress deflates and I wake up cold and aching on the wood floor. I refuse to look at this as a metaphor.

DAY 13: PHILADELPHIA

Population: more runaways, Los Angelinos, and liberal theorists

I have a reliable digestive system. Every morning, I take a poop. This morning is no exception. However, I will not poop in Pete's apartment. For reasons that should be clear. I hope the classroom where I will teach my workshop has a bathroom.

The classroom turns out to be in the apartment's basement, and it has a bathroom. But the bathroom door leads right into the basement where the workshop will be going on. So as I'm going through my morning routine, I can hear the students in the basement wondering where I am. I clear my throat, give some sign I'm around. Then I exit, and one of my future pupils immediately goes to use the bathroom. The cat is out of the bag, and he left a poop in the there.

Overall, the workshop is a hit. Only a half-dozen students, but by now, I am a well-oiled machine. With no gas in the tank, we cruise through 'til noon.

Em texts me to say she doesn't think she can see me when I get back. This hurts worse than I thought it would. I guess because I didn't think about that as something that would happen. I understand it, but it hurts because I was hoping I could see her, go to the zoo with her, because I love her and our time together. But she says that will be too sad. She is right, but I hate goodbyes. They are sad and final, and so I try to eliminate them from my life. Em and I differ on our philosophy of not being together. I'd like to see her. Isn't that one perk of mutually ending a relationship? We can still be in each other's lives? Em feels differently. She says that anything that feels close to the rhythm of a relationship will be too hard. I believe that if we grew together sweetly and softly, we could grow apart the same way, and that severing our connection will be the ultimate pain. Like so many of the trials we go through as adults, there's not a scientific measure for the best or the least painful approach. That's the rub. Knowing either choice will be painful, but squabbling over the degrees doesn't seem like an effective use of time. So we agree not to see each other when I get back. At least, not intentionally. At least, not right away. But I will see her again. I'm sure of it. Whether the context will make it difficult is anyone's guess.

I go on a walk and get something to eat while Josh teaches his workshop. I am in waking hibernation, sleeping walking, despondent. Eating to sustain myself, but closed off from the world to protect against the forces of an intimate nature.

We say goodbye to Pete, and he gives us a hearty handshake so reminiscent of a coach, I half expect it to be followed by him saying "Good game out there." We're headed to Philly, where we're staying with the owners of the Good Good Comedy Theatre. Even though we've got a whole other city, workshop, and show, I'm already wrestling with anxiety for New York. I reserved a room with a single bed, thinking my air mattress would be enough. But it's not. The strain of the road has made me desperate for the comfort of a private bed. Not to mention,

Josh has been furious about every single bed we've had to share, and it's only been a couple. On the train, I contemplate contacting the hotel in New York and getting a second room—a lot to spend for three days, but only a little to spend for a friendship.

Am I bad at partnerships? I'm sensible when I shouldn't be. Impulsive when it's disastrous, and sensitive 110 percent of the time. Is this nature or nurture? Are all only-children like this? Or just the ones who technically have half-sisters, but the age discrepancy left you growing up mostly alone? Is it something I did? Would another child in this case be closer to their siblings? To their mother? Their father?

I'm filled with a lonely dread as we depart the DC train depot and head for Philly. I try to lose myself in a TV show. I go with *Casual*, an LA show about relationships. It's normally one of my favorite shows because it's sad and funny, it's about relationships without happy endings, and it takes place in Los Angeles.

I am a sucker for shows that take place in LA. Devouring LA-centric shows has a two-prong effect. Prong one is validation. A story centered in LA reassures me I made the right choice. If *Entourage*'s Drama can find success in LA, or Issa can grow up despite her flaws, then surely I'll find what I'm looking for. It's shallow and unfounded, but I fully buy into the bullshit that if the entertaining and interesting story takes place in the city I moved to, then I must at least be pursuing something of note. This is ridiculous because there is a show about everywhere, because shows are designed to feel relatable. The only reason there are more LA shows is because it's cost-effective.

The second prong is escapism. Even shows about the hardships of LA don't include the traffic. It might be a minor detail to further antagonize or irritate the protagonist, like when the boys go to the valley to see *Aquaman*. But when people want to get somewhere in LA, they get there and we are there with them. But the truth is no Sunday Funday in real life will ever be as friction-less as the ones in *You're the Worst*. The characters have their own drama, but they don't drive around looking for parking, or take a Lyft with a man showing you a trailer for his movie on his iPhone. Although, maybe they should, because that was a remarkable experience for me, and the amount of coke snorting and sexual spankings that guy squeezed into his homemade trailer was impressive. But mostly, and for good reason, those parts are cut out. Because otherwise, those parts would take up the whole twenty-one minutes.

Here is a brief list of LA shows I love, and the briefest review of what they showcase about the city I call home:

> *Californication* – I like that much of it takes place in Venice. And yes, there are a lot of beautiful women on this show. This kind of show will never be made again, and it will never have a reboot. For good reason. It objectifies women and makes drunk sex-addicted writers seem cool. But it does this with competence (at least for the first season, and perhaps the last). And so, as someone who lives in California, wants to write, and is attracted to the female form, this show is enticing. It is bad for you. It's what conservative adults meant when they said TV will rot your brain.

> What to watch: Season 1. It's a complete story about a failure who can still be a good dad.

Insecure – This show is magnificent. The stories are intentionally polarizing, without a clear right or wrong, and the characters are both enlightened and foolish. And of all the shows on this list, it is the only one told primarily from the perspective of people of color. This is important because it is educational. I know that might seem boring, but I assure you it isn't. The term *education*, much like the term *diversity*, often gets diluted to nothing more than a buzzword. It's shorthand for something important, but it's used with such regularity, its value gets overlooked in favor of its presence. Businesses pay lots of money to have their employees educated on what constitutes sexual harassment because sexual harassment is costly, not necessarily because it's painful and dehumanizing. Studios, theatres, and other entertainment enterprises push for diversity not because having stories told from different perspectives is critical to community growth and human value—which it is—but because they are told diversity means more eyeballs, and that means more zeros on the end of their checks. So when I say *Insecure* is educational, I mean just that. It is teaching me how alike and unalike I am from people who have had a different experience in this country. It's also not the show's job to educate. It's job is to make HBO money. That's what it is paid to achieve. So the fact that it educates while also being incredibly funny and sharply written makes it storytelling of the highest caliber.

What to watch: Season 2 is a masterpiece, but Season 1 makes it all matter more. So watch the whole thing.

You're the Worst – This show also makes drunk sex-addicted writers seem cool, but it also deals with PTSD and depression in a way that offers truth and weight to the subject. I like when they have brunch and run around the neighborhoods I've seen. They also have a nice improv storyline.

What to watch: All of it. But dip your toe in with S01E09, "Constant Horror and Bone-Deep Dissatisfaction."

Entourage – This show is awful. It's sexist and homophobic, and that's just by design. Hollywood is disgusting. It's not all repugnant, but it's far more upsetting than we want to admit. Vince and the boys remarkably showcase the bad and the ugly as the good. This show is like a bag of chips. It's easy to burn through, bad for you, and hard to stop. I can't believe it's an HBO show. I would watch a spin-off with Ari Gold and Billy Walsh in a heartbeat.

What to watch: Just about any episode with Billy Walsh. My favorite is "Adios, Amigos," but "Sundance Kids," "The Release," and most of season 4 all have plenty of Billy. And "A Day in the Valley" is essential LA.

Casual – This is what I'm currently watching, and it is melancholic and tragic and hilarious. I suggested my dad watch it, and he got worried about me because I found it funny. This show does an excellent job of highlighting the struggles people with no problems have. It takes white affluent folks who live in sunny LA, work very little or not at all, and makes them wallow in loneliness or self-loathing. In the wrong hands, this would make us hate them even more. But this show humanizes them by making their misery a consequence of their actions. They don't struggle with health or wealth, but they actively can't get out of their own way, and they're are no more enlightened than the rest of us. Maybe their smooth journey even robs them of insight, which allows us to sympathize with their ignorance and empathize with their self-inflected misery. Despite their best efforts, they hoist their pathetic bodies on their own petards. It's effortful failing, my personal darling, and it's comforting to know those ahead of us haven't unlocked eternal elation. LA can often make me feel quarantined. It's as if everyone around me is doing well, and I'm rolling around in this bubble of self-doubt and incompleteness that is successfully preserving me from any professional success or interpersonal growth. But this show reminds me LA is just one of those toy guns that when you pull the trigger, it cranks out bubbles.

What to watch: It builds nicely, so if you want the full feeling, go start to finish. But the back half of Season 2 is so sad and loving.

Southland – This is the best cop and LA show you likely have never seen. They eat at Yuccas and bust criminals on Sunset and La Brea. It's handheld shooting to give a documentary effect. This, combined with intense narratives and characters who feel as real as the locations, make this show unbelievably good.

What to watch: Season 5. It's dark, emotional, and tense in a way you would not expect from TV in 2013, on TNT.

Curb Your Enthusiasm – I almost didn't include this show because I figured the location had nothing to do with what I liked about it. The show is pretty, pretty, pretty good because Larry David is pretty, pretty, pretty good. But then again, I didn't really enjoy the New York season—the Viagra episode and the Michael J. Fox episode being the exception. I think the supporting cast, the LA locals, are critical to the show's enjoyability. Gotta have Ted, and Mary, and Wanda, and Funkhouser.

What to watch: Season 6, with "The Blacks" is my favorite. I love the *Seinfeld* plotline of season 7, mostly contained in episodes "Reunion," "Table Read," and "Seinfeld."

Episodes – This little hidden gem is worth your time simply because I'm fairly sure you haven't watched it, and each season is fewer than ten half-hour episodes. It's low stakes, lots of laughs, and you could get by with just watching the first season in a day. It's a perfect blend of American and British comic sensibilities. There is a lot of dry and raunchy wit matched up with Matt LeBlanc doing a great asshole version of himself. It does a fun send-up of LA and Hollywood, and the first two seasons end with some brilliant British-style physical comedy.

What to watch: Season 1. Season 5 is also spectacular. I think you can skip to it if you're on the fence, but if you really liked the first season, you won't regret the whole run.

Here's where I'll give you a minute to go to social media and call me out for not including *BoJack Horseman*. It's fine. I have it coming. I know it's good, but it always takes me awhile to embrace an animated show when I don't find the animation visually appealing. Also, I'm not a big Will Arnett fan.

I get nothing from *Casual* at that moment, and this devastates me far more than it should. I suddenly feel nothing for anything, and I wonder if I should just get off this train in Philadelphia and keep marching until I grow tired. And after those two blocks, I'll just hole up somewhere with a comfy bed until I'm forgotten about. I can't imagine anything worse, but right now it feels liberating. I'll pass worry, pass anger, pass grieving, right into ambivalence. The kindest thing I can say to myself is that this evaporation would take a lifetime.

The cruelest estimate would be a few years. I give it eighteen months because self-loathing can sometimes take the pressure off of trying to be my best. I opt to just put my head down, gather my belongings, and step off the train and onto the Metro. I don't have the guts to leave it all behind. I worry about how I treat other people, and abandonment feels like it might have a profoundly negative impact on the ones being left. And perhaps that's self-aggrandizing. Fantasizing about leaving is literally my escapism. In the same way books or video games take someone out of their day-to-day life without ever really transporting the individual. I can't see myself ever doing it, but it's a fun world to faux-explore.

It occurs to me, but not until much, much, much later—we're talking three drafts later—that this fantasy of leaving a trip that is all about leaving has come up multiple times. I never do it, and every time, I chastise myself for not being bold enough to do it. And I'm not sure if this desire to disappear into an unknown city is organic, or if I got addicted to the mild sensation of the fantasy. With hindsight, I think I was mostly just reacting to the disappointment I felt that this trip was not doing what I had envisioned it would. I'd thought this meager trip touring the country and doing comedy would complete me. With my relationships ending, I felt less than whole. I was now without someone and with nothing. But if this trip could prove to enrich my life by being the successful outcome of all my hard work and dedication, then maybe that's who I would be. A lone entertainer, content in my ability to create. My relationships may be gone, but the experiences and enrichments I got from them would get me through this next endeavor, and the dream of touring on my art would be enough to make me see myself for who I am.

That hasn't happened. I can't see who I am. So I want to run away to a place that might show me. But I can't escape.

That's the thing about life. Even running away from it is just a continuation. You can't not write your life's story. Running away, starting over, turning over a new leaf—those are all just chapters. When you really think about it, it's no wonder it's cliché to say, "I've got a great book in me, I know it." Because you do. You are the book. Even if it's a tragedy or a how-to on living a stable, uneventful existence, it's your original tale. Even the lies we tell are true, because they are what that character did. So me, my character, never really goes anywhere, even when he does, and yet he continues to try, which is just so him. At least my protagonist is consistent.

We walk from the Philly Metro station to the Good Good Comedy Theatre, and I am sweating so much I feel like I've been turned inside out, with all the liquid in my body being soaked up by my clothes. I look behind, half-expecting to see footprints of sweat. We meet our host, Katie, at the theatre, and she is kind. Do I have a weakness for kind women? We run tech and then get the keys to her apartment so we can drop our bags off before dinner and our workshop and show.

Like an old married couple, Josh and I hardly speak to each other over dinner. It's a sign we've grown closer to each other over this trip. No longer trying to impress one another, and confident that the other one is here to stay. He is on his phone looking for dates, and I'm mentally trying to categorize this experience. It is the time of my life. I'm just not sure what time. I'm at the tail end of an almost three-week train tour across the country that allowed me to improvise and teach with my best friend. I'm steadily writing what will be my first book, and I'm gleaming with a brief insight into who I am. Or at least, who I am not. Progress, by any measure. If anything were to make me feel ecstatic, this would be it, but I haven't felt that joy in a minute. Perhaps it's because I've been practicing even keel for so long, I don't quite know how to let go and outwardly express. I made the call down to my feelings a week ago, but I'm still on hold. Or maybe I'm just very sad still.

It's possible that no amount of self-identification, or career success, or relationship-building, or country-touring could overcome grief. For starters, grief is a motherfucker. And for another thing, the feelings aren't mutually exclusive. For better or worse, humans can hold more than one feeling at a time. Not well, and not easily, but we can. And perhaps I am. This recognition of all the privilege and wonder in my life is the joy. It might not be palpable, but I'm not *not* seeing it. I'm not in a convertible, top down, on the way to see Van Halen, but I'm not listening to "Bright Eyes" in the parking lot, either. If the characters in *Casual* are the chimpanzee on the self-actualization timeline, void of self-awareness and their good fortune, then I'm that hideous species just ahead of them, bummed over the realization of loss, but I'm taking steps forward, my hand clenched around some motherfucking wheat. Emotional evolution, here I come.

I teach another workshop; maybe the best yet. I have one student who has never done improv before, and a few who are advanced. I find a nice balance, and the feedback is great. Some students come to the show, and one even hangs out after the show. She is an attractive woman, probably ten years younger than me, and I notice she doesn't shave her armpits. This is a turn-on for me. It was my only criticism about *Wonder Woman*. That island was so isolated from everything that the women had never seen a watch before, yet they all had smooth underarms. Give me those hairy pits. But I suppose the movie isn't about turning me on. In fact, I think it was made with the opposite intent in mind.

Anyway, Deb we'll call her, and her male friend Jones, come out to food and drinks with us. Deb and I talk about a term she calls "liberal in theory." She uses this term to describe people who support progressive movements and social justice, but do so only on social media and in bar debates, without ever really making the effort. This ever so slightly opens the window to talk about education, and so I sneak in, unlock the front door, and wave in the demolition team. And like that, we're talking alone. This is not intentional, but I seem to be able to clear a room or get time alone with someone by talking about our country's lack of investment in morality. Most dudes I grew up around played sports or had money, and that seemed like a cool party trick. Gather round while they talk about the playoffs or their parents' vacation home in Telluride. Whereas, I prefer the less popular, "Self-reporting for individuals with learning disabilities is so low, probably because of shame or insecurity, that we don't really have accurate data on how many graduate, or even attend a university." That usually clears the room, and the person left has my undivided attention.

We leave the bar and walk past the Liberty Bell for a picture. You can't see the crack unless you wait in a lengthy line during the day, so we sneak a pic from the untainted side. The bell cracks but remains intact, so we celebrate it. It would be nice if that sentiment bled into a few more of this country's principles. Then we go to an apartment party. I oscillate between talking to this woman and sitting quietly on the couch. It's not so much that I'm only interested in her, as it is I'm limited in my ability to connect socially. I put my arm around her at some point, which she verbally acknowledges, and that's enough for me to not try again. I put it out there. She can now determine where the night goes. She determines it goes for cheesesteaks. Actually, it's Josh who determines this, but her and Jones come along.

We get another moment to ourselves, and nothing happens. Later, Josh interrogates me in the Lyft on the ride home. I tell him nothing happened. He admonishes me. I don't care.

I'd been treading water 'til my arms went numb. Now that I'm on a raft alone, I think I should rest before I go swimming again. For the second time in as many nights, I sleep on an air mattress that deflates over the course of the evening.

DAY 14: NEW YORK (1/3)

Population: dicks and not dicks

New York! We made it. Just about. We're on the train from Philly to NY. So many people are waiting for and seated on the train. I enter the car marked "Quiet Train," thinking it will be empty, but it's packed. I can't wrap my mind around this. Why would the quiet part be full? Is this the social utopia I've been looking for? Are New Yorkers not the loud, opinionated characters portrayed in movies and television? If it's quiet, how will I know if they're "walking here?"

The answer, it turns out, as told to me during our New York episode of our podcast two days later, is that weary nine-to-five commuters proposed it—a chance for some respite in between presumably their husbands shouting about the Knicks, and their bosses screaming about needing more pics of that menace Spider-Man. New York is just as I imagined.

All things considered, this last leg of the trip is painless. We get to the hotel—the moment I've been dreading—and they let us check-in early.

"I have one queen for you," the hotel clerk says.

Josh looks at me like he might hit me.

"Any chance there are two beds available?" I plea.

There are not, but we get upgraded to a king. I tell him I'll sleep on the air mattress. I'm not sure if me sleeping uncomfortably every time we're not on the train makes up for all the work he did, or the uncomfortable sleep he had on the train, but I suppose it can't make things worse.

I must go to the fitness center. I feel fat and gross. Always. On this trip, I feel it more. The placebo effect of those supplements has worn off. My relationship with exercise is that we've been casually dating since high school. I know that it's never made me look ripped, and I can count on my three fingers the number of times people have said I look like I work out, but I bet in an alternative universe where I don't exercise, I look very unhealthy.

I was not born with good genes. There is a picture of my grandpa and his two brothers on the beach with their shirts off. They are all young men, maybe in their late twenties, and my grandpa's brothers all have early muscular bodies, like how Superman was drawn to fight Nazis. But not my grandpa. He looks more like how Jimmy Olsen was drawn—a journalist writing about Nazis. "You don't remember what that looks like because nobody wants to read about a schlub writing about his boring opinions in an ever-exciting world," the writer of this book wrote unironically. My grandpa, and—thanks to Darwin's work on traits—also me, have bodies built just well enough to hold our organs and transport our heads. My head is in good shape: no glasses, no cavities. My body, however, could use braces. So it's off to the gym I go. Before I leave, I make a joke to Josh that I'll be gone, so he should feel free to freely feel himself. He tells me I'm a gross idiot.

In the fitness center, there are a couple of elliptical machines, free weights ranging from ten to forty pounds, and some version of a Bowflex. Standard gym equipment. I use it all, but lightly. I'm just looking to get my heart rate up and maybe pump blood into my muscles so they don't atrophy and get replaced with some version of a fried potato. The thing I appreciate about the gym is that it is where I go to not think. I didn't realize this for a long time, and I have to imagine many people go to the gym precisely to be with their thoughts. Not me, though. I go, put on some music, and just completely zone out. And it feels spectacular. Especially since I've been carrying around grief, sadness, exhaustion, guilt, and anxiety for two weeks. I tried not to pack any of that for this trip, but it seems like I keep getting care packages sent from my life back home. But in the gym, they don't like you to have excess baggage, so it all takes a back seat and I listen to Jay-Z. I will listen only to Jay-Z and Joey Bada$$ while I am in NY because they are essential NY rappers. So for a New York workout, I select Jay-Z's "Public Service Announcement," "Lucifer," "U Don't Know (remix with M.O.P.)," "Hello Brooklyn 2.0," "Oh My God," and "Kingdom Come" (I will die alone arguing that Kingdom Come is a great Jay-Z album). I can feel the supplements and blood coursing through my veins, and I feel great. It's a short, exhilarating, and mindless twenty-minute workout. It makes me feel unstoppable, which is usually an excellent sign that something bad is coming. Or someone.

I keep my headphones on as I leave the fitness center, get into the elevator, and walk to my hotel room. I place the plastic key in the slot, turn the handle, and hear a scream. When I look up from the handle, I catch a blur of Josh fleeing from the bed to the bathroom, with his laptop lying open on the bed, porn displayed on an incognito tab.

Muffled from behind the bathroom door, "You fucking idiot! You're a fucking moron! Who works out for only half an hour, you fucking idiot?! Five seconds earlier, and you would have walked in on me cumming! Fucking idiot."

I'm paraphrasing. It may have been a few less "idiots," and a half-dozen more "fucks," and he may have said "climax," but you get the point. He was aroused and then terrified.

Meat boy masturbates, nearly meets his maker.

I have to place my hand on the desk chair because the combination of my heavy breathing from the workout and my deep laughter makes me light-headed. This is the second time I've walked in on someone masturbating, and I don't know if that is a lot or a little. I've never walked in on sex, oddly enough. The time before was in college, and the kid was a friend but not my dormmate, but he was using my computer to jerk off with. I guess he had used my computer for something, and my porn was not hidden well enough, so it's almost a crime of circumstance. I don't know if it was the first time he did it, or the fifteenth, and I guess I don't even know if it was the last time he did it. All I know is, I went to my dresser, head down, and got out a pair of socks and took them with me into another room. It was only when I was sitting on the couch with a pair of socks I didn't need that I had realized what I had done. The kid came out and said, "You caught me jerking off, ha-ha." I had to give it to him. It was a subtle delivery that fell right on the line of "I'm joking, of course I wasn't," and "I'm just saying exactly what happened." I think the guy is a restaurant manager and swinger now, and I'm confident that kind of doublespeak probably makes him very successful at both. "I catch you high at work again and you're canned," or "We should have sex with more people than just each other."

Josh did not have that subtle delivery. He called me a *fucking idiot* twelve times. If you're wondering, like I was, why I was the idiot, it was because he had not planned on jerking off until I planted the seed for him to spill his seed, and I upset him that I was not gone longer. I posit he should have started earlier. We do not see eye to eye on this. However, we both agree he has laid claim to the bed, because he came on it, and because after laughing that hard, I could pass out exhausted on a bed of nails.

This is my fourth trip to New York. Once, I went to see Rage Against the Machine perform at Rock the Bells when I was twenty-two. And the other three times have been for the Del Close Improv Marathon. And you know what? Counting the brief glimpse of Josh's freshly flogged phallus, I've seen a man's dick every time I've been in New York. Does this make me special? Or just a real New Yorker?

At a bit show at the first improv marathon I performed in, a man named Tim stripped down naked and gave another man Alex a lap dance. Bit shows are stupid ideas performed by large groups of people at 1:00 a.m. Sometimes brilliance comes out of bit shows, as in a legendary set where all the improvisers played Batman, but one improviser played Batman as if he were an improv student. And sometimes it's forty people doing dumb character lap dances until one person does it actually naked.

At another improv marathon, someone took a picture of their dick on my cell phone. So I suppose that could happen anywhere. I guess I got lucky for the sake of the streak. If luck is how you would categorize it.

This brings us to the last, but not least, epic dick shot I saw at Rock the Bells. The lineup was as follows: headlining was Rage Against the Machine, preceded by Wu-Tang, preceded by Cypress Hill. So if I was to get a good spot for Rage, I would have to get that spot for Cypress Hill. This presented a slight inconvenience because I dislike Cypress Hill. Rapping about getting high has never interested me, and B. Real's high-pitched nasal has never sweetened the deal. But there I was, near front row as they inflated a forty-foot Buddha with a pot leaf on his stomach, and taunted a man by the name of BoBo to hit a twelve-foot glass bong. *This can't get worse*, I thought. But then a mosh pit broke out in front of me, because nothing says Buddhist stoner like running in a circle, kicking and punching strangers. Like white blood cells, everyone in the immediate vicinity spotted one entity not like the others. A skinny, bearded man double-fisting bottles of Bud Light was marching around with too much aggression, even for a mosh pit. A circle designed for fighting to music still has rules, and this guy was not abiding. People gave him a little extra breathing room. This fella was working shit out.

What happened next happened in probably under a minute, but I felt like I was watching a Nichols Refn film. The bearded man's belt came unbuckled and escaped every loop holding it captive. It fell to the ground and slithered away with some helpful kicks from the mob. All the while, "Insane in the Brain" played. The belt, I would learn, was both for aesthetics and utility. Beardy's skinny jeans slipped down. The look on Mr. Beard's face distorted from anger into panic, but he was too locked into this mosh pit to make his way to the exit. He kept getting pinballed back into the middle. His hands, still holding beer bottles, couldn't corral his jeans. The denim escaped out the barn door and lay at his ankles, revealing tight white briefs. James Bearden's body then collided with some fellow mosher, and the force was such that it knocked the underwear away from hairy scary's body, exposing his entire dick and balls. Now this is important. He wasn't pantsed, nor did his genitals exit out the intended dick hole. No, sir. Rather, the force he was hit with sent the mass of his underwear to the side, releasing his wiener and nuts out the leg hole. And I swear to you, in a packed outdoor concert at Randall's Island, the only thing you could hear in that split second was two dozen people cry out in horror. I glanced up quickly, and the once furious bearded man was a lost little boy who wet his pants trying to find the bathroom in a Pier 1 Imports.

And that concludes this tour of dicks I've seen while in New York. If you're wondering, Rage Against the Machine put on the best show I've ever seen. I felt abducted and probed by rock gods. And still, I can't recall their set with as much clarity as that angry dolt's ding dong.

After a nap, I do a show with a team I have been coaching for the last year and a half. I regularly pressure the teams I coach into letting me perform with them. This habit is fairly new. I used to hate it. I felt this pressure to be outstanding. Or at least, to be a model of what I instruct. But I did it because I always thought it was cool when my coaches played with me, forgetting how nervous it made me. So the shows tend to be bad. Them nervous, me self-conscious. But then I kept doing it because I figured I would get better at it. And I did. And then the more I did it, the less rare and foreign it felt. It was fun, above all. Which is the goal. There is this comically juvenile hierarchy in the comedy improv community in Los Angeles. Not comically in that it's witty or satirical, but comedic in hysterical that it would be allowed to calcify. It may exist in all comedy communities, or all improv communities, but I can't say because this is the only one I know. It reminds me so much of high school that I wonder how long it will be until we add detention.

Honestly, every other high school component I considered for hyperbole already exists. We have proms and homecomings, but we call them mixers. We have a cafeteria and extracurriculars like volunteering at food banks, rec basketball leagues, and scavenger hunts. There's getting cut from varsity (the theatre's house teams), and there are house parties where a few people sneak away to do coke. Dating is the only other thing outside of comedy that anyone talks about. There are advanced classes, and a principal, except we call her an artistic director.

Anyway, somewhere along the way, we stopped checking to see if these carryovers from high school made sense and we just did all of them, so there's this weird class system from freshman to varsity to alumni. People don't sit at different tables at lunch, but they sit at different tables at the bar, or they take part in the digital equivalent, making exclusive groups online and posting private events. There isn't a selection process like in PE, but people get very selective when picking teams. It all contributes to that unnecessary exclusiveness. We're adults playing make-believe, and we can't stop pretending that it matters. But it doesn't. Not in any career or legacy sense, anyway. But it matters in how it makes people feel. I think it's important to play with the people I coach, or people who are more green than me. Because that's all it is. Experience. The people coaching me are only doing so because they arrived on the scene earlier. Without a doubt, I am giving guidance to people who would be much more comedically fine-tuned than myself had they just packed up and moved out to LA earlier, or had their parents got pregnant in the '70s.

Anyone can get good at improv. The skill is not that rare. Which is why it doesn't pay. And so, consequently, when improvisers defy the odds and spin their skills into gold via TV and movies, they find little reason in staying out till 11:00 p.m. to get on stage in front of an audience of eight, usually made up of the other performers. Unless for the love of it, or to remind those still in the glorious trenches that we're all in this together if we choose to be.

The caste system is artificial. It's just something else we make up. So I say, let's make something else up. And I'm not alone. There are some thoughtful individuals who always make time to play around at jams or indie shows. Maybe it's for their own selfish reasons, or maybe it's because they care to remind everyone that any of us can make it. You don't have to become anyone else to level up. Watching or playing with someone who appears "ahead" or "satisfied" is one way to keep the perspective that they're up there making it up as they go along, just like you. The people I idolized coming up turned out to be just as flawed as me. Regretfully, I didn't find that out soon enough, and I may have shed parts of myself or stayed back, rather than put myself out there, because I had this distorted version of how much more skilled and put together everyone around me was. When, in reality, we're all just different models of the same imperfect system. Unique, yes. But also, no one is special. And the bummer is that we experienced that system during high school, the time in our lives when we're most pliable and absorbent, so it felt essential to our existence. Years later, we're still seeking that environment to define us. The problem is, when we find that environment, we revert to the people we were back then: selfish, inexperienced, insecure hormone junkies. The behaviors that come along with that time in your life are not always pleasant. And that's okay and natural. What's not okay is when those behaviors bubble up to the surface long after we've learned empathy, compassion, and consideration. It's not intentional, it's habitual. And habits are hard to break.

Try as we might, the themes from *To Kill a Mockingbird* never penetrate the psyche the way learning to alienate someone in the cafeteria so you yourself don't get alienated does. Because adolescence and community are about survival and acceptance. Sure, books can teach it in the ethereal, but they're no match for shaming someone or being shamed into sitting alone outside because you wore Walmart brand knock-off Airwalks.

I actively choose to live in the Los Angeles improv scene, and I've carved out my little nook and I love it. It is infinitely more supportive, collaborative, funny, inspiring, and encouraging than any other scene I've spent time in. If it wasn't, I wouldn't actively return to it, build inside it, and celebrate its growth. But it can be toxic, too. I suspect all adult worlds are just replicas of their former high school predecessors, as that is part of the intention behind educating humans at that stage of development, to affect them before they age into rigidity. So it might be unfair to say the Los Angeles improv scene is more toxic than other niche communities, but comparison isn't the point. Identification is. So that change can occur. Ubiquity does not equate to normalcy. We can be better. Together.

That's one thing improv has taught me. I once read that sports teach resiliency. Players learn that one game does not define them, because there will always be another one. My sports career is almost non-existent, so I never learned that lesson. When you play only one game, it can define you. Poor athlete. But eight years of having fun, despite saying, "Yes, and," and when the big game comes, having a room full of my peers and teachers respond with, "No, thank you," taught me I am not defined by one move, one scene, one set, or one show. I got better over time by being aware, listening, responding, and reacting. So I am confident that the system that taught me can teach itself. It starts with calling out what is unusual, and ends with a group game where everyone's voice and choice is honored.

The show is in this echo chamber of a theatre, and we are working against the vapid space the entire time. It is not a memorable show in either a good or bad way. We all go out for Ukrainian food, and for the first time in two weeks, I have a meal with people who aren't Josh or his family, or strangers. I think the term is *friends*. I don't really have a feeling about this either way, except it's good to sit with people I know, who I'm not tethered to in every other capacity. I should restate that this is not a reflection of Josh. My introverted leanings just make it difficult for me to coexist or cohabitate for extended periods of time. I would not make a good penguin, despite my marching away tendencies.

I get drinks at a bar called Molly Wee because I am told the "party space," the reserved dance hall on the twelfth floor of an office building where the improvisers are encouraged to drink, sucks and there is a line. The drinks hit the spot, and it is like I am back in LA with everyone I know, except no one lives here. We're on a field trip. And we've ditched the scheduled activities to get drunk. Don't tell our parents. In this analogy, it would be the UCB founders, or I guess our actual parents. We are forever children, hiding our shenanigans from the chaperones.

I have not seen Josh in hours, but he tells me he thinks he will get lucky. So I go home around 12:20, and I blow up the mattress for the third time. At 3:00 a.m., Josh enters alone. I fall back asleep, but in two hours I reawaken and crawl into the bed. To hell with his masturbatory musk; I need a mattress made of more than hot air and desperation.

DAY 15: NEW YORK (2/3)

Population: grown-ups, twentysomethings, and Chad

First night on a bed in a week, and I feel like the Incredible Hulk. I am Popeye, and a solid night's sleep is my spinach. You might think being able to sleep anywhere immunizes me against bedless rest, but really it exposes my flaw. I am a tired human most of the time. But right now, I have the energy of Babe the Blue Ox on Red Bull. I am up and marching to a show I am performing in at 9:40 a.m. The team I am performing with comprises nine people, seven of who have flown out here. But only myself and one other person show up for it because improv is not about homework, preparation, or planning; it is about spending $700-plus to fly across the country to do what you could do in LA with the same people in LA, but for a slightly less familiar, comparably sized audience. The illogic to this can't stop us now. The show goes well. But my restedness has worn off. I go back to a vacant hotel room to sleep. Josh is gone teaching a class. Today will be uneventful, I decide.

Two hours later, I am up and carrying a bag of dirty clothes to a proper laundromat. For the size of my bag, I am doing far too much laundry, but I hate carrying around dirty clothes. Or having dirty clothes. I do laundry all the time. Far more than I do any other cleaning. My apartment is cluttered; there is always a stack of mail on the table and dishes in the sink. It's not disgusting, but it is disproportionate to my laundry routine. There's something about having my favorite clothes always available. I have them more ready to wear than they are worn. I almost never wear my favorite clothes, and when I do, I usually wash them immediately. When I go on vacation, I usually will never take all my favorite clothes. I will take one favorite shirt and a pair of jeans, and the rest will be clothes I am fine with losing. By this system, I inadvertently wear my least favorite threads far more than my favorite threads. So then, I'm most comfortable in those clothes, and they, in turn, sort of become my favorite. I don't have as much control over what I like as I think. I think none of us do. I will want to like a movie so badly, but it will disappoint me, and I can't force myself to like it. On the other hand, I will expect not to like *Bladerunner 2049* because I didn't like the original, only to later vote it as one of my favorite movies of the last ten years, if not all time. It is disorienting to have conscious wants and uncontrollable likes.

My sisters' dad will give me advice on this subject two months after I unpack from this trip, and two months before he packs for his last trip. He will tell me he has a $200 cowboy hat and a $300 pair of boots he was always saving for a special occasion. And then he got diagnosed with Parkinson's and he became immobile, so wearing the hat required help, which outweighed the feeling of wearing it, and his feet swelled, so the boots no longer fit. "Save nothing for a special occasion," he'll tell me.

I go see another team I coach back in LA perform. I'm in New York City, as far from my home as I can be without a passport, and I'm doing exactly the same thing as I do on the West Coast, except I'm not getting paid, and the theatre space is worse. After four thousand miles, I may not have any better sense of who I am, but I at least know I'm pretty much the same wherever I go. It appears to be the age-old case of taking the boy outside himself, but not taking himself outside the boy. I thought I was more pliable than this. More apt to change. But I'm rigid in that I won't venture far from being flexible.

The team, they crush. I'm laughing. I'm proud. I regret nothing.

I have lunch with my former roommate and current friend. It's him, a few mutual friends, and his girlfriend. To see him with his girlfriend, who he moved in with after moving out, makes me feel behind. They've been living together for nine months, and he seems to have evolved more in that time than the eight years we lived together. That's not a knock against his life while we lived together, and maybe it's mostly that I saw him every day, so I didn't notice the change. It's almost as if we're meeting for the first time. He seems more self-assured, more sturdy. Just more himself. I think *adult* is the term. I'm impressed, if not a little shook. How did he lap me in our respective quests for self-actualization? I went back to school, got a career, purchased health insurance. And now I'm crying on trains and barging in on my best friend jerking off. Is this the me I've cultivated?

Dinner consists mostly of catching up on people's travels. My travel is the longest to recap, not to mention my breakup and loss of my grandpa. Therefore, we talk about it the least. There's always more to talk about when nothing happens, than there is to talk about when everything happens. Trip to Fiji, who has the time? Saw a dude's dick at a concert? Pull up a chair. If something happens to you, write a book. You only have to tell it once, and people can learn about it at their leisure and to the depth they want, and at the level you're comfortable with.

Josh is meeting up with an old friend, Nick, who is a food critic. So after dinner, I jet across town to meet up with them for my favorite meal: second dinner. We get cold noodles. Everything we order is a first for me, and it's all delicious. This reminds me of getting food with one of my closest friends, Farley, who is a food writer in Los Angeles. In regular intervals, I'll receive a text from him inviting me to lunch at a place I've never been before. A few hours after saying yes, I'm introduced to new food, filled in on the city's expanding cuisine-iverse (he does not use this term, nor would he approve of it), and encouraged to think about eating as an exercise in cultural education as much as a necessity to staying alive. Even new foods in new neighborhoods with new people reinforce the same ol' me.

I have another show. A bit show, but no one shows their dick. It, like most of my experiences with bit shows, feels dumb and excessive. Improv is one of the most frivolous excesses of the privileged. And bit shows, they're the gout of improv, the king's disease, unhealthy excess. Improv costs hundreds of dollars and an immense amount of dedication, and at the end, you have nothing tangible to show. A memory or experience, yes. But even an impressive improv show is difficult to recount, and the retelling is extremely diminished. So it exists, and then it's gone. Unlike a sketch, or a play, or a book, or even live storytelling, it's never done again the same way or with the same intent, or the same characters. It's not rehearsed or polished. It's just dumped onto the stage in front of an audience, and with any luck, people will laugh and gasp, and hopefully leave fulfilled. Both performers and audience.

A bit show is all of that, but somehow matters less, costs more, and wastes more time. A bit show comprises a premise, sometimes involving props, and is somehow agreed upon that it's not "real" improv. It's Batman-prov, or strip-prov, or banana-prov, and it takes place between the hours of midnight and 4:00 a.m. usually. Not only do we have the time and money to waste on "meaningful" improv, we also have the time and money and hotel beds to waste on "meaningless" improv.

After this bit show where someone got taped to a chair and was fed socks and Snickers, I make my way to the party space. I immediately hate it. I am in a rare cynical form. It reeks of an arbitrary distinction for comedians who are all similar when compared against the vast vocations the rest of the world has to offer. You can only get into the party space if you have a performer wrist band. Once you get to the space, there is another VIP section for people with a more exclusive wristband. This wristband is for teachers and performers who have earned a certain level of celebrity. I drink a couple beers and wait in a line to go out on the balcony. There is a line because the balcony is apparently reserved for people who smoke or like to stand in exclusive lines. I fall into the latter because I don't smoke, but waiting in a line gives me something to do. Why am I here? Why do I insist on dragging myself out to an event I know I won't like? I'm my own worst date. "Oh no, I brought me to a party. I know I hate how I hate how self-conscious parties make me feel. Why did I do this to me?" Because occasionally, life-changing good comes out of it.

Nine years ago, I was sitting in my car, parked on the street, before my first improv class, contemplating dropping out before attendance was taken and driving the fifty miles back to my apartment in Upland, where I was living with my dad. I remember thinking, *I can just go home and watch TV, because that's safe and comfortable and enjoyable.* But I didn't. Instead, I went in and said my first "Yes, and." And now, here I am, thousands of dollars and tens of thousands of hours later, drinking beers in different parts of New York City, talking to friends and peers I know solely because of improv, and I am answering their questions about what it's like to tour the United States on the perceived merit of my improvisational skills. By generous measurements, I am a success. But I don't feel like one. I feel like a fraud. I sleep on a queen-size bed but am the king of imposter syndrome. And I sleep alone.

I gratefully accept an invitation to play with a second team I coach, and I flee the party space. I take possibly my last Lyft of the trip and barely make it, and my team—well, not *my* team, but *the* team—is drunk and delighted to see me. And I am delighted to see them. I do well when I understand my role. We have a silly set and then go for shots at a nearby bar at 1:45 in the morning. We drink pickle backs, and I realize that I am ten years the senior of everyone on the team. I could have taught these people when they were in high school, and I was teaching high school.

I flip the lens another angle and recall being twenty-three. It was 2005, and I was in the home stretch of college. That upcoming year would get weird. But perhaps that is a story for another book. My twenties were a struggle for me to navigate—often fun, but also untenable—and so I appreciate everyone doing their best. You'll never know as little and do as much as you do in your twenties. It's a glorious train wreck, and these friends of mine are doing it with style and grace.

After leaving the bar by myself, I text Josh I'm coming back, and he advises me not to. It is now 2:30 a.m., and I am on the streets of New York, slightly drunk, alone, and trying to figure out what to do. I text a friend of mine who I know has a room with two beds, but he doesn't text me back because it is, as I said, 2:30 a.m. I consider seeing if the hotel where we're staying has another room, but I suspect they don't because they didn't earlier. I also have it in my head that I won't be able to run my card again, and I can only use the one card there because I only have one credit card that says *Jacob*, which is what my driver's license says. I check hotel apps, but it's past midnight, so HotelTonight will only let me look at rooms for the next day. Hotels.com, however, shows me three rooms that are still available, but I have to rent them for two nights if I want them for the current night. I say *fuck it* because now it's 3:00 a.m. and I'm not near my hotel, and I'm fucking tired, and I don't give money the respect I should, and I think going to the room with Josh might be enough to really sour our friendship. After two weeks together, we're on thin ice. So I do it. I drop $800 I definitely don't have, for peace of mind and security.

When I arrive at the hotel, the concierge tells me they don't have any rooms. I say I just booked one, and he says I did it through a third party site and they overbook. I literally throw my hands up and say, "I give up." I turn around to exit, then turn back toward the concierge and ask if he can help me. Here I am, at the end of my rope, surprising myself and asking a stranger for help.

"I can rent you a room for a no-show," he casually says.

So it would appear they do have empty rooms, just not available rooms? Whatever. I'm at his mercy.

I call up Hotels.com and cancel. They say they need to talk to the concierge, and I say I'm looking at him, but they can't take my word for it, so they put me on hold.

The front desk phone rings, and the concierge and I share a look that says, *How dumb is this?* He picks it up and tells them he is overbooked. Then the operator takes me off hold and relays to me what I heard in-person, and they cancel my reservation. I pay $200 instead of $800, but I still feel like I got taken for a ride.

The room is exquisite. On the nightstand is a bag of cookies and an envelope with the name Chad on it. I open the envelope and read the handwritten note. The hotel thanks Chad personally for staying with them. I flash to my Lyft driver who operated the parking lot structure and said he had had people leave their cars in his parking structure, and then die, and then the cars would get left there, only to be claimed by the next of kin. I am Chad's next of kin. I hope he is not dead. But if he is, his death was not in vain. I eat the cookies in bed and sleep like a 1920s orphan brought in from the cold.

DAY 16: NEW YORK (3/3) TO LOS ANGELES

Population: paraders, food critics, wise guys, and Lemon

For two weeks, I woke up every morning either next to Josh or right next to Josh. This morning, I wake up alone. Minus the three-hundred-plus strangers also staying at the Redbury. I finish the cookie from the night before, take a gloriously long shit, a slightly shorter shower, pack up the complimentary toiletries, and set out for my last day of a two-week run away.

If you include the running to the show at midnight, Chelsea to East Village, then back to the sex den, formally my hotel, and then aimlessly searching for a hotel—all of which the pedometer on my iPhone does—I will walk twelve miles on my last full day in New York City. And in these last twenty-four hours, I will be comforted by the familiarity of friends old and new and grateful for the time with them. I will travel for two weeks to appreciate the connections I have already made.

My last day in New York coincides with Pride. This puts the whole city in a joyous mood. Maybe not the whole city, but all the good parts. It feels warm to walk around. I am no stranger to Pride, and every year, it feels more like a celebration, and I have to assume that's because every year, we usher out more intolerance and welcome more acceptance. It must have been so scary to march that first time, and I'm sure it still is. But as an observer and supporter, I feel a touch of second-hand pride. Perhaps that's part of the idea. It's pretty hard to hate something that makes you feel good, and it shouldn't be hard to hate something that makes someone else feel good, especially when it doesn't impact you. It feels good to identify with an open and loving generation. It's a real testament to the movement and its positivity that the decision was made to pass on the love and not the hate. This is a good day to be my last day in New York.

I walk and I walk and I walk. I'm walking here. And I'm sitting here, at a little brunch restaurant. I order a Bloody Mary and a breakfast sandwich, and I eat it alone and watch the parade. The breakfast sandwich is rich and runny, the Mary thick and spicy, and the parade a combination of it all. I have always enjoyed Pride. I think it's important, but I also just think it's cool to see people being themselves in such vibrant ways. I have slight envy for being able to boldly be yourself that way. Sure, I have found a way to do it on stage, but I get to hide behind the theatrics. And I guess maybe some people here do that, too. I mean, there has to be some more introverted folk in this parade who feel that this is their chance to be themselves, even if it's not who they want to be all the time. I'm not referring to their sexuality, but their individuality. I don't know what it's like to be ostracized. At least, not in any serious way. But on a tiny level, I can relate to indulging in who you are—or in my case, who I think I might be—even if factors (external for some, internal for others) don't make it easy. I almost feel bad at how much joy I am taking from being an onlooker. It's unfair to receive the joy without having to endure the pain, but that's what I'm getting to do. I am a parasite of privilege on an organism of bravery and freedom of expression. Thank you, Pride.

I make it to one theatre for our second to last show. This is a Puddy show. Puddy is the third improv team someone asked me to join in LA, and it is the only one still going. It is comprised of Josh and two more friends, Wayland and Clay. All three guys were "grades" ahead of me when I was coming up. They were on teams before I even knew you could audition to be on teams, so playing with them always makes me feel like my raffle number got picked for a spot on some celebrity basketball tournament. It's a blast, and it feels like dumb luck I ended up with them.

I can remember when I got the email asking me to join. I was on the couch, and I nearly vaulted through the ceiling. It's a feeling I've tried to pass on by asking people coming up behind me to play with me. Who knows if it recreates any of the same sensations? Maybe that's not what people want. I could ask, but that seems somehow delusional. "Would you like it if I asked you to play with me?" What kind of megalomaniac does that? It felt good when it happened for me, so that's my model. And I think it's working because people continue to be receptive to my requests. But there have been instances where I get a relationship wrong, tip the scales of perception unfairly. That I was wrong about wanting to connect with Em and see her after this trip makes me question every instinct I've had about all my relationships. It's like that sentiment about receiving one thousand positive reviews as a band or an author, only to obsess over the one negative criticism. Thank god there's not a website for reviewing social interactions.

Wayland and Clay aren't here, so it's the Jake and Josh show. We are both pretty strung out, and without the anchors of some sturdy guests, we're flailing. It's not a bad show, but it definitely feels like last call. The show ends at 2:40, and we have to get across town and set up for our final podcast recording of the trip at 4:00 p.m. Another race against the clock, but we make it. We have two wonderful guests, and one of them explains the quiet car to us. We have a blast of a last show. We are using the UCB's equipment, and there's a little branded display, so it feels like an odd joint venture. We're guests in someone else's house, but we are the life of the party. I have an incredible time and really feel the joy of this trip as we laugh, and shout, and make jokes about James Bond fighting too loudly on the quiet train. I'm reminded of why I do all this. Because it makes me fucking happy to laugh with my friends. It's that simple. For all the metaphors and analogies and pondering and loathing, it can be as simple as connecting over a joke with someone you've known for years, or someone you just met.

Josh's friend Nick, the food critic, comes to our show and is interested in hanging out. I insist on getting ice cream because I've been trying to get some since I got to New York, and at this point in the trip, I've decided I'm entitled to a sweet frozen treat. We walk the High Line, a beautiful garden walkway high above the city, with art installations, craft tables, hipsters, and loners. There is something distinctly New York about every inch of this city. Even a person sitting and reading *The Hollywood Reporter* while listening to "California Love" seems like they would be out of place in Culver City. The edges are more distinct around them.

I spend the walk asking Nick about everything food-related. He is an expert paid to talk, and I am a fan delighted to absorb. I seize the opportunity for a familiar role. Thank you, Nick.

I peel off and go home for a nap. Josh returns with a woman just as I am waking up, both of us using the hotel room for our most primal urges. Señor Siesta y Señor Fiesta.

I meet up with a collection of friends to take a late-night stroll for some dim sum. The only thing I can guarantee to adore about a vacation is that I can categorize multiple meals as sightseeing. I can justify eating six times a day and spending money I don't have if it's under the umbrella of a cultural experience.

The walk takes thirty minutes, which is ten minutes short of the length needed for my friend to tell a story about eating at a restaurant owned by the mob. The details are lost to the night, but the plot points are that the restaurant was a front, and the meal they ate was the only one prepared that day. Even when I'm not on the podcast, I'm just trying to hear people's stories. But I'm off the clock, so I don't make jokes. I listen. Thank you, friends.

I walk back with the group and split off to go home for some rest before our 4:00 a.m. call time to take a cab back to the airport. Josh does not come home before I close my eyes.

The first thing my eyes focus on is the fumes of alcohol wafting through the room. Josh is drunk enough to make me fail a breathalyzer. He has somehow got his hands on an extendable paper tube toy. You know, the ones that are coiled up, and when you whip them, they extend twelve inches? He has one of those, and he whips it at me while I'm in bed, while I get dressed, while I call downstairs for a shuttle to the airport, while I get told the shuttle isn't running but they'll call us a cab, while I learn that the cab is a private car service, while I say fuck it and agree to the car service because I'm tired and disoriented and Josh is hitting me, while we wait for the car service, while we're in the car, while we're in line at security, while we wait to board, and finally, while we're on the plane. At one point, he whips it at me over the head of the woman sitting between us on the plane. I want to strangle Josh. I want to watch his eyes pop out of his head. I want to kick his corpse under a truck tire. But I do nothing because he is filming the entire experience. I am filled with a rage I did not know was present in my body. I am John Wick, and my dog is my personal space, and Josh is bashing its head in with this paper funnel. I am tired. I am ready to go home. At this moment, I hate the only person I feel close to. I wonder why this is the feeling greeting me at the end of my journey.

The woman sitting between us on the plane has three carry-on bags, and she places one on my legs. I fall asleep cursing both friend and stranger.

We're back in LA, and I am beaming with anticipation to open my apartment door, to greet my cat, and to lie down in my bed. Josh and I take the Flyaway to Union Station, and we say our goodbyes. It's short and strained. I know we'll be fine, but for now I just need to flee once more and return to base.

I cuddle up with Lemon, my cat, who at this moment, I love more than anything else in this world. I have grown to love her more every year we live together. It is a love I did not know I was capable of, and I'm surprised every morning to find my adoration has increased. She purrs as loud as a lawnmower, and it soothes me to sleep. Thank you, Lemon.

In four hours, I get up and go to the sink, and there is my grandpa's mug sitting in there, left for two weeks. It says his name on it, and has a picture of two Air Force jets. I wash it out and just fall apart.

I am crying and I can't stop. It's as if I have been physically flexing every muscle in my body for seventeen days, fighting to keep the sadness away from my chest, and I just let go. It feels like a pack of wild dogs were unleashed on my heart, tearing pieces off, fangs gnawing at chambers and valves until there's nothing left but a blood-soaked rib cage. I realize now that this trip was a distraction. It took seeing the whole country by train, meeting and playing with a dozen strangers, and putting myself so far outside my comfort zone with little to no respite, just to keep my heart from breaking wide open. I did not heal on this trip, I merely induced an emotional coma. I have lost my roommate to growth, my grandpa to the grave, and my girlfriend to generational disagreement. The most present and consistent relationships in my life have been severed, and I feel stained and empty like the mug in my hands.

UNPACKING

Inventory: swimming trunks, stamps and envelope, twine and a pocket knife, and you

I wrote the following between June 30 and February 10, 2018.

My trip ended some time ago, and yet here I am, lounging at the pool at the Roosevelt Hotel in Los Angeles. Why? Because sometimes what feels like home is anything but. And so I lean into escapism once more. One of the greatest gifts I have ever received when I was a teacher was not a Starbucks gift card—despite every parent seemingly finding it perfect. It was another teacher clueing me in to the easy accessibility of hotel pools during the weekdays. These pools are relatively unoccupied during the conventional work hours, but the business is still paying to keep them maintained and supervised, even when there isn't much profit to be had. This leads management to consider the feasibility of selling a fifteen-dollar cocktail in the middle of a hot day if they throw in a pool and lounge chair for free. And I've been buying this combo for years now. Except, this time, I am a guest at the hotel. A getaway from my home, and a respite from a getaway. I am a guest in my town, a stowaway in my life.

The idea was always to end this story when I got back to LA. To leave it as conclusive as I could, acknowledging the inevitability that nothing is finite. Except for death and sincerity. And ironically, it's death that keeps this narrative chugging on long after the train has pulled into the station. And sincerity that has nagged me into putting it on the page.

On a Monday in the near future, Mike, my inverse step-dad, will stop eating and drinking and will take a cocktail of pain medication to help him drift off to sleep and then to die. It's been hard on everyone, as is the burden of death, but there's been an added element of emotional despair. Death by choice can make you feel so helpless, even if it is actually more within your control. Some death sentences are so certain, the idea that "nothing can be done," can offer a modicum of liberation. The end as a choice requires an acceptance of exhaustion, an embracing of peace. I don't know how to do that. And so, perhaps that's why I'm here. Being a guest at a hotel gives me the illusion of total control. Or perhaps my home is just not the sanctuary I need it to be right now. I'm not sure if it's the repetition of unusual sleeping quarters that's made the single-serving sleeping situation more comforting, or that everything in my apartment reminds me of my former room-mate, or my ex-girlfriend, or my dead grandpa.

Fuck, this is hard. This literary pilgrimage, this cultural investigation, this examination of self, it takes its toll. Holding so much out in front of me gets heavy, but I don't know how to put any of it down. The pressure builds, but when I open the valve, it seeps out. I wanted to construct a mechanism that helps me burn clean, but the cogs are heavy and I'm grateful for spurts and strains. I wanted to write a book at a point when I was lost, and end it at a point when I found something. But it feels as if I've built a Rube Goldberg machine with no finished product in sight.

I've written approximately ninety-eight thousand words since they cremated my grandpa, but I haven't written one word to him. When he was alive, and before I moved within a two-hour drive of him, we wrote each other month after month. From the time I was seven up until 2007, I kept him abreast on school, and work, and dating. He would do the same, substituting out school for golf, work for volunteering at a bookstore, and dating for dating. He was a softer mirror, a look into my future without dread or anxiety.

My therapist suggested that now would be a good time to write him. She said it would be a way for me to keep the relationship going. It seemed like a sensible thing to do, not because I am spiritual by nature, but because it's not like I have a lot of other options. I feel vulnerable, weak, homesick. And anyone who has gone to camp, or a new school, will tell you the cure for homesickness is to reach out and touch the one place you know you're loved. So I sit at this hotel, sun on my face, pool at my feet, and I write my grandpa.

And the fever breaks. Shortly after the letter, life falls back into place. First, I get some sleep, then I teach improv. I eat meals at home, and occasionally have a night out. I develop a comfortable, if not ideal, living situation with a roommate who indulges me in my quiet time. I fly to Colorado to see my dad. I go up north with my sisters, who are visiting with their dad. I start dating someone who makes me laugh, and considers me, and challenges me.

It's true what Jeff Goldblum says: "Life finds a way." I was far from extinct, fortunate not to be experiencing homelessness or outright defeat, but my grief led me to flee, which led me to be depleted, which led me adrift. And now…now I'm pretty much back on my bullshit. Not settled. Closer to broke than bliss. But better.

Then Mike dies.

He dies before the ball drops on 2017. I speak at his memorial, and just like when I spoke at my grandpa's, I get overcome with nerves. I become self-conscious that wanting to speak has more to do with me than with the deceased or the grieving. In fact, I would have preferred not to speak at either service, except I felt I owed it to both men to tell them what they meant to me. And in that, I reach my destination.

Mike gave no fucks what you thought of him, but he gave every fuck to think about you. He wasn't judgmental, but curious. Deeply interested. And it didn't matter what you were like or what you were into, he would talk to you about it because—and this is just me speculating—he wasn't concerned with who he was; he was interested in who you were.

My grandpa wasn't that different. He took a more malleable approach. He was a spiritual father to my uncle, a fierce debater to my father, a lover of cards and games to my cousins. And to me, he was quiet company. He, too, was not interested in the impression he left on you, but in nourishing the relationship you had with him.

When I speak at my grandpa's funeral, I tell this story. I once helped him and his girlfriend pick up a flat-screen television from the Marine base shopping center. He and his girlfriend would often call on me to drive them some place, or set up the answering machine, or carry in cat litter. Innocuous errands that made me feel important. On this occasion, I stuffed the TV in my trunk, but it would not fit. We took our chances and began the drive back to their retirement village. On the 5, the trunk popped open, and it slammed up and down on the TV box. We pulled over on the side of the highway. I was visibly nervous and sweating from my forehead and behind my ears, worried that the TV would be damaged, or that it would damage my car, or that we would get a ticket. My grandpa, at ninety-two, took a spool of twine out of his pocket, along with a small pocketknife. He cut a length of rope and tied it to the trunk hatch and to some hooks in my trunk. He said not to worry, that we'd be fine, and he put a calm hand on my shoulder. I suppose when your past includes being in World War II, discount shopping does not sound the same alarms as a Nazi invasion.

At the start of our mission, I remember foolishly thinking I was the hero, come to save the day. But in truth, and of course, it was my grandpa who wore the cape. I don't know about God and footprints in the sand, but I know my grandpa flew me out of more than one crumbling building.

Mike, AKA Uncle Mike, AKA my sisters' dad, AKA my inverse stepdad; and Nick, my grandpa, AKA Ol' Nick, AKA my ace in the hole, AKA my friend, taught me that, life doesn't require a sense of self. That knowing who you are isn't that big of a deal. They both knew who they were early in life. Mike, a tough as nails adventurer with a big heart that never let him drift too far from his daughters. And Nick, a driven company man, dedicated to doing his best work for his country, and ensuring that his family would be taken care of. And maybe that's what made looking after others easy for them. Once they had themselves figured out, they could focus on those around them. Or maybe they realized that life is short, and worrying about yourself is not worth the trouble. So pick a lane and make sure you've got enough room and seat belts for your loved ones because it's a bumpy ride and the trip will be over before you know it, and you don't want to be left alone, unpacking a box of dirty mugs to clean.

There are two kinds of people in this world. There are those who want you there for them, and those who want to be there for you. In other words, heroes, and the rest. The rest is totally acceptable. We all fit the category at one time or another. Most often as babies and kids, but also in line at the grocery store or waiting to see a doctor. I have been unbelievably lucky to have been born into a family surrounded by so many people showing me how to be heroic, not concerned with carving out their own identity but instead with being available. I had my mom from the cradle, my sisters from afar, my dad when I was at my lowest, and Mike and Grandpa at their end. I just spent three weeks and thousands of dollars trying to figure out who I was without those in my life who were there for me. And it turns out that who I am is less important than who I am there for. I don't need to be full to be an above-ground pool. I need to be an above-ground pool for people who need one. Knowing me any better will not fill me up, because being full isn't my identity. My identity isn't as important as my purpose. My years of teaching and improv and this tour have taught me I can be there for others, that I can say, "Yes, and," and make someone feel heard, feel safe, be supported. I'm not sure who I am, but I am at my best when I make myself available. A pool is a pool, even if it's not full, so long as it can be filled. Fulfillment. Get it? Of course you do. It's a bad joke. But hey, that's about as much as me as I know. Bad jokes, sad stories, too much talk about butts and penises and boobs. And hopefully, taking on the mantle left by Mike and Grandpa, a little bit of a hero. I won't always succeed at it. In fact, I'm sure I'll fail at it. But it will be an effortful failure. The kind I have plenty of experience in, and the kind that has taught me everything I need to know about myself to be myself.

Dear Grandpa,

My mailbox is empty. I get bills, and packages, and the occasional postcard, but nothing from you. That's to be expected since you passed away over a year ago, but I can't help myself from hoping that maybe one last letter, something that got lost in the shuffle, will arrive with my name on it in your handwriting. A sign that I'm not without you. For twenty-five years, I knew that if I sent you a letter, I could expect to hear back in ten days. Like the sun rising every morning, that consistency gave me comfort in a world that was unpredictable. Your endless love was there to pick me up when I stumbled. How do I write to you when I know you can't write back. How do I risk getting knocked down when I know you can't pick me back up?

I know I'm supposed to be accepting and logical about this. You were ninety-four, after all. You weren't going to be around forever. But I'm not ready to say goodbye. I'm not ready to live a life without my grandpa, without my buddy. I was always able to do things with you in my corner: move, go to college, move, go back to college, teach, try, fail, learn, succeed, repeat. Whatever I did, no matter how scary, I could look behind me and see you there, giving me the confidence to believe in myself.

Sometimes I have dreams where you're still here, or dreams where you come back. They were most vivid just days after you passed. In one dream in particular, we were sitting at your dining room table at the Del Mar Beach Club. You told me not to worry because I had "honest grit," and that I would be okay. I think I know what you meant, or what I meant in my projection of you. I think you meant there was a truth in me, a genuineness that would keep me resilient, that would protect me from the bricks and bastards thrown my way, if I could manage to hold on to the values that you instilled in me. Valuing family, integrity, drive, and kindness. I trust that you're right. I need you to be. Because there's a whole ring in front of me, and my corner is empty.

I'm so grateful for your fingerprints on my life. I can't make new memories with our experiences together, but I can have new experiences with your memories. The grief washes over me when I consider that every moment we had together will have to be shared with more and more moments where you're no longer around. For 99 percent of my life, you were there, even if just a subtle presence, with me knowing that if I picked up the phone you were on the other end. As I get older, the lunches I have on Sundays without you will far outweigh the ones with you. There's nothing to do about that. The frustrations and finality of that closes in around me. This must be what grief is. The inability to fill the emptiness or console the loneliness. Accepting that you're gone is when I need your comfort the most. And so I will reach back into the past and bring those memories of us together close to my heart. I anticipate new jobs, new friends, new loves and heartbreaks, and unfamiliar experiences as life rolls on. I will think of our time together as I encounter each unknown day ahead. Having you in my past fills me with love in my present and confidence in my future.

I teach improv full-time now. From my living room in your rocking chair, I sit there and read like you did, and wait for my students to brighten my front door like I did with yours. While the time we had together is fixed, the time I have with your influence and unconditional love is ever-expanding.

Dad and I are closer now, and we're brought even closer by your sayings—a code between us. We're each other's "ace in the hole." We remind each other, "Illegitimi non carborundum" (Don't let the bastards grind you down). When we need a laugh, we remind ourselves that this is all a "hardware store, with screws on the left, and nuts on the right." My favorite, "Keep your eye upon the donut and not upon the hole."

I also have your teapot. There's nothing special about it except that it was yours. It's stainless steel and it sits on my stove, as it used to sit on yours. I recall it on the stove in your house on Cozumel Court, when I used to fly out as a teen on my own and visit, and we'd go putt golf balls. You had a modest house with two bedrooms and a garage and a patio. You'd fix up the second bedroom for me, and there would be a package on the bed with a Hawaiian shirt for me to wear. You'd tell me you bought matching ones for my dad and uncle. I used to lie in that bed before going to sleep, thinking about how you spent your time alone, driving around, shopping, and preparing for my visit, and I could feel my heart grow.

I recall the teapot on the stove in your apartment at the retirement home, or the "graveyard with lights," as you called it. With your two bedrooms, your covered parking spot, and your rented storage locker, there was your unexceptional teapot. Every time I came to visit, you would be in your rocking chair, reading Nora Roberts, and you'd get up and give me a big hug and kiss me on the cheek. You'd give me a folded napkin with cookies you'd stolen from the dining hall. I would giggle thinking of you pulling off heists for me.

I remember the teapot on your stove in your studio with no bedrooms, no dining room, just a bed, a bathroom, and a small kitchen. You'd often be asleep when I arrived, and you wouldn't get up because you needed a walker, so I'd come to you for a hug and a kiss on the cheek. We'd go downstairs and you'd ask me to check your mail. You no longer had the energy to run errands for yourself, let alone bop around on account of me.

Every couple of years, for the last ten years of your life, you parsed down, and you went out less, but you were no less there for me, and you kept the teapot. You may not need a garage, or storage, or room for guests, but you need hot water. And you need companionship. We all do. And so in the morning, I boil water for my coffee. I am alone in the kitchen with your teapot, and I think of all the times you were alone in your kitchens with your teapot. I am mostly happy alone, but I think of how you must not have been, because you worked hard to have a family and keep them close. So hard, in fact, that I didn't have to work at all for mine. They were just there when I got here. I am sure I take them for granted, and I worry someday I will be alone not by choice, and I will be sad. But I have your teapot, and knowing that we both had it when we're alone staves off the loneliness. Because I'm not lonely. I don't visit my mailbox as much because I don't need to, much to the chagrin of my postal worker. You're no longer a letter away. You're right here.

I pour a cup of coffee in a mug with your name on it, sit in your chair, and enjoy our new time together over a big donut with barely a hole in it. I love you, Grandpa.

ACKNOWLEDGMENTS

Thank you to my grandpa for being my lighthouse, my life preserver, and my raft. Thank you to my mom for being my hero and my dad for his unconditional love. Thank you to my sister Nicola for being there when it was darkest, and thank you to my sister Michelle for inspiring me to be there for others. Thank you to Mike for loving me as a son. Thank you to Em for helping me be a better person and accepting me when I wasn't. Thank you to Josh for believing in my voice and for making this whole trip possible. Thank you to my editor, Sarah, who went above and beyond in helping me write a stronger book. Thank you to Avalon for putting up with me and giving me hope and guidance along the way.

Thank you to Gilli, Ryan, John, John, Erin, Dickie, Hannah, Farley, Brian, Dave, Joe, Reyana, Amy, Jessie, Ginny, my cousins, my uncles, my aunts, my nephews and nieces, Dani, Suzie, Alma, Leysan, Genetra, Andrew, Ben, and the music of Nipsey Hussle. THANK YOU to everyone who believed in me enough to help get this book made, and an extra special thanks to all the parents of all my friends who loved their kids enough to go out on a limb for them and buy a sad memoir from some weird, oversharing comedy nerd.

GRAND PATRONS

Allegra MacGregor
Amanda Bonar
Amber Williams
Ashley Christiansen
Ben Axelrad
Brian Palatucci
Farley Elliott
Christopher Satriano
Claudia Satriano
Dan Lippert
Dani Shank
David Hunsaker
Dickie Copeland
Eric Pastore
Gabe Durham
Harrie Lydon
Jeffrey Levy
Jesse Merrill
John Orlando

Katie Surh
Leysan Dickenson
Mark Wilson
Mark Borders
Toni Borders
Mark David Christenson
Mark Jabbour
Nicola Rushford
Natalie Johnson
Jacqueline Orellana
Paul Schlesinger
Peter Hong
Robert Pulido
Robbie Rittman
Ryan Rosenberg
Susan Burgess
Tyler Schnupp
Karima Tatum
Will Hines
Will Stephens

INKSHARES

INKSHARES is a reader-driven publisher and producer based in Oakland, California. Our books are selected not by a group of editors, but by readers worldwide.

While we've published books by established writers like *Big Fish* author Daniel Wallace and *Star Wars: Rogue One* scribe Gary Whitta, our aim remains surfacing and developing the new author voices of tomorrow.

Previously unknown Inkshares authors have received starred reviews and been featured in the *New York Times*. Their books are on the front tables of Barnes & Noble and hundreds of independents nationwide, and many have been licensed by publishers in other major markets. They are also being adapted by Oscar-winning screenwriters at the biggest studios and networks.

Interested in making your own story a reality? Visit Inkshares.com to start your own project or find other great books.

CPSIA information can be obtained
at www.ICGtesting.com
Printed in the USA
BVHW032014240621
610386BV00006B/27